THE BANKING REVOLUTION: SALVATION OR SLAUGHTER?

"Explodes the view that technology is an enabler of profit. Instead it exposes that technology is a two-edged sword – offering companies survival over their competition, but reducing profit through the commoditisation of services. Technology is the great equaliser – optimising value to the customer and constraining value to the shareholder. **This book demonstrates that technology does not create value – it distributes it.**"

ROBIN BARRETT
Senior Vice President, Technologies International, American Express

"A thorough review of the competitive trends in Financial Services with some provocative conclusions. **A must for anyone with an interest in the future of UK Banking.**"

PATRICK O'SULLIVAN
*Chief Executive, Eagle Star Insurance Company Ltd
(Formerly Chief Operating Officer, BZW)*

"**A serious, thoughtful and very interesting book,** predicated on a serious and interesting problem: how can general managers and technologists jointly identify new business opportunities created by technology? The book succeeds in helping to bridge that gap."

ANDREAS PRINDL
Director, Nomura Bank International plc

"A thought provoking read which not only provides an excellent primer on the evaluation of the application of technology to banking in the UK but also **challenges conventional wisdom as to what changes technology might bring in the future.**"

JOSEPH DE FEO
President and CEO, The Open Group

"After reading this book, I felt vindicated. **The technology management frameworks presented in the book are very relevant to my real world experiences in the top management relationship with the IT function.** The challenge is to find a Chief Information Officer who can adequately manage technology while actively buying into, understanding and implementing the business strategy programmes."

MALCOLM S. MCDONALD
Chairman and CEO, Signet Banking Corporation

"**A fascinating account of the winners and losers in the banking industry's struggle to master and profit from today's revolution in information technology which they neither created nor are able to control.** This book will be a valuable asset to the top managers and strategists of both banks and their regulators trying to cope with the technology revolution they face. I suspect this book will be even more valuable to competitors waiting in the wings to take advantage of bank's relative inability to deploy their resources flexibly, as so vividly illustrated by the authors."

JAMES M. UTTERBACK
*Professor of Management and Engineering, Massachusetts Institute of Technology
Visiting Professor, Harvard Business School*

ABOUT THE AUTHORS

Mark Carrington is a founding partner of Mitchell Madison Group and is based in London. In his sixteen years as a management consultant, he has covered the full gamut of technology management issues and has served a wide range of international banking clients in wholesale and leasing finance banking, treasury, investment banking, retail banking, credit cards and investment management.

Prior to Mitchell Madison Group, he was at AT Kearney, Perot Systems Europe, McKinsey & Company, Deloitte Haskins & Sells and Price Waterhouse. He graduated in Business Science and Law at the University of Cape Town and has an MBA from the University of Witwatersrand. He is also a qualified management accountant.

Philip Langguth is a founding partner of Mitchell Madison Group and is based in London. In his twelve years as a consultant, he has served client executives in the US and Europe in wholesale and retail banking, investment management, and securities services, as well as the technology providers. He has had extensive experience through a wide range of engagements in strategy development, risk management, and organisational and operational effectiveness, giving him a unique ability to bridge the gap between the business and IT worlds.

Previously, he was at McKinsey & Company in London and New York, and JP Morgan in New York, where he was responsible for the bank's electronic banking services. He holds a BA with Joint Honours from the University of Durham and an MBA with highest distinction from Rutgers University Business School in the US.

Thomas Steiner is a founding partner of Mitchell Madison Group and is based in New York. Previously, he was a partner at McKinsey & Company, for a decade, where he was a co-leader of the Information Technology practice, and also a partner at AT Kearney and leader of the global Financial Institutions group. He has served client executives of leading banks as well as technology providers on a wide range of management issues. Over the past 20 years he has worked with more than 100 institutions in 24 countries.

He is the lead author of *Technology in Banking: Creating Value and Destroying Profits*, published in 1990, and *Systems Technology and the United States Commercial Banking Industry*, published in 1987. He is an honours graduate of Dartmouth College and has a JD degree from Harvard Law School and an MBA from Harvard Business School where he was a George F. Baker Scholar.

THE
BANKING
REVOLUTION
SALVATION OR
SLAUGHTER?

**How technology is creating
winners and losers**

MARK ST. J. CARRINGTON

PHILIP W. LANGGUTH

THOMAS D. STEINER

FINANCIAL TIMES
PITMAN PUBLISHING

LONDON · HONG KONG · JOHANNESBURG
MELBOURNE · SINGAPORE · WASHINGTON DC

FINANCIAL TIMES MANAGEMENT
128 Long Acre, London WC2E 9AN
Tel: +44 (0)171 447 2000
Fax: +44 (0)171 240 5771
Website: www.ftmanagement.com

A Division of Financial Times Professional Limited

First published in Great Britain 1997

© Mitchell Madison Group 1997

The rights of Mark St J Carrington, Philip W Langguth and Thomas D Steiner
to be identified as the authors of this work have been asserted by them
in accordance with the Copyright, Design and Patents Act 1988.

ISBN 0 273 63055 5

British Library Cataloguing in Publication Data
A CIP catalogue record for this book can be obtained from the British Library.

Figures 2.10, 8.1, 9.3 and 10.1 adapted and reproduced from *Technology
in banking: creating value and destroying profits* by Thomas D. Steiner and
Diogo B. Teixeira, Business One Irwin, 1990, with permission of
The McGraw-Hill Companies.

Figure 2.13 adapted and reprinted from *Innovation: the attacker's
advantage* by Richard N. Foster, by permission of International Creative
Management, Inc. and Macmillan General Books. Copyright © 1986
Simon & Schuster.

Figure 2.14 adapted and reprinted by permission of Harvard Business
School Press, from *Mastering the dynamics of innovation* by James M. Utterback,
Boston, MA, 1994, p. xvii. Copyright © 1994 by the President and Fellows
of Harvard College; all rights reserved.

10 9 8 7 6 5 4 3 2

Typeset by Northern Phototypesetting Co Ltd, Bolton
Printed and bound in Great Britain by Biddles Ltd, Guildford and King's Lynn

The Publishers' policy is to use paper manufactured from sustainable forests.

FOREWORD

The financial sector is the most advanced and dynamic sector of the British economic portfolio. It is a major employer. It is an increasingly important contributor to the country's position in international commerce. In spite of the historic weakness of sterling, it occupies a pre-eminent position in the financial activities of Europe. It provides an array of financial services unsurpassed anywhere in the world. These achievements are the result of fifteen years of internationalisation, liberalisation, re-regulation, innovation and growth. New and especially American entrants to the market have strengthened the City of London's standing and capability by the transfer of skills and technology. London's international position has never been more robust or broadly based.

Within the established domestic heart of the traditional financial system the process of change has been more difficult. The great retail banks, Barclays, Lloyds (now Lloyds TSB), Midland (now owned by HSBC) and NatWest still handle 80% of all financial transactions and they are key to the understanding of the future of the financial sector as a whole in the United Kingdom. Their adaptation to a more competitive and uncertain world is incomplete and problematic. The roots of these difficulties lie in the changes brought about by the increasingly rapid development of telecommunications and electronic data processing. Banks are essentially information handling systems. Cheap, timely, accessible and copious data has eroded the rents formerly available to them as the owners of information. The increased capability and capacity of information systems have radically changed the scale, scope and economics of the whole banking sector. Regulation has adapted and reformed so as to allow the exploitation of the new possibilities made available by these changes.

This new environment is characterised by a new and very expensive underlying technology with complex economics and no established models of success. Banking is now a capital intensive business with high fixed costs and low marginal costs. The risks have altered and the absolute and relative value of all the components of the business have changed with them. The responses to this change in the drivers of investment and organisation have been varied and consistent patterns have been hard to identify.

The industry has developed various and divergent strategies: consolidation, efforts to 'unbundle' the business into discretely managed activities, and the extension of diversified service portfolios. But these have not always been clearly related to long-term objectives and their effect on profitability has not always been obvious or favourable.

In one sense, it is easy to generalise about the likely longer run outcomes for the industry. The need for scale will produce a steady trend towards disaggregation, leaving an industry structure characterised by a small number of large scale processing providers. The advantages of specialisation will drive the dissolution of the business into self-standing activities and to the proliferation of a large number of small auxiliary service providers. The migration of margins closer to the customer will provide opportunities to large and experienced retailers with loyal client bases. In more operational terms, for the traditionally entrenched players, it remains unclear whether and to what extent existing elements of vertical integration can be maintained, what competitive advantages can be sustained in which services and which market segments, who will survive, to what extent and where.

The faint outlines of a pattern can be seen emerging. Traditional banks have assumed that their scale and the consequent size of their investments in technology will protect their core business and have supposed, rightly or wrongly, that the key to success is an increase in their service range. The middle-size banks and the demutualising building societies have pursued, through mergers, the scale they believe that they need to support their information technology investments. Players in other retail sectors, like the supermarket chains, have seen that processing scale is no longer required when they can buy access to unbundled payment systems.

But a more detailed understanding of the way in which the sector develops necessarily remains a matter for investigation and debate. This book offers important help in this task. It provides a comprehensive analysis of the major services and distribution methods in the sector suggesting the nature of their economics and their effect on existing banking practices and structures. It sets out a theory of technological innovation adapted from work in the manufacturing industry and shows how it can be applied to anticipate the nature and timing of technological innovation and used to defend the business from incomers. It also suggests the nature of the managerial and cultural changes that will be needed for traditional banks seeking to develop and protect their investments in information technology and to maintain the breadth of their service provision.

In the end, economics will determine the future. But the financial retail markets are not perfect, and thoughtful strategies will make it possible not only to manage the defence of existing positions but also to generate and shape opportunities not yet identified. The development of some of the more important components of those strategies may be stimulated by the analyses and experience on which this book is based.

Angus Walker

CONTENTS

ACKNOWLEDGEMENTS

Usually acknowledgements made for the labour that goes into writing a book go to the families and loved ones who have lost the author for long periods of time. This book has been different – the real effort has been made by the large number of our colleagues who have been co-opted into the programme and whose analytic ingenuity we have drawn on.

Special recognition should be given to Kevin Mellyn, who broke the back of the history of UK banking and who contributed much thinking to emerging developments in the banking arena, in particular the concept of 'back to the future' that is discussed in the Epilogue of this book; to Nick Robinson and Will Chalmers who laid the foundations of the data analysis, to which Rosemary Coventry, Matt Hollier, Jean Huang, Michael Maybaum and Darren Montgomery all contributed subsequent time and effort updating, cross-referencing and validating; to Gordon Buchanan, for his innovative work in the application of technology to customer targeting and lifecycle management that we have drawn upon in Chapter 8; to Moritz Schlenzig, for his contribution to the section on inventing the future bank, in Chapter 9; to Asiff Hirji, who did much of the research on supermarket banking for Chapter 6 and who synthesised our thinking for the Epilogue; to Sandy McGuffog, who provided the overview of the CHAPS process in Chapter 3; to Andy Gueritz, who helped us to organise our thinking in Part 3 and drafted many of the chapter summaries; to Anne Jordan, Sarah Kelly and Kerrie Musgrave in our Information Services group, who frequently came up with creative ways of finding even the most obscure information; to Marco Shirodkar who spent many an evening making our graphics look interesting and user-friendly; to Sarah Coombes, whose diligence and persistence helped us keep the administrative tasks in the publication process under control; to Sandy Rose, for his comments and editorial contribution; to Tom Metz, for his advice and assistance; to Angus Walker, for his patience and valuable counsel; and to Mark Thompson of Financial Dynamics, our public relations adviser, who somehow managed to keep us on course and maintained a sense of humour when many of the deadlines came and went.

We owe a special debt to Sue Starks, our editor, without whose tolerance, patience and determination none of the successive drafts would have been completed; and to Constantine Psaltis, who brought the final version to fruition, working tirelessly over many evenings and weekends after finishing his client work, refining, revising and co-ordinating the many parties involved.

Mark St J Carrington
Philip W Langguth
Thomas D Steiner

INTRODUCTION

It is commonplace today to say that banking is undergoing a radical transformation. The symptoms are obvious: new products, new players, new channels are appearing daily. This transformation is taking place across all sectors of the banking industry. The retail sector, with its sheer size and competitive intensity, is the main arena of change and the main focus of this book, although many of the themes and our technology management thinking are applicable to securities houses, insurance companies and investment firms.

In this environment of change, information technology is one of the major issues on any bank Chief Executive's agenda, thrust into prominence by the massive and increasing magnitude of its costs at a time when competitive pressures have never been greater. On the one hand, IT seductively promises great benefits in terms of productivity improvements and new product or service offerings. Indeed, the enormous technology investments in UK banking since 1980 have led to a significant reduction in employment, despite rapidly growing volumes (Figure I.1). On the other hand, top managers are finding it increasingly difficult to judge

> **Banks urgently need to improve their ability to think strategically about IT investments. Only those banks that use their technology resources effectively have the opportunity to secure real competitive advantage in this fast-changing industry through real product or service differentiation.**

how much value is actually created and translated into profits by these investments. Most institutions lack a framework within which general managers and technologists can jointly identify new business opportunities created by technology and discuss the relationship between business opportunities and technology choices. They lack the appropriate metrics and management information systems, a phenomenon exacerbated by IT devolution in many of the large clearing banks. And when Chief Executives try to challenge the level of spend, they find themselves unable to do so effectively, frequently faced with choices they do not know how to make. Over time, this gap in understanding is growing. Too often, decisions are taken that fail to increase shareholder value and may even destroy it.

Fig I.1 UK commercial banking institutions' assets, IT spend and employees

1980–2000   1980=1x

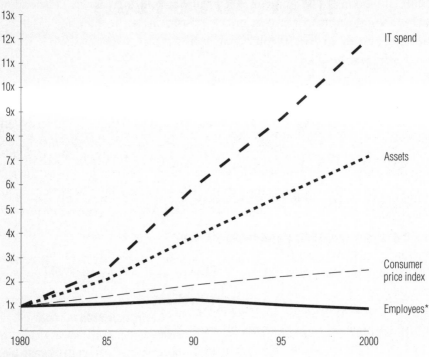

* Full-time equivalent

Source: Mitchell Madison Group (MMG) analysis

This book aims to bridge the gap in understanding by providing both general managers and technologists with an insight into what technology is doing to the UK commercial banking industry and offering some guidelines on the management of technology in banks. This is especially relevant now that top management, looking at the truly remarkable performance of the UK banking industry in the last four years (Figure I.2), have started to wonder: is this the salvation that IT promised us, or is it the lull before the slaughter?

In 1990, Tom Steiner, together with Diogo Teixeira, examined the impact of IT on commercial banking in the US in *Technology in Banking* (Business One Irwin, The McGraw-Hill Companies). In it, they described how IT could simultaneously increase value for the users of bank services while destroying the profits of the providers. In short, technology made possible the provision of enhanced services at lower cost; however, it also enormously increased capacity and diminished labour, thereby ultimately working in favour of consumers rather than shareholders or workers. The 1980–90 time period in the US was marked by a substantial technological shift in banking. The joint impact of a four-fold increase in IT spending with an eight-fold increase in price/performance of technology created a massive, up to 25- to 50-fold, change in services, capacity, labour usage, and prices in the US.

Not surprisingly, as information technology has become more prevalent, growing from 8% of operating expenses in 1980 to 16% in 1996, the pace of consolidation in financial services has accelerated. For example, the US commercial banking industry has progressed from a highly fragmented industry structure to one that a few very large players dominate. In 1980, the ten largest firms controlled 24% of industry assets; by 2000, the ten largest will control 50%. Although the UK is already highly concentrated, substantial merger activity has occurred and will continue to occur. The

Fig I.2 Shareholder value created/destroyed

UK commercial banking sector, 1980-96   Percent

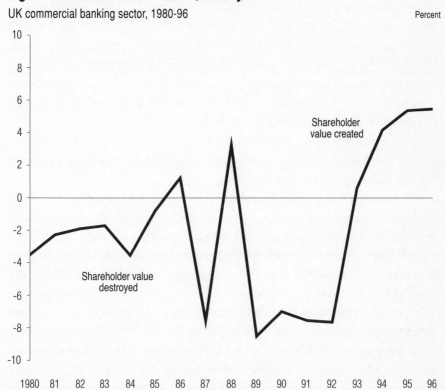

Note: This chart shows the sector's return on capital against the return shareholders require, as determined by the comparable return of risk free investments (government bonds) and the relative risk of investment in this sector

Source: MMG analysis

3

mergers of Chase – Chemical, Wells Fargo – First Interstate, BancOne – First USA and Nationsbank – Barnett in the US, and Lloyds – TSB and Halifax – Leeds Permanent in the UK have significantly concentrated power in the banking industry.

This is a global phenomenon, as technology does not 'respect' political lines, and so we see a continuing pattern of global consolidation. Consistently, technology does not 'respect' regulatory lines either and, as a result, cross financial industry consolidation has occurred and will continue to occur. For example, the Lloyds – C&G and Abbey National – N&P mergers in the UK are merely typical of what will continue to occur as product and channel lines continue to blur. The power of IT to proliferate both channels and products vastly exceeds the ability of politically focused regulators to compartmentalise.

Finally, the dividing line and the balance of power between the financial services users of technology and the providers of IT are shifting. The enormous increase in market capitalisation of the technology providers since 1990 speaks clearly of their relative power (both financial and brand). Interestingly, many providers now have such consumer visibility (e.g., Microsoft, IBM, Netscape) that joint ventures are truly balanced in terms of relative appeal to consumers. This trend deserves close discussion in coming years as it could have vast implications for the restructuring and reshaping of the financial services industry.

All of these factors contribute to a very great need to evaluate and assess IT as a major strategic force partially harnessed inside a firm and partially beyond the direct control of any firm.

In this book, these ideas are further developed in the context of the UK banking industry. The major UK clearing banks rank among the top banks worldwide in their spending on information technology. No country has a greater concentration of sophisticated technology users of such scale in its financial services sector. This situation is in sharp contrast to the highly fragmented financial services industry in the US at the beginning of the 1980s. One of the purposes in writing this book is to test whether the ideas developed in the context of the US industry have a broader application in other geographies and market structures. Focusing on the UK has made it possible to refine the concepts and demonstrate their applicability outside the US. It is the conclusion of this book that banks urgently need to improve their ability to think strategically about IT investments. Only those banks that use their technology resources effectively have the opportunity to secure real competitive advantage in this fast-changing industry through real product or service differentiation.

The book is in three parts, intended to group the main themes addressed and to separate the general discussion from the review of specific lines of business, which some readers may choose to read selectively based on their particular area of interest.

Part 1 (The transformation of banking) sets out this book's main propositions. It describes how, since 1980, banking in the UK has been transformed by new rules and new technology. The relationship between the two is complex. Regulatory changes have affected industry structure and economics, and have themselves been stimulated and necessitated by technological changes, which are still continuing. The first part of the book explains these changes and describes their effect on banking as a whole.

Part 2 (How lines of business are being transformed) reinforces the propositions presented in the first part with specific evidence from the main lines of business and delivery channels in retail banking. It discusses the major changes in each business line and the role of IT, both today and in the future, highlighting the resulting management challenges. Skipping over this part would not take away from the overall proposition, although for some readers the business-line discussion should bring added insight.

Part 3 (Succeeding in the technology revolution of banking) returns to the main propositions and sets out suggestions and approaches for dealing with the central question: what can be done? It offers approaches that bank management can adopt to meet the challenges posed in the short term by the apparently inexorable rise in IT spending and provides a framework for charting a course for the longer term.

PART

1

THE
TRANSFORMATION
OF BANKING

Since 1980, banking in the UK has undergone tremendous structural change. This has been primarily the result of new regulation and new technology, which itself precipitated the change in regulation. Some of the most important regulatory changes were:

- the abolition of credit controls on sterling lending, which was followed by the expansion of the banks' direct consumer lending, credit card and mortgage businesses
- the opening up of membership in the payments system, thus ending the clearing banks' traditional monopoly
- the deregulation of building societies, which allowed them to offer a wider range of services and forced the entire industry to offer interest on the vast majority of its accounts
- the 'big bang', which allowed commercial and foreign banks to participate in the securities industry
- the change in the rules governing capital adequacy, which forced banks to set aside and allocate capital according to the different risks inherent in their activities.

These regulatory changes facilitated the entry of banks, building societies and other non-bank providers into each other's traditional markets, and allowed the expansion of these institutions into other financial services, such as insurance, securities, estate agency, pensions and unit trusts. The demutualisation of building societies, in their attempts to break free of the remaining constraints in competing with banks, was also eased, as was a new wave of mergers and acquisitions leading to further consolidation.

Over this same period there has been a surge in business volumes. Since 1980, total industry assets have grown six-fold, representing a more than two-and-a-half-times increase in real terms, and the volume of non-cash payments has also grown to more than two-and-a-half times its 1980 level. Spending on IT grew at an even faster pace – rising to £4 billion or a more than four-fold increase in real terms from its 1980 level – as institutions attempted to keep up with or get ahead of competition (generally through productivity improvements) and create some sort of differentiated service.

The effect of the structural changes, the increase in business activity and the enormous technology investments is proving to be the same for banks in the UK as it was for their counterparts in the US a decade earlier – productivity has increased greatly and customers receive significant additional value from their banking relationship – but banks are finding it increasingly difficult to sustain consistent profitability. While employment has shrunk since 1989 – its peak year – by almost 90,000 full-time equivalents and is continuing to contract, and thousands of branches have been closed, operating cost/income ratios have barely improved for the players most actively replacing labour with technology.

A close look at recent profitability figures reveals that unusually low loan loss provisions – rather than increased efficiency – almost exclusively account for the recent improvement in financial performance. IT investments, while generating some cost savings, have not produced the expected gains in profits. Competitive intensity, abetted in part by the technology investments themselves, has pushed banks into passing cost savings along to customers through reduced product prices. As competition increases, this trend is set to become more pronounced. As banks continue to increase systems intensity, defined as the proportion of expenses accounted for by IT, shareholders will not benefit. Indeed, they may ultimately be hurt, insofar as the new investment decreases information asymmetry and enables more borrowers to bypass banks and interact directly with ultimate investors. But if banks eschew additional investments the shareholder will likewise be hurt since new players, taking advantage of the more advanced technologies, may also be able to muscle the banks out of the market. The challenge for banks is to identify and gravitate towards those technology investments that hold the promise of true product innovation and can foster a stronger market franchise.

Chapter 1 discusses the changes and challenges faced by the banking industry since 1980. Chapter 2 then describes the role technology is playing in the transformation of the industry.

BANKING SINCE 1980: CHANGES AND CHALLENGES

During the 1980s and the first half of the 1990s, banking in the UK has seen momentous changes. The industry is dominated by a few banks of increasingly significant scale. Before 1980, the banks and the building societies were highly insulated from competition by their size or by the existence of a quasi-cartel in deposit banking or mortgage issuance; these two groups developed differentiated roles and offered very specialised and exclusive financial products and services to their different customer groups. Now the industry is operating in a new competitive climate, under very different new rules, and with new economic and technological forces acting on it. These changes have altered the structure of the industry and have accelerated the process of industry consolidation. As a background to the discussion of the role of technology in banking, this chapter outlines the changes in the industry since 1980, beginning with a description of the main players in it.

THE BIG FOUR AND THE REST

British banking can be described in terms of four sectors, defined mainly by the customer segments served and the products or services provided: retail personal, serving the transaction and credit needs of individuals; small business and mid-corporate, traditionally akin to retail due to the similarities in product delivery; wholesale credit, serving the transaction and credit needs of large corporations; and securities and investment banking, providing trading and corporate finance services and operating, by the nature of the market, mostly on an international basis. These four sectors are often grouped into two major arenas of activity: retail, covering retail personal and small business/mid-corporate; and wholesale, covering wholesale credit and securities/investment banking.

The British commercial banking industry serving these sectors has tradi-

Fig 1.1 Institutional structure of UK banking industry
1980–97

UK Commercial Banking Institutions			Foreign banks/ UK merchant banks
Big Four	**Other Retail**	**Building societies**	
Key Players			
• Barclays • Lloyds TSB (Lloyds Bank[1]) • Midland[2] • NatWest	• Abbey National[3] • Bank of Scotland • Clydesdale[4] • Co-operative Bank • Girobank[5] • Royal Bank of Scotland • Yorkshire Bank[4] • (TSB[6])	• Alliance & Leicester • Bradford & Bingley • Britannia • Halifax • Nationwide • Woolwich • (Cheltenham & Gloucester[6]) • (Leeds Permanent[7]) • (National & Provincial[8])	• Foreign banks (e.g. JP Morgan, Citibank) • UK merchant banks (e.g. SBC Warburg, Schroders)
Profile			
• Grew up as a series of mergers in 1960s and 1970s • Have large branch networks and coverage across the whole of England & Wales • Significant slices of all markets give advantages of installed base and position but make them potential loser in increasingly competitive environments	• Abbey National historically a building society, but increasingly behaving as a bank since demutualisation, and attacking Big Four aggressively • 3 Scottish banks hold similar positions in Scotland to the Big Four in England • Smaller banks focusing on geographical or product niches	• Focused on personal sector, traditional products are mortgages and savings • Increasingly focusing on transmission and non-mortgage lending • Top players have recently demutualised, but retain building society profile	• London is most active international banking centre in the world: wholesale and investment banking tend to be international rather than domestic

New 'personal financial services' entrants

e.g. • Direct Line   • Sainsbury
     • Marks & Spencer   • Tesco
     • Prudential   • Virgin

1 Until 1995
2 Owned by The Hongkong & Shanghai Banking Corporation
3 Was a building society until 1989
4 Owned by National Australia Bank
5 Owned by Alliance & Leicester
6 Until 1995. Now merged with Lloyds
7 Until 1995. Now merged with Halifax
8 Acquired by Abbey National in 1996

tionally been structured around three groups of institutions, as illustrated in Figure 1.1: the 'Big Four', a set of full-line/full-customer banks, which are widely known as the clearers because of their long lasting domination of the clearing system; the 'Other Retail' banks, which have in some cases also covered wholesale activities, but have tended to focus on a geographical or socio-economic niche; and the building societies, a large but rapidly consolidating number of deposit-taking institutions serving the residential mortgage market, traditionally as mutual organisations but increasingly as public shareholder-based companies.

We have defined these categories to note the deep behavioural differences that have existed in the market for over a century, not to describe how the structure of the market and the behaviour of its participants will evolve in the future. In fact, the lines between these groups are increasingly blurring. Big Four banks are now well-established players in the residential mortgage market. Other Retail banks are merging with Big Four banks or building societies. And building societies themselves are discarding their traditional narrow focus and are demutualising to become banks. Clearly the effect of the recent mergers (as well as future ones) will be to consolidate the industry into fewer and fewer institutions that offer increasingly similar and overlapping product lines.

The Big Four banks are Barclays, Lloyds TSB (Lloyds Bank until 1995), Midland (owned by The Hongkong and Shanghai Banking Corporation) and National Westminster. They have dominated banking in recent decades, accounting for over two-thirds of retail current accounts and of the expense base of the industry (£16.2 billion out of a total of £23.6 billion in 1996): in terms of operating expenses, the average Big Four bank is eight times as big as the average Other Retail bank and nine times the size of the average top-six building society. They own 56% of the 15,500 branches in the banking system, averaging about 2,200 per bank. They also do the vast majority of the industry's work, mostly by transmitting value among accounts, either by internal accounting or through the payments system: in 1996, 8.3 billion non-cash payments were made in the UK; directly or indirectly, the Big Four processed more than three quarters of these. They are the operational backbone of the UK financial services industry.

The Other Retail banks include three Scottish clearing banks (Royal Bank of Scotland, The Bank of Scotland and Clydesdale Bank), Abbey National (formerly a building society, but has now broadened its activities well beyond savings and mortgages), Yorkshire Bank, the Co-operative Bank, and Girobank (owned by Alliance & Leicester but operating as an independent bank serving the business sector). Clydesdale and Yorkshire are both owned by National Australia Bank, but they are different organisations and have not been consolidated. All the banks in this category are basically retail branch banks, averaging 380 branches in the UK (ignoring Girobank, which uses the 20,000 outlets of the Post Office) and accounting for about 17% of industry spending. Until 1995 this group also included TSB, a retail bank descending from the regional Trustee Savings Banks and focused primarily on the lower income slice of the personal and small business sector. Despite superior efficiency and cross-selling capabilities, TSB failed in its attempts to become a full-line bank, and finally joined the Big Four by merging with Lloyds in 1995. Lloyds TSB Group has maintained the separate TSB brand and branch network for the time being, but internally has consolidated its operations into its new Retail Financial Services division.

The building societies vary greatly in size: of the total of 76 societies in 1996, six accounted for 78% of operating expense in this group. These were the Halifax (including the former Leeds Permanent), Nationwide, Alliance & Leicester, Woolwich, Bradford & Bingley, and Britannia. This group also included, until 1995, Cheltenham & Gloucester, which has now become the mortgage lending arm of Lloyds, and National & Provincial, now acquired by Abbey National. Building societies have traditionally dominated the market for savings and domestic mortgages, and are now direct retail competitors of the banks, offering current account services and making other types of loans within limits. The top six building societies average 490 branches each and accounted for about 11% of industry spending (£2.6 billion) in 1996, with another 3% accounted for by the smaller building societies. As more and more building societies are demutualising, but are retaining in the short to medium term their focus on savings and mortgages, this group is defined for the purposes of this book more by the customer and product focus of its members than by their legal status. Increasingly, however, the boundaries between Other Retail banks and building societies are becoming blurred, and very few institutions appear to be resisting the trend towards becoming full-line retail banks, some national in scope.

While retail is the primary focus of institutions in every group (and virtually the sole focus of building societies), the Big Four also specialise in wholesale banking (Figure 1.2). In fact, they are dominant players in the UK wholesale banking sector – which also includes, as we discuss below, several significant but much smaller UK merchant and foreign banks – and accounted in 1996 for 90% of wholesale activities, in operating expense terms, by UK commercial banking institutions (Figure 1.3). Most wholesale customers bank with one of the Big Four, although the Scottish clearers dominate the wholesale market in Scotland. Retail market shares are complicated as many customers bank with all three types of institution. For example, they might use a Big Four bank for cheque and other payments, a building society for savings and mortgages and Girobank for some bill payments. Others may use one institution for all their banking and other personal financial needs, although this is a recent development, and still rather rare.

Fig 1.2 Matrix of involvement

	major focus
	primary or substantial
	medium
	limited
	minimal or none

	Retail personal	Small business & mid-corporate (commercial)	Wholesale credit	Securities & investment banking (international)
Big Four	●	●	●	◑
Other Retail	●	◔	◔	○
Building societies	●	○	○	○
UK merchant banks	○	○	●	●
Foreign banks	○	○	●	●
Nature of competition	8–15 significantly sized players	4 main players in England & Wales; 3 players in separate Scottish market	Highly competitive with numerous British and foreign investment banks	

Fig 1.3 Total UK banking operations – breakdown by operating expense

1996   Percent

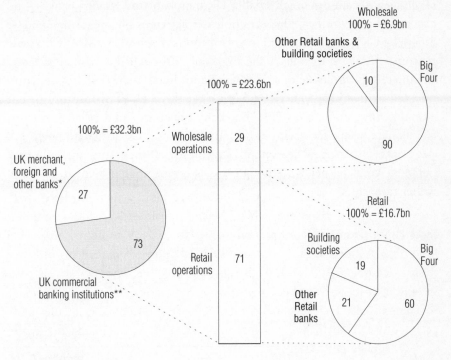

* Mainly wholesale banking
** As defined in Figure 1.1
Note: Analysis shows total worldwide operating expense of UK registered institutions and their subsidiaries, but not their parent companies if overseas

Source: MMG analysis

Beyond the institutions we have described, the UK is, of course, host to a large number of other banking institutions, the most significant being American and Japanese investment banks as well as UK merchant banks (an increasing number of which are now owned by the large continental European banks). These institutions focus on the international capital markets for which London is a primary global centre. Notwithstanding the size and importance of these institutions, this book focuses on the UK commercial banking industry and on its primary arena of activity, the UK retail banking market.

In this arena, another set of players is becoming increasingly important. Companies with significant customer franchises but no traditional involvement in banking are now offering banking products, such as savings accounts, personal loans, or even cheque accounts, usually as part of a 'personal financial services' package that also includes other financial products, such as investments, life insurance and general insurance. While their share of the market remains small for the time being, their challenge to traditional players is another illustration of the increasing competitive intensity discussed in later sections.

SURGE IN BANKING ACTIVITY

Institutions in all three categories grew very strongly between 1980 and 1996. Their total assets increased six-fold, from £189.5 billion to £1,145.1 billion, a compound annual growth rate (CAGR) of 11.9% (Figure 1.4).

The main force driving this expansion was rapid growth in the ownership of financial accounts, which began in the 1970s and continued throughout the 1980s. As recently as 1975, only 9 million households (45%) had a bank account – mainly salaried and professional people, and those with unearned incomes. Most of the working population was paid weekly in cash, and paid most of their bills in cash. Since then, however, the 'un-banked' have declined dramatically: by 1996, 94% of the adult population in the UK had some form of account, with 83% having a current account (Figure 1.5).

Several factors contributed to this surge. The post-war 'baby-boom' generation grew up, started jobs and bought homes. The banks themselves stimulated demand for banking services by adding attractive new products, such as credit cards and cheque cards, and by relaxing standards for opening cheque-book accounts. And new providers entered the banking game; by 1996, most top building societies offered current accounts.

This once-only transformation of 'un-banked' into 'banked' households will be essentially complete in the next few years. In other words, the market for current accounts, the engine of recent banking growth, is almost saturated.

This broadening of access to financial services resulted in a steep rise in transaction volumes. Non-cash payments increased more than two-and-a-half times between 1980 and 1996, rising from 3.01 billion to 8.16 billion in 1996.

Not surprisingly, this surge in banking activity has driven up industry operating expenses, from £5.4 billion in 1980 to £23.6 billion in 1996, a CAGR of almost 10%. Industry employment, however, rose only slowly up

Fig 1.4 Commercial banking activity growth

Assets, 1980-96

£ billions

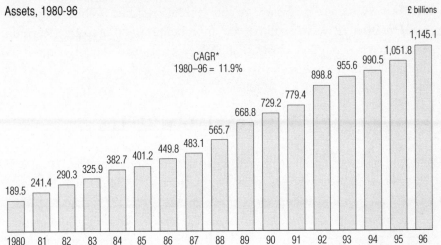

CAGR*
1980–96 = 11.9%

189.5 241.4 290.3 325.9 382.7 401.2 449.8 483.1 565.7 668.8 729.2 779.4 898.8 955.6 990.5 1,051.8 1,145.1

1980 81 82 83 84 85 86 87 88 89 90 91 92 93 94 95 96

Non-cash payments**, 1980-96

Billions of transactions

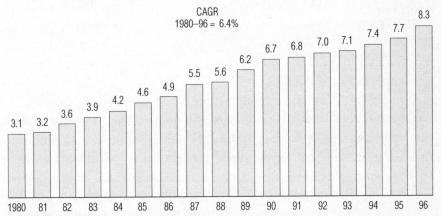

CAGR
1980–96 = 6.4%

3.1 3.2 3.6 3.9 4.2 4.6 4.9 5.5 5.6 6.2 6.7 6.8 7.0 7.1 7.4 7.7 8.3

1980 81 82 83 84 85 86 87 88 89 90 91 92 93 94 95 96

* Compound annual growth rate
** Excludes PO order book payments and cash acquistions

Source: BBA, BSA, Housing Finance Statistics, APACS, MMG analysis

to 1989, and has since been dropping, ending 1996 only marginally above its 1980 level (Figure 1.6). This reduction in staff numbers has to some extent been forced on the banks, as staff have become increasingly scarce and therefore expensive (for example, as the number of school leavers has declined), but has largely been driven by cost-reduction initiatives aiming to improve poor financial results.

It is the substitution of technology for labour over this period, with the resulting gains in productivity, that has allowed the industry to handle the

Fig 1.5 Growth in account holding

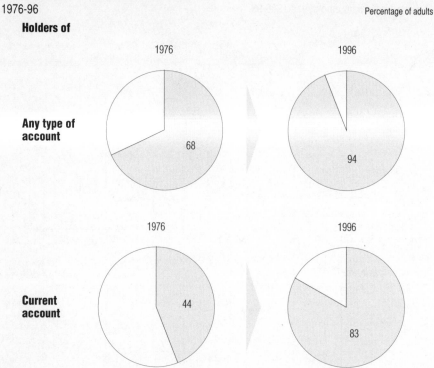

1976-96   Percentage of adults

Holders of

Any type of account

1976 — 68

1996 — 94

Current account

1976 — 44

1996 — 83

Source: APACS

big increase in volumes while reducing staff numbers. What has been called the 'retail banking revolution' could not have happened without IT. The pattern and effects of this technological revolution are explained further in Chapter 2.

The increase in banking activity and the influx of new technology, however, could not have influenced banking in the 1980s as much as they did without the fundamental changes in the 'rules of the game' that took place over the same period.

CHANGES IN THE RULES

Previously, the different types of institutions in the UK banking system specialised to a large degree by product. Through their membership and ownership of the Clearing House (the centralised, self-regulated system for exchanging and settling cheques), the Big Four effectively controlled the payments system, enjoying a virtual monopoly on wholesale and retail cur-

Fig 1.6 Commercial banking industry employment*

Full-time-equivalent employees 1980-96   '000, percent

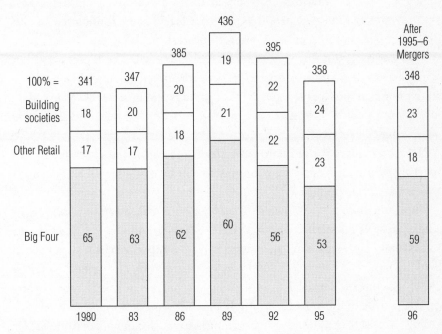

CAGR
1980–89 = 2.8%
1989–96 = -3.2%

* Domestic employment by UK commercial banking institutions
Note: Abbey National is shown in building societies until 1989

Source: BBA, BSA, MMG analysis

rent account balances and related lending. They did not, however, compete for savings accounts, made few consumer loans (except through their finance houses) and wrote very few mortgages.

The Other Retail banks were niche players. TSB was a collection of savings banks, offering consumer loans and limited payment services, Girobank offered a limited payments service based on current accounts through the Post Office, and the Co-operative Bank was linked to the consumer co-operative movement. Yorkshire Bank was a regional branch banking franchise jointly owned by the Big Four.

The building societies effectively ran a mortgage cartel and dominated retail savings, but offered only the most limited payment services through agency arrangements with the banks. The Big Four and the building societies avoided direct competition with each other, even though their retail customers overlapped to a large extent.

Stockbrokers and jobbers, merchant bankers, discount houses and other City institutions had well-defined, and to a certain extent exclusive, wholesale markets. Insurance companies, estate agents, solicitors and other independent financial advisors also served distinct consumer markets. This sharp separation in roles, products and clients had some foundation in law, but depended more on custom and self-interest.

And yet, by 1990, this picture had largely changed. The Big Four, Other Retail banks and building societies were all directly competing for consumer deposits and loans, especially for savings and mortgages. Many were also selling pensions, unit trusts, insurance, securities, estate agency and other financial services.

What changes in the regulatory environment during the 1980s led to this blurring of the previously clear boundaries in financial services? There are five in particular (Figure 1.7).

First, *the ending of 50 years of exchange control, and the abolition of credit controls on sterling lending* (1979–80) helped push the Big Four to shift their focus away from wholesale and international business to branch banking and their personal and smaller corporate customers. Without exchange controls, large UK companies could borrow in any currency in any capital market in the world. The Big Four's lucrative near-monopoly of providing overdraft credit and other advances to large companies came under attack from the emergence of sterling commercial paper and other sources of cheaper finance. Although the Big Four dominated sterling commercial paper, its returns were slight in comparison to returns from traditional bank lending. On the other hand, they could now lend their sterling resources freely to the personal sector, and did so by expanding direct consumer lending and the credit card business, and by entering the mortgage market.

Second, *the opening up of membership of the payments system* after 1985 was a key step in enabling other institutions to offer current account services in competition with the Big Four. In 1970 there were only six members of the Bankers' Clearing House (the Big Four, Coutts and Williams & Glyn's), which was operated and owned by its members (in contrast with the system in the US, where the Federal Reserve Banks in effect, created the national payment system). In the mid-1970s the Clearing House banks admitted three Other Retail banks (as participants, not members) – the National Girobank, the Co-operative Bank and what was then called the Central Trustee Savings Bank. This was mainly done to

Fig 1.7 Phases of competitive development

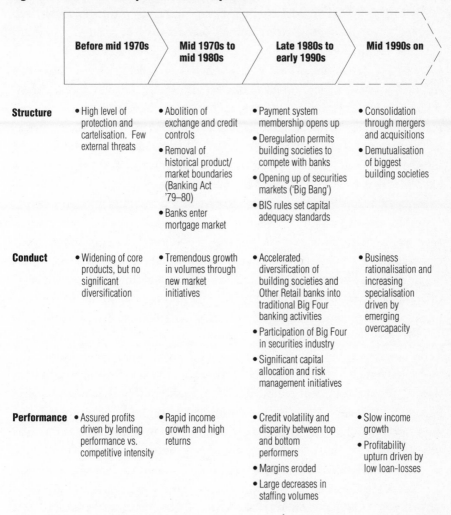

	Before mid 1970s	Mid 1970s to mid 1980s	Late 1980s to early 1990s	Mid 1990s on
Structure	• High level of protection and cartelisation. Few external threats	• Abolition of exchange and credit controls • Removal of historical product/ market boundaries (Banking Act '79–80) • Banks enter mortgage market	• Payment system membership opens up • Deregulation permits building societies to compete with banks • Opening up of securities markets ('Big Bang') • BIS rules set capital adequacy standards	• Consolidation through mergers and acquisitions • Demutualisation of biggest building societies
Conduct	• Widening of core products, but no significant diversification	• Tremendous growth in volumes through new market initiatives	• Accelerated diversification of building societies and Other Retail banks into traditional Big Four banking activities • Participation of Big Four in securities industry • Significant capital allocation and risk management initiatives	• Business rationalisation and increasing specialisation driven by emerging overcapacity
Performance	• Assured profits driven by lending performance vs. competitive intensity	• Rapid income growth and high returns	• Credit volatility and disparity between top and bottom performers • Margins eroded • Large decreases in staffing volumes	• Slow income growth • Profitability upturn driven by low loan-losses

spread costs, especially of the new automated Clearing House BACS (Bankers' Automated Clearing Services), which the members had jointly developed. Eventually the monopoly on payment systems enjoyed by the Big Four began to spring leaks. The Co-operative Bank, lacking in volume of its own, began to offer access to clearing on very attractive terms to building societies and other competitors, such as Citibank. The Child Report (December 1984), which recommended opening access to the clearing system, simply recognised reality. Now, several Other Retail banks, notably Abbey National, and the largest building societies, have joined the clearing system and offer current account services.

A third important regulatory change was *the building societies' deregulation* of 1986. This broadened the societies' access to wholesale funds, and enabled them to change from mutual associations into publicly owned banking companies, and to offer a wider range of financial services – notably, interest-bearing current accounts. The fullest example has been Abbey National, which demutualised in 1989, converting its status from building society to bank, and which has progressively tackled the core banking markets by offering current account services and reducing prices on overdraft facilities. Most of the other building societies have also moved into banking, and increasing numbers are now following Abbey National's example by demutualising, the most notable being Halifax, the Woolwich, Alliance & Leicester and Northern Rock.

Today, the distinction between a bank account and a building society account, once so clear cut, has blurred in the minds of consumers, especially younger ones. As a result, most banks have been forced to pay interest on current accounts, in addition to offering a plethora of high-interest savings accounts. The proportion of all accounts held in banks that received interest almost doubled from 40% in 1988 to 78% by 1996.

Two other important changes should be mentioned. The 'big bang', the 1986 *opening of the securities markets* and implied reorganisation of the Stock Exchange, allowed the Big Four (and a range of foreign banks) to participate in the securities industry, offering them what they hoped would be access to a major new source of profitability, but proving a mixed blessing, especially given the crash of October 1987. Also, the *BIS capital adequacy rules*, together with a more strenuous and formal regulatory regime through the Banking Act of 1979 and the Financial Services Act of 1986, increased the pressure on the Big Four to build capital and to allocate it according to the different risks inherent in their activities and assets.

These are radical changes for any 'traditional' industry to absorb. What has been their effect on the relative economic strength of industry participants?

INCREASING COMPETITIVE INTENSITY

Traditional role of banking challenged

Despite the dramatic growth in their assets since 1980, banks and building societies as a whole faced increasing competition from other channels for the use and provision of funds, and saw a significant reduction in their share of financial activity in the economy over the same period (Figures 1.8 and 1.9). The trend towards financial disintermediation, which removes the banks from the equation and brings the borrowers and lenders of funds together, had started before that period, helped by the development of the wholesale and retail financial markets. The period since 1980, however, brought an acceleration in this trend. Helped by deregulation and advances in information technology, non-bank channels grew rapidly, at the expense of banks and building societies.

Fig 1.8 Shift in personal sector financial assets
1980-96   £ billions, percent

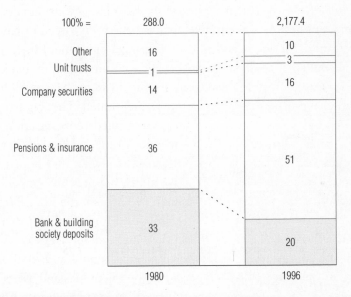

Source: Office for National Statistics, MMG analysis

This trend is threatening banking's traditional role and, while it still allowed the industry to grow significantly, it increased the pressures on banking institutions by broadening their competitive arena. The Big Four and the other institutions realised that business was being lost not only to other banking players, who might have been facing similar financial pressures and therefore might pose less of a threat in bad times, but also to players as diverse as pension funds, unit trusts, and the stock market.

Many banks and building societies responded to this trend on the per-

Fig 1.9 Shift in corporate sector financial liabilities
1980-96

£ billions, percent

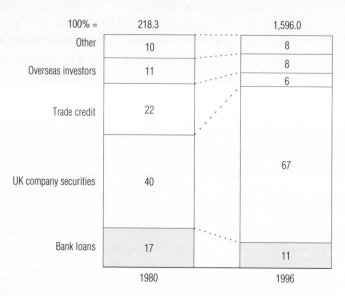

Source: Office for National Statistics, MMG analysis

sonal side by launching products that minimised financial intermediation and generated mainly fee income, such as unit trusts. Similarly, on the corporate side, banks – especially the Big Four – tried to capture more non-interest income by expanding their investment banking activities. While these efforts were in some cases successful, they did not have a significant effect on the loss of share of financial activity by banking institutions, and by 1996 this share stood at less than two-thirds of its 1980 level.

Big Four under attack

Between 1980 and the mid 1990s the Big Four's dominance of the UK banking industry, in terms of asset share and branch networks, was gradually eroded.

Although their assets were growing strongly, at a CAGR of 12.4% between 1980 and 1990, the Big Four were simply not expanding at the rate of their competitors (Figure 1.10). The Other Retail banks increased assets at a CAGR of 21.9% and the building societies at a 15.0% rate between 1980 and 1990. And between 1990 and 1995, before the addition of TSB and Cheltenham & Gloucester, the Big Four's assets grew at an annual rate of only 5.7%, while the rest of the industry grew at a rate of 9.5%.

One institution in particular has emerged to join the Big Four clearing banks in a 'Big Five', as they are increasingly called. Abbey National, with £116 billion in assets in 1996, is 21% larger than the smallest of the Big Four, Midland. While each of the Big Four grew its assets at a CAGR of between 9% and 11% between 1980 and 1996, Abbey National grew at 18%. Abbey National is now the twenty-second largest European bank in terms of first tier capital, and the fourth largest UK bank if the Midland subsidiary of HSBC is viewed separately from its parent.

On a smaller, but still significant, scale TSB had assets of £30.3 billion in 1995, making it over 40% of the size of Lloyds. Between 1980 and 1995, TSB's assets grew at a CAGR of 11%, and it expanded aggressively into wholesale businesses. However, its efforts to become a full-line provider on its own merits were not successful and in 1995 it was absorbed into the Big Four by merging with Lloyds.

Within the building society sector, there has been rapid consolidation

Fig 1.10 Share of industry assets

1980-96

£ billions, percent

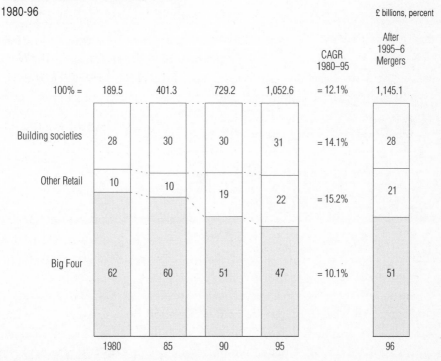

Note: Abbey National shown in Other Retail from 1990; CAGRs are calculated with Abbey National in Other Retail throughout, for consistency

Source: BBA, BSA, MMG analysis

around the six biggest institutions. Each of these has £12 billion or more in assets, the largest – the Halifax – having over £102 billion. Between 1980 and 1996, the number of societies fell from 273 to 76 while the group's assets grew by a CAGR of 12%.

As competitors have grown more rapidly, the Big Four's share of the industry expense base has declined, from 75% in 1980 to 69% in 1996, despite the recent Lloyds mergers.

The relative decline of the Big Four shows clearly in their branch networks (Figure 1.11). In 1972 the Big Four controlled virtually all high-street banking in England and Wales, owning 11,509 branches (65%) out of a total of 17,691 in all of the UK. In a paper-based world, convenient access to a local branch was, and still is, the key to collecting deposits. In 1980 they owned 54% of the total, and by 1995 47%, although this share grew back to 56% with the addition of TSB and Cheltenham & Glouces-

Fig 1.11 Branch networks

1980-96

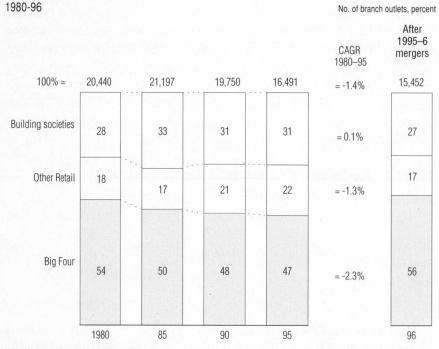

No. of branch outlets, percent

Note: Abbey National shown in Other Retail from 1990; CAGRs are calculated with Abbey National in Other Retail throughout, for consistency
Branches exclude Girobank post office outlets

Source: BBA, BSA, MMG analysis

ter to Lloyds Bank. The Big Four shed over 2,800 branches between 1985 and 1995, and all have programmes to reduce the number of their full-service branches further. In contrast, the building societies added 1,300 new outlets from 1980 to 1987, but they had to rationalise subsequently, shedding over 900 branches. The Other Retail banks were split between the Scottish clearers plus TSB, which followed the pattern of the Big Four, shedding branches aggressively since 1980, and the rest, who had until recently been either maintaining or even increasing their branch networks.

The Big Four's branch networks are still massive. However, in an industry where the branch has always been the basic business unit and the key element in the distribution system, the relative decline of the Big Four is significant.

Profits volatile

The pre-tax profits and rates of return in the industry reflect its increasingly competitive environment.

Between 1980 and 1986, pre-tax industry profits grew steadily at a CAGR of 16.4%. Profits fell between 1986 and 1992, to give a negative CAGR of -3.7%. The massive provisions, especially for less-developed country (LDC) debt, in 1987 and 1989, and the unusually low provisions in 1988 by the Big Four, caused sharp swings in performance in those years (Figure 1.12). Since 1992 profits have recovered and the Big Four have seen a period of sustained growth, as they have emerged from the recession, which exposed their poor lending practices (e.g., to small businesses), and have required little additional provision for bad debt.

Table 1.1   Pre-tax profits – compound annual growth rate (%)

	1980–86	1986–92	1992–96
Big Four	13.2	–13.8	50.1
Other Retail	16.3	–0.1	37.6
Building societies	28.0	7.7	16.7

The trends are similar for all three categories of institutions, but most severe for the Big Four, as shown in Table 1.1. Although LDC loan loss provisions distorted their results in the late 1980s, the Big Four earned over £200 million less in 1992 than in 1980.

Fig 1.12 Pre-tax earnings
1980-96

£ billions

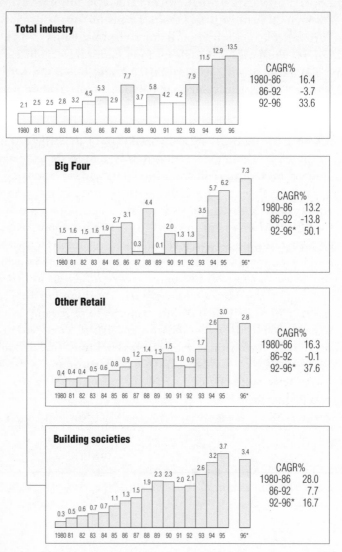

Total industry

Year	Value
1980	2.1
81	2.5
82	2.5
83	2.8
84	3.2
85	4.5
86	5.3
87	2.9
88	7.7
89	3.7
90	5.8
91	4.2
92	4.2
93	7.9
94	11.5
95	12.9
96	13.5

CAGR%
1980-86 16.4
86-92 -3.7
92-96 33.6

Big Four

Year	Value
1980	1.5
81	1.6
82	1.5
83	1.6
84	1.9
85	2.7
86	3.1
87	0.3
88	4.4
89	0.1
90	2.0
91	1.3
92	1.3
93	3.5
94	5.7
95	6.2
96*	7.3

CAGR%
1980-86 13.2
86-92 -13.8
92-96* 50.1

Other Retail

Year	Value
1980	0.4
81	0.4
82	0.4
83	0.5
84	0.6
85	0.8
86	0.9
87	1.2
88	1.4
89	1.3
90	1.5
91	1.0
92	0.9
93	1.7
94	2.6
95	3.0
96*	2.8

CAGR%
1980-86 16.3
86-92 -0.1
92-96* 37.6

Building societies

Year	Value
1980	0.3
81	0.5
82	0.6
83	0.7
84	0.7
85	1.1
86	1.3
87	1.5
88	1.9
89	2.3
90	2.3
91	2.0
92	2.1
93	2.6
94	3.2
95	3.7
96*	3.4

CAGR%
1980-86 28.0
86-92 7.7
92-96* 16.7

* Due to the 1995–6 mergers, subgroup data for 1996 are not comparable with previous years. CAGRs for 1992–96 have been adjusted accordingly

Note: Abbey National is shown in Other Retail throughout for comparability

Source: BBA, BSA, Housing Finance Statistics, MMG analysis

To some extent these trends were the result of the consumer boom of the mid-1980s and the subsequent recession, but they also reflected increased competition. Up to the early 1990s, the Big Four were losing ground to other institutions in terms of profitability. In 1980, they accounted for 69% of industry profits; by 1992 only 30%. In 1992, building society profits were more than 60% above those of the Big Four, and Other Retail banks earned 70% as much as the Big Four. One Other Retail bank, Abbey National, made more money than three of the Big Four in 1992, and 44% as much as all four combined.

The Other Retail banks and the building societies not only increased the absolute level of their profits, but also maintained or improved their rate of return on equity for most of the 1980s. Although their impressive returns faltered in the early 1990s, in common with the rest of the industry, the decline suffered by the Big Four was steeper (Figure 1.13). The improvement seen since then, especially of the Big Four, is remarkable (Table 1.2).

Table 1.2 Pre-tax return on equity (%)

	1980	1986	1992	1996
Big Four	24.0	25.6	7.3	30.8
Other Retail	24.6	23.1	10.6	29.1
Building societies	17.4	24.3	17.2	20.3

In terms of return on assets, the pattern is similar. During the recession all categories of institutions showed declines from the 1980s level, but the Big Four did worse than the other two categories. By 1996, returns on assets had picked up, although they were still generally at or below their 1980 levels (Table 1.3).

Table 1.3 Pre-tax return on assets (%)

	1980	1986	1992	1996
Big Four	1.25	1.20	0.31	1.28
Other Retail	1.44	1.45	0.56	1.24
Building societies	1.43	1.72	0.83	1.28

Fig 1.13 Pre-tax return on equity

1980-96

Percent

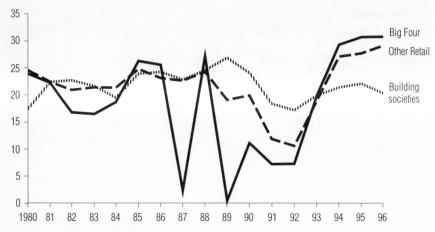

Note: For building societies, total reserves are used as equity

Source: MMG analysis

Recent profitability figures are making many top executives across the industry, and especially at the Big Four, feel that their investments in IT, cost re-engineering and improved risk management are paying off. In fact, the recent profit upturn is traceable primarily to just one factor – the decline in loan loss provisions. There does not appear to be a fundamental long-term shift in industry economics.

Pre-tax return on assets improved for the industry between 1992 and 1996 by 77 basis points (0.77%) and for the Big Four by 97 basis points, a truly extraordinary recovery. However, the reduction of loan loss provisions accounted for 91 and 110 basis point increases respectively (Figure 1.14). In other words, operations were in fact less profitable in 1996 than in 1992 and were rescued by the dramatic decline in loan losses.

Of course the decline in losses is not to be ignored. To the extent that it is the result of improved credit risk assessment techniques and processes, it could have a long-term effect on banking economics. It is more likely, however, that the banks are experiencing the results of the end of a prolonged and acute recession that cleared many bad loans from their books. There is, as yet, no evidence that other bad credits will not reinflate loss totals during the next down phase of the credit cycle.

Should loan loss provisions return to their ten-year average rate, they

Fig 1.14 Sources of change in pre-tax return on assets

1992-96   Basis points

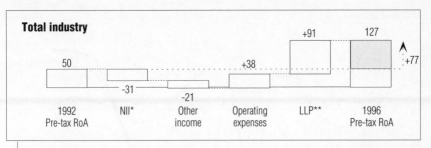

Total industry

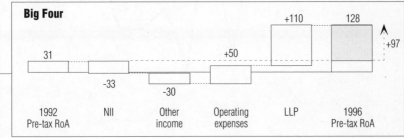

Big Four

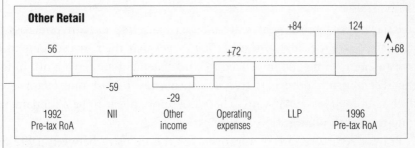

Other Retail

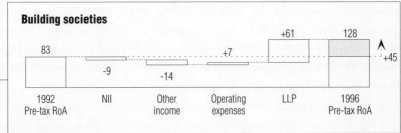

Building societies

* Net interest income
** Loan loss provisions

Source: MMG analysis

Fig 1.15 Loan loss provisions/assets ratio

10-year overview, 1987-96

Basis points

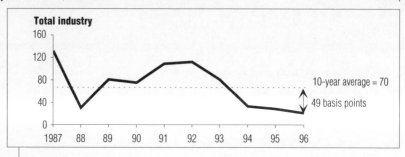

Total industry

10-year average = 70

49 basis points

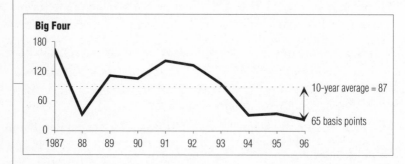

Big Four

10-year average = 87

65 basis points

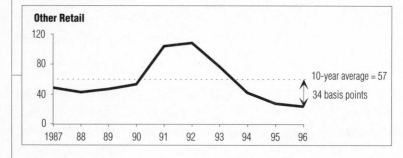

Other Retail

10-year average = 57

34 basis points

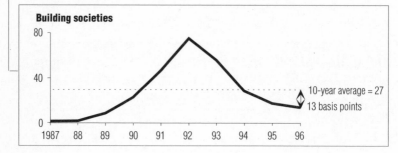

Building societies

10-year average = 27

13 basis points

Source: MMG analysis

would strike a whole 49 basis points from the return on assets of the industry and 65 basis points from that of the Big Four (Figure 1.15). Return on assets would then fall, especially for the Big Four, back to levels similar to those observed in the early 1990s. The large investments in IT and cost reduction would have had little value other than to have made possible the processing of increased industry volumes. The situation for the Other Retail banks and the building societies was directionally similar but not as pronounced as for the Big Four.

It is possible that a structural change in the economics of the industry and especially the Big Four has set in: basically, income growth may be decelerating at a rate that may not be countered sufficiently in the medium term by their efforts to contain costs. It is no surprise then to see the banks and building societies looking to merge; mergers provide a further source of cost reductions.

Revenue growth slowing

If we take a closer look at the drivers of profitability, we see two significant forces at work. First, the Big Four's net interest income growth, in absolute values, has slowed (from a CAGR of 10.6% in 1980–8 to one of 3.0% in 1988–96, not accounting for growth from mergers and acquisitions). During 1989–94, when the trend towards paying interest on current accounts began, net interest income for the Big Four increased by only £325 million or 0.6% CAGR; the modest increase in growth in 1995–6, to just over 4%, has only partly offset the slowdown over the previous period. As a result, the Big Four, which began the 1980s with net interest income at 3.7% of assets, ended 1996 with net interest income at 2.4% of assets, giving a negative CAGR for the net-interest-income/assets ratio over this period (Figure 1.16).

A second factor affecting the performance of the Big Four is the slowing of the growth in non-interest income (mainly fees and commissions), which had been strong in the early 1980s. Between 1980 and 1988 the Big Four expanded non-interest income at a CAGR of 16.4%, but this declined to 8.5% between 1988 and 1996 (not accounting for growth from mergers and acquisitions). The reduction in average inflation from 6.1% to 4.6% accounts for part of this slower growth, of course, but clearly not for the biggest part.

To be sure, the Big Four also slowed the rate of growth of expenses. Their operating expenses grew by a CAGR of 12.3% between 1980 and

Fig 1.16 Change in Big Four profitability

1980-96   Percent

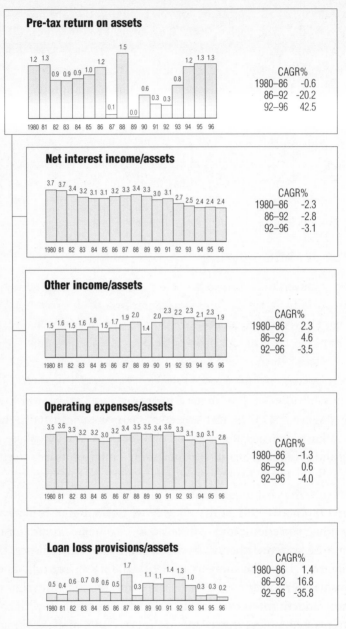

Pre-tax return on assets

	CAGR%
1980–86	-0.6
86–92	-20.2
92–96	42.5

Net interest income/assets

	CAGR%
1980–86	-2.3
86–92	-2.8
92–96	-3.1

Other income/assets

	CAGR%
1980–86	2.3
86–92	4.6
92–96	-3.5

Operating expenses/assets

	CAGR%
1980–86	-1.3
86–92	0.6
92–96	-4.0

Loan loss provisions/assets

	CAGR%
1980–86	1.4
86–92	16.8
92–96	-35.8

Source: BBA, Annual reports, MMG analysis

Fig 1.17 Average rate of year-on-year change in Big Four revenue and cost

1980-96   Percent

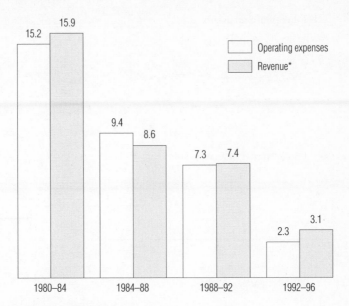

* Net interest income + other operating income

Source: BBA, Annual reports, MMG analysis

1988, but growth fell to 4.8% between 1988 and 1996. However, the slower growth of costs just about compensated for the slower growth of revenue (Figure 1.17). In fact what has happened is that the Big Four appear to have managed to control costs to an extent, but these are still growing and revenue pressures are increasing rapidly and are offsetting any savings.

As a result, the cost/income ratio of the Big Four dropped only slightly between 1980 and 1995. At the same time, Other Retail banks and especially building societies improved their cost/income positions considerably and therefore widened the gap between their ratios and those of the Big Four (Figure 1.18). The mergers of 1995 and 1996 brought operations with considerably lower cost/income ratios into the Big Four, thus producing a step-reduction in cost/income to 64%. But the gap with the other players remained much greater than in the early 1980s. In the sixteen years since 1980, the economics of the Big Four have not only failed to improve fundamentally, but have actually deteriorated relative to their smaller retail competitors.

Fig 1.18 Cost/income ratios

1980-95   Percent

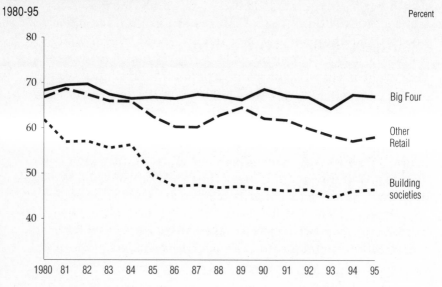

1996 (after mergers)   Percent

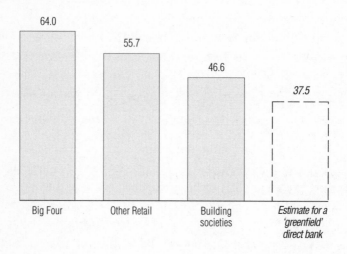

Source: MMG analysis

UNCERTAIN OUTLOOK

Relentless increase in competition

Competitive intensity is not showing signs of decreasing. Aggressive new product initiatives are being launched almost daily, and new players, ever more unconventional, are entering the market. The Big Four now have to compete with Direct Line's mortgages, Prudential's current accounts, and Marks & Spencer's and Virgin Direct's savings products; they have to sell credit cards against US non-banks undercutting them significantly on price; they have to sustain income streams in products like mortgages and insurance against specialists and direct providers with often a much lower expense base; they have to face the Scottish banks, who are finally finding a potentially powerful way to enter the English market, through alliances with supermarkets; and they have to find a way to compete with looming dangers like the Internet, and electronic commerce.

Clearly, the high levels of recent profits are encouraging new players to enter the market, especially as they realise that they can probably compete from a lower cost base than the established players. The cost/income ratio of these new players, whose strategy is often to set-up 'greenfield' direct banking operations, is likely to be below 40%, whereas even after decades of aggressive investments in technology to improve productivity, the comparable ratio for the Big Four seems to be stuck above 60%, with that of the Other Retail banks and building societies in the range of 45–55% (Figure 1.18).

Given these increasing pressures, it is not surprising that investors and credit agencies alike agree that banking is no longer the stable industry it was sixteen years ago. Share return volatility has never returned to the low levels of the early 1980s, when some shares were actually less volatile than the market as a whole (Figure 1.19). And NatWest and Barclays, the two biggest institutions, have not recaptured triple-A ratings, despite exceptionally high profits in recent years (Figure 1.20).

Consolidation to the rescue?

The UK banking industry saw, in 1995 and 1996, a series of high-profile mergers. In 1996, three of the top six institutions were involved in merger activity that increased their size considerably and set them further apart

Fig 1.19 Big Four share returns volatility* compared with London stock market

Share return indices vs. FTSE-All Share return index, 1980-96

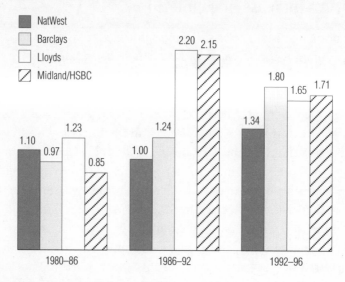

* Relative volatility is measured as the ratio of variation coefficients

Source: Datastream, MMG analysis

Fig 1.20 Standard & Poor's credit ratings

The cases of Barclays & NatWest, 1983-96

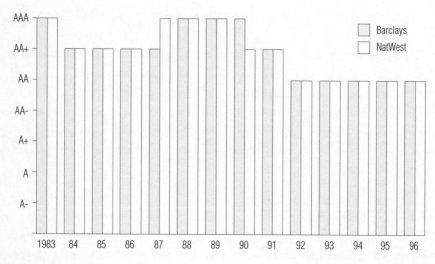

Source: Standard & Poor's

Fig 1.21 Total assets by institution

1996   £ billions

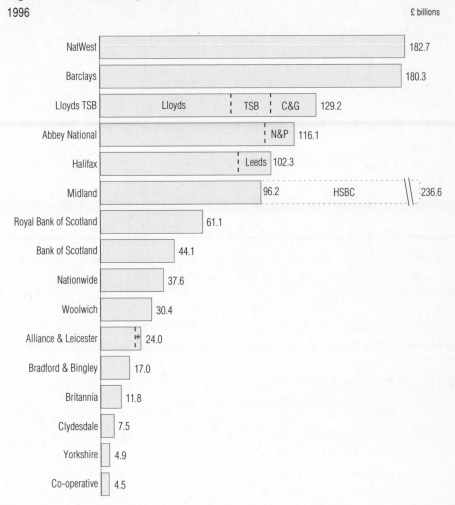

* Girobank
Source: Annual reports, MMG analysis

from the smaller players (Figure 1.21). These in turn have now become more susceptible to takeovers, and further consolidation could follow.

In their consolidated form the Big Four account for 69% of the industry's spending versus 63% before the mergers, and 70% of IT spending versus 65% (Figure 1.22).

Fig 1.22 Top ten institutions' share of commercial banking industry*

1995-96   Percent

☐ Big Four

Assets

Pre-1995/96 mergers	47	78
Post-1995/96 mergers	51	86

Employees

Pre-1995/96 mergers	53	79
Post-1995/96 mergers	59	83

Operating expenses

Pre-1995/96 mergers	63	86
Post-1995/96 mergers	69	90

IT spend

Pre-1995/96 mergers	65	87
Post-1995/96 mergers	70	90

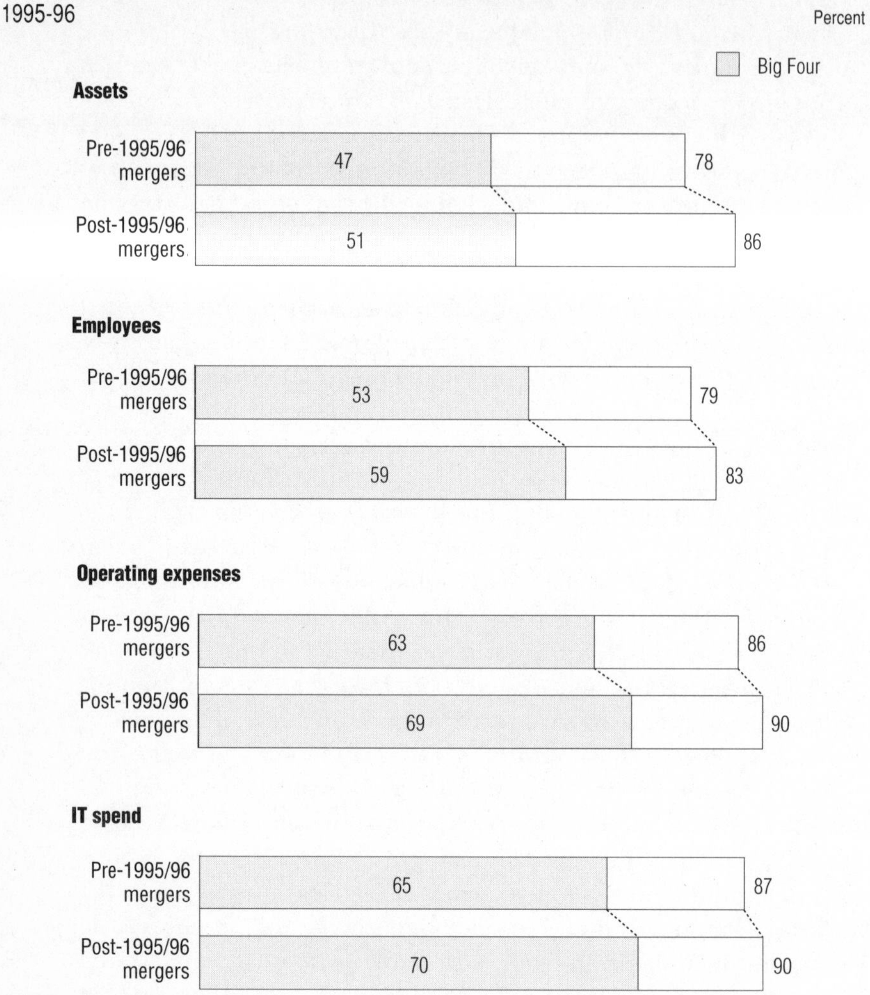

* Top ten in terms of assets:
  Pre-mergers – Big Four, Abbey National, Halifax, Royal Bank of Scotland, Nationwide, Bank of Scotland, TSB
  Post-mergers – Big Four, Abbey National, Halifax, Royal Bank of Scotland, Bank of Scotland, Nationwide, Woolwich

Source: MMG analysis

This trend towards consolidation is raising hopes in the industry. Executives are looking to the US, where the recent mergers within states ('intra-market') appear to be enabling new large players to use their market power to sustain relatively high prices for their services. It is not clear, however, whether the mergers in the UK will have the same effect; the pre-merger situation was not as fragmented as in the US and a lot of the merger and acquisition activity in the UK may actually be increasing rather than decreasing competition, by creating large credible alternatives to the Big Four. On the cost side, senior executives are hoping that increased scale will enable them to invest in new technologies that will lead to a lasting reduction in the cost base – e.g., imaging, which is expected to lower substantially the cost of item processing. At the same time, mergers may make further cost reductions possible by eliminating overlapping facilities – e.g., branches and data centres. In the US, some intramarket mergers have succeeded in effecting economies equal to 35% of the cost base of the acquired institution; and such savings are net of investments required to raise the acquiree's capabilities to the level of those of the acquirer. Nonetheless, the capacity of banks to drive such savings to the bottom line is, as we have already suggested, questionable. The critical skill for banks will be the ability to identify and manage effectively those technology investments that can generate sustainable shareholder value.

The next chapter examines in greater detail how these technology investments transform banking.

HOW TECHNOLOGY TRANSFORMS BANKING

In the previous chapter we saw that, despite recent profitability, banks, especially the Big Four, are coming under increasing pressure to contain costs in response to greater competitive intensity. Automation is an important weapon in this struggle. IT systems related to banking, including processing and communications devices, have now improved to the point where they permit a fundamental change in how banking services are produced and delivered. Machines can work much more quickly, accurately and cost-effectively than human beings in many banking tasks. As in many other industries, technology is now clearly displacing labour in banking. Does this spell good news for bank profits?

The experience of the US banking industry indicates that it may not. In the States, as in the UK more recently, a big increase in systems expenditure has been followed by a reduction in industry employment. However, there was also a sharp drop in profits in many lines of business that is unexplained by purely cyclical factors. This apparent link between automation and reduced profitability represents a warning signal for the UK industry.

An examination by product line and by business suggests that the automation of banking is happening in four stages, starting with customer account records – the most labour-intensive activities – and moving towards integrated systems that will link all aspects of customers' relationship with the banks. At each stage, new competitors armed with new technologies may appear. By being aware of which stage their businesses are in, management can understand the process and formulate appropriate responses. A useful way of looking at this problem is an 'S-curve analysis', which shows how a hitherto successful business may have to become a 'defender' in the face of new 'attackers'.

THE TECHNOLOGY INVESTMENT DRIVE

An early success story: using IT to automate cheque clearing

Throughout the 1960s and 1970s the London Clearing House banks were applying IT to their internal operations, and were especially effective in co-operative improvements to the Clearing House-based payments systems, notably BACS, for regular automated payments (and later CHAPS, for high value, same-day clearing). Each of the Big Four banks used early mainframe computers in a similar way – namely, to get the current accounts in the branches off paper ledgers and on to electronic ones. In addition, each bank established a computerised cheque clearing department near the London Clearing House, where current account ledgers were updated just before cheques were exchanged. The current account was thus closely tied to cheque clearing, both functionally and physically.

Although the branches were no longer maintaining the current account ledger, they were still paying and cashing cheques and receiving deposits over the counter. As late as 1978, nearly two-thirds of bank staff (120,000 people) were employed in this way in the six Clearing House banks, at a cost of £800 million a year. The traditional system of transporting cheques to the London Clearing House for exchange and getting them back to the branches on which they were drawn was still in place. A customer's current account was specific to that customer's branch of deposit, both in law and in practice, and the decision to pay or bounce a cheque lay with the bank manager.

The next step was the partial automation of the cheque clearing process with MICR (magnetic ink character recognition) technology, which was initially directed towards the bank clearing departments that stood between the thousands of branches and the Clearing House itself. These departments were the hubs of the system, but also its choke points. In the 1970s the 10,000 branches of the Big Four were taking in over ten million cheques a day, of which two-thirds had to be exchanged through the Clearing House. At least one-and-a-half million cheques passed through each bank's central clearing department in a five-hour cycle (300,000 an hour). Without high speed reader-sorter technology, these volumes could not have been handled.

However, even with automation at the hub, the cheques still physically moved to and from the thousands of branches, where they were hand-sorted and filed. This highly labour-intensive activity convinced the Clearing House members to use technology to replace cheques in the payment system as much as possible, and to automate the handling of cheques in branches. Did early success in cheque-clearing carry through into other stages of automation, and into other lines of business? Part 2 of the book traces these efforts in detail.

To a large extent, the clearing banks are still running on the applications systems they built in the 1970s, and continue to benefit from the efficiencies created by automating the costly paper-based clearing. On the whole, the 1970s was a decade in which the clearing banks as a group looked to technology to ease their common cost problems, rather than using it to establish competitive advantage in products or services. As a result, the co-operative use of technology by the Clearing House banks has made the UK the most successful of the cheque-writing countries in slowing and eventually displacing the growth of paper-based payments. This early success was followed by further IT expenditures on a big scale. The inherent profitability of these moves would have brought significant benefits to the banks, had Midland not introduced free banking on accounts in credit – a strategy which its competitors had to follow.

IT expenditure up, bank employment down: profits?

Four UK banks are in the world's top fifteen banking IT spenders (Figure 2.1). The two largest UK spenders, Barclays and NatWest, respectively spent around £1 billion ($1.57 billion) and £850 million ($1.35 billion) in 1996. Apart from the US, no other country in the world has four banks on the technological scale of the major UK clearers. Systems intensity for the industry as a whole – the proportion of expenses accounted for by IT – has more than doubled since 1980, from 7.6% to 16.2%. For the Big Four, systems intensity approached 17% in 1996 and is continuing to grow towards the 20% mark.

The Other Retail banks and the building societies in the UK are not in the same league as the Big Four in terms of IT spending. Of the £3.82 billion spent by the UK industry on IT in 1996, the Big Four spent 70%, the Other Retail banks 17% and the building societies 13%. The two smaller categories lag the Big Four in systems intensity, and will continue to do so, given their simpler mix of businesses and lower processing demands. How-

Fig 2.1 Top bank IT spenders

1996

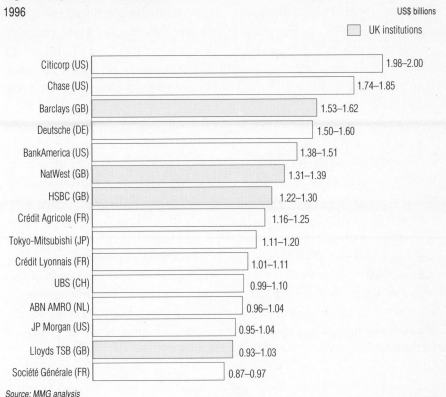

US$ billions

☐ UK institutions

Bank	US$ billions
Citicorp (US)	1.98–2.00
Chase (US)	1.74–1.85
Barclays (GB)	1.53–1.62
Deutsche (DE)	1.50–1.60
BankAmerica (US)	1.38–1.51
NatWest (GB)	1.31–1.39
HSBC (GB)	1.22–1.30
Crédit Agricole (FR)	1.16–1.25
Tokyo-Mitsubishi (JP)	1.11–1.20
Crédit Lyonnais (FR)	1.01–1.11
UBS (CH)	0.99–1.10
ABN AMRO (NL)	0.96–1.04
JP Morgan (US)	0.95-1.04
Lloyds TSB (GB)	0.93–1.03
Société Générale (FR)	0.87–0.97

Source: MMG analysis

ever, they are increasing their systems spending more quickly than the Big Four (Figure 2.2) and are becoming significant IT participants.

To a large degree, this technology expenditure is a direct substitute for other spending, especially staff costs. This relationship has been the same since the beginning of the industrial revolution – and what was true for steel, cars and computers is now coming true for banking (Figure 2.3). The relationship between IT spend and employment in UK banking falls into two phases (as shown in Figure 1.6). Between 1980 and 1989 employment grew modestly, at a CAGR of 2.8%, in spite of the rapid increases in banking activity described in the previous chapter. Employment peaked in 1989, and since then has fallen, by 88,000 full-time equivalent employees, to 348,000 in 1996 – a figure lower than in the mid 1980s. Employment at the Big Four alone decreased by 82,500 full-time equivalent employees, a drop of 31% since 1989 (Figure 2.4). All the Big Four have announced plans to reduce staff even further over the next few years, as have Other

Fig 2.2 UK banking IT spend
1980–96

£ billions, percent

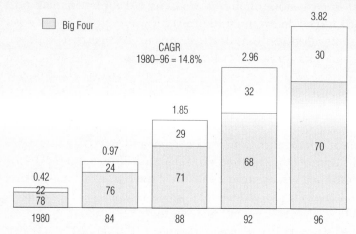

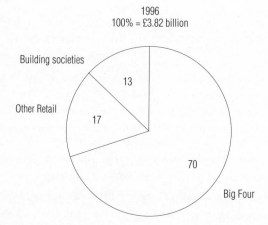

Note: 1996 shares are not directly comparable with earlier years due to mergers across groups
Source: MMG analysis

Retail banks. Even building society employment, which had continued to increase when the other groups were shedding staff, has now been decreasing for a number of years and is likely to accelerate its decline as the current round of building society consolidation gathers pace.

This job loss would probably have occurred earlier but for the protected market positions of these banks in the 1980s, the increase in business volumes, their traditional reluctance to make people redundant, and the effectiveness of staff unions. However, it is now clear that technology is

Fig 2.3 Industry employment life cycle

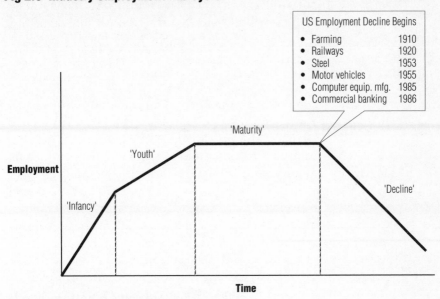

US Employment Decline Begins

- Farming   1910
- Railways   1920
- Steel   1953
- Motor vehicles   1955
- Computer equip. mfg. 1985
- Commercial banking   1986

Fig 2.4 Labour displacement – Big Four

Full-time-equivalent employees, 1989–96

1989=100

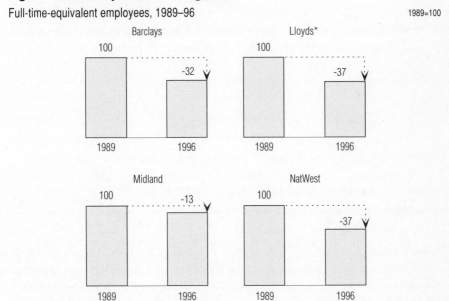

Total fall of 31% equivalent to 82,500 full-time jobs

* Lloyds is shown on a comparable basis to remove effect of additional TSB and C&G staff

Source: BBA,, MMG analysis

replacing jobs, and enormous IT investments are being made to increase productivity. IT spend per employee is now almost ten times its level in 1980 (Figure 2.5). And indeed, when measured as volumes processed per employee, productivity has been growing rapidly: in 1996 banks processed more than two-and-a-half times as many payments per employee as in 1980 (Figure 2.6).

Fig 2.5 IT spend per full-time-equivalent employee

1980–96   £'000s

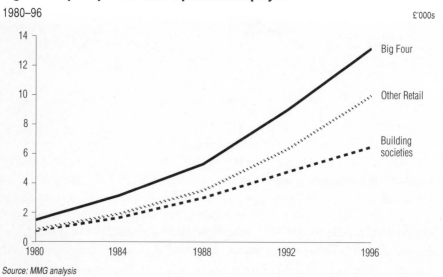

Source: MMG analysis

These advances in productivity have helped control the growth of costs. Yet, while exceptionally low loan loss provisions have driven recent profits up, revenue growth is being driven down by increasing competitive pressures. Increased operational efficiency, the main objective of IT investments, does not appear to be bearing fruit for bank shareholders. In fact, as we saw in Chapter 1, the Big Four's operations, indeed the operations most aggressively targeted with IT investments, have not become much more profitable since 1980, with cost/income ratios stuck well above 60%. At the same time, the operating profitability of Other Retail banks and building societies, whose investments in IT lag significantly behind those of the Big Four, has improved, in some cases considerably.

The Big Four, together with their competitors, would be right to wonder whether their huge investments in IT are therefore a waste or whether they will eventually lead to increased operating profits. Neither of these interpretations is correct. As we saw, the banks' investments in IT are indeed

Fig 2.6 Payments processed per full-time-equivalent employee
1980–96   000s

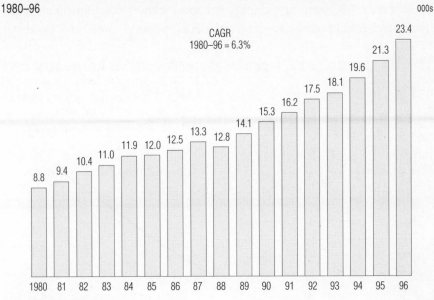

Source: APACS, BBA, MMG analysis

improving productivity. Without those investments, banks would, of course, be left behind in the competitive game and their profitability would suffer as their costs became increasingly higher relative to the industry's. However, IT investments on their own do not lead to increased profits.

First, on their own they, of course, increase costs rather than reduce them, not only because of the high hardware and software costs, but also because of the expensive skilled personnel that must be hired to support the technology. Aggressive and focused efforts by the banks are required to take full advantage of any efficiencies so that other operating costs can be reduced or eliminated. The Big Four banks still have a significant part of the operational infrastructure that they had decades ago, when they were the only payments processors, despite the fact that they have invested sub-stantial amounts in technology that could make that infrastructure obsolete or would require different processes to deliver its full potential, as described in Part 3.

Second, even if banks manage to address the high fixed infrastructure costs and to control their IT spending on a more rational and aggressive basis, IT spending will not on its own improve long-term profitability. It is the thesis of this book that technology investments set in motion a competitive cycle that generates increasing value for customers, but can eventually destroy industry profits rather than improve them. The experience of the US banking industry reinforces this view.

The US experience: IT replaces people, attacks profits

Between 1980 and 1996, IT spending in the US banking industry grew from $3.5 billion to over $20 billion. As a result of this massive increase in technology spending, the US banking industry has been shedding labour (Figure 2.7). Employment in the US industry was at its peak in 1986, at 1.56 million people. By 1996, 214,000 people (almost 14%) had lost their jobs. By the end of the century, employment will almost certainly be below its 1976 level.

Fig 2.7 US banking industry employment and IT spend

1980–96

US$ billions, '000s

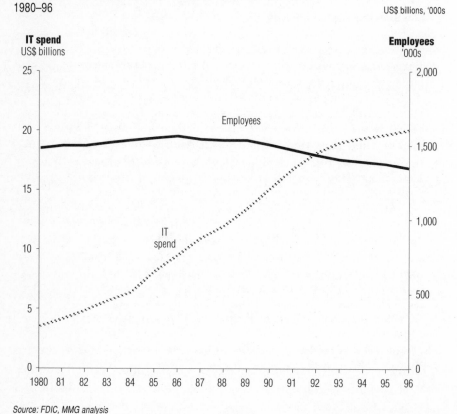

Source: FDIC, MMG analysis

In a few lines of business in the US banking industry systems intensity has now reached 60% and IT has replaced human labour as the dominant means of production. However, the crucial question is: who will benefit economically from this substitution? The evidence is that in these lines of business profitability has actually decreased, and it is the customers or users of bank services, not the banks themselves, who have benefited from the gains in efficiency. One striking example is the international funds-transfer business of the leading New York correspondent banks. Although this is a wholesale rather than a retail or commercial activity, it may point the way for UK banking businesses.

Before the 1970s, making dollar payments for banks outside the US involved a long paper-intensive process. During the early 1970s, official cheque delivery and exchange was automated with CHIPS (Clearing House International Payments System), but the clearing cycle was not changed and otherwise the system remained essentially manual. CHIPS was implemented shortly before the Bretton Woods system of fixed exchange rates was abandoned in 1972, which resulted in a global boom in foreign exchange and Eurodollar trading. Spurred on by this surge in dollar clearing, the US banks invested in automating their internal processing and information systems to interface with CHIPS. They also developed and aggressively marketed proprietary systems for reporting balances and initiating payments, in an attempt to gain market share. IT was being used to transform the process of dollar clearing.

Growing at a compound rate of over 20% a year in volume, and even more in value, dollar clearing became one of the most profitable businesses in international banking. In 1981 – a year of exceptionally high money market rates – the eight leading providers earned pre-tax profits of about $1.2 billion from clearing for overseas correspondents (Figure 2.8). By 1990, however, these same banks as a group made virtually no money from dollar clearing, and several of them suffered large losses. What went wrong?

Automation was very effective. Between 1980 and 1990 funds-transfer volumes in these banks more than doubled, from 73 million transactions a year to 166 million, while total costs increased only 15%, as staff numbers were reduced. As a result, average unit costs were cut in half, from $9.20 per transaction to $4.60 during the decade. The leading CHIPS banks can today process up to three-quarters of all payments with no human intervention whatever, eliminating the source of most errors and most costs.

Fig 2.8 International funds transfer

US case, 1980–90

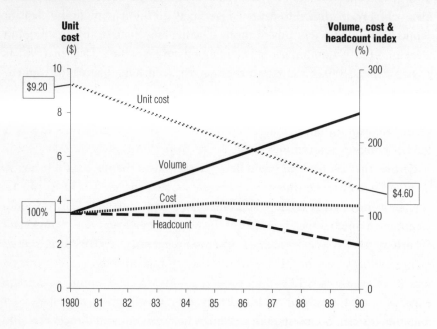

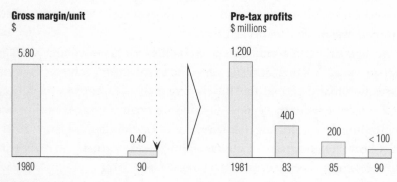

Source: FDIC, MMG analysis

That precisely is the problem: technology made the system too efficient. The automation that drove out human error also provided customers with greatly improved control over their accounts and, perhaps more important, greatly facilitated their ability to switch providers. The transition in late 1981 from next-day settlement to same-day settlement in CHIPS enabled customers to eliminate the high credit balances which had made the semi-automated business of 1981 so lucrative. Profits plunged by two-thirds in two years. As profitability declined, virtually all the leading dollar clearing banks continued to automate, both to cut costs further and to complete development programmes. Systems intensity rose from 15% in 1980 to over 50% in 1990. Efficiency increased, but so did the processing capacity of the systems, and this led to price wars.

International funds-transfer has now become a largely fixed-cost business. All leading competitors have built systems of virtually unlimited capacity, which undermines their ability to price their services profitably. Transfers that cost $9.20 could be priced at $15 or more in 1980, but in 1990 a payment which cost $4.60 might at most have a 'list price' of $5, and customers with large volumes of routine payments could normally negotiate a much lower price. As prices kept being driven down (they have now reached levels as low as $1 to $2) the room for profit margins became a fraction of what it was before the early 1980s. In addition, customers no longer left economically attractive balances which could supplement earnings. Nor could technology investment be cut back: the Federal Reserve imposes strict systems requirements on the banks, to minimise the risks involved in clearing hundreds of billions of dollars through CHIPS each day.

In short, the drawbacks of this massive over-capacity more than offset the immense improvements in efficiency achieved. US dollar clearing is not an isolated example, but rather an example of what has happened and will happen to many other banking businesses. Technology attacks these businesses first for three reasons: the profitability of each transaction is high, the number of major players is small, and the basic transaction is simple and labour intensive. Similarly declining profitability can be seen in other highly-automated wholesale businesses in the US, such as cash management and securities processing. Profitable a decade ago, these businesses are currently break-even or low-margin activities for most providers, loss-makers for others. Like funds transfer, they are characterised by redundant electronic capacity, which banks are selling at cut-throat prices.

Could all this happen in the UK? In particular, are the UK banks currently experiencing an irreversible decline in banking jobs, rather than merely a cyclical dip in employment? And, perhaps more important, will they also find, as in the US, that increased efficiency benefits bank customers rather than bank shareholders?

Fig 2.9 Concentration of retail banking industry

Top-five share of country's total retail banking assets*, 1996   Percent

Canada	77
UK	63
France	49
Germany	42
Japan	41
Italy	36
USA	28

* Covers country's commercial banks and savings institutions. Excludes investment banks and foreign banks

Source: MMG analysis

The two banking industries are very different. The UK has one of the most concentrated financial systems of any major country, while the US as a whole has one of the most fragmented (Figure 2.9). Large-scale processing businesses are less important to the Big Four banks in the UK than they are to the largest US banks (with a few exceptions, such as correspondent banking to Midland). Retail lines, which are very important to the Big Four, may in some cases be less vulnerable in the short term, especially in cases like deposit accounts, where – unlike other retail lines like credit cards – pricing is not transparent and switching providers may involve an element of risk. And systems intensity in the UK processing businesses has not yet reached US levels. But the displacement of labour by technology is a universal phenomenon, and has begun to transform banking across all lines of business, both retail and wholesale. So, if, as we believe, the UK is likely to follow the same path as the US, what shape will this transformation ultimately take?

UNDERSTANDING HOW TECHNOLOGY TRANSFORMS BANKING

The four stages of automation

Technology in banking progresses through distinct stages, each of which addresses different aspects of the business. People and paper are displaced by machines and software to some extent during every stage. But the distinctions between the stages are critical. Knowing which stage a line of business is in enables management to predict how much time is left before the conditions that encourage price wars are fully in place.

Fig 2.10 Simplified banking business system

| Stage: | C | B | A | A | B | C |

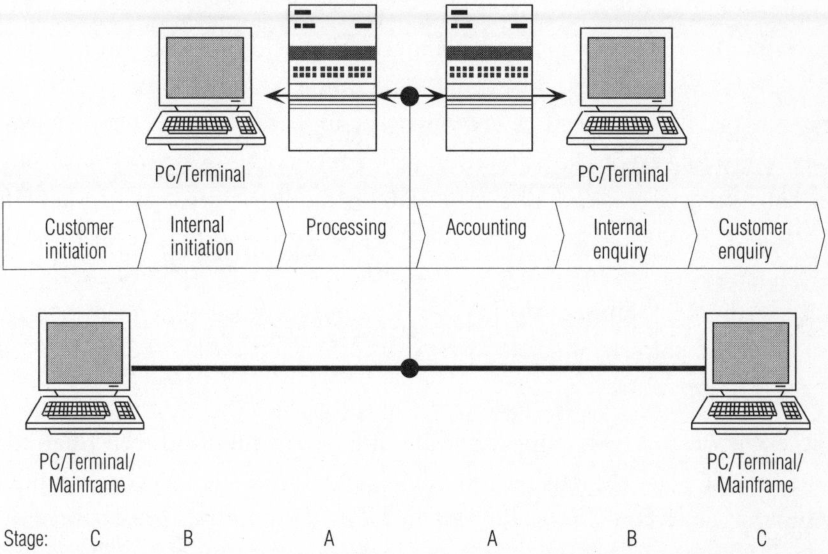

From Thomas D Steiner and Diogo B Teixeira, *Technology in Banking*, (Business One Irwin, 1990) with permission of The McGraw-Hill Companies.

To understand the four stages clearly, it is helpful to view each banking business as a 'business system'. Figure 2.10 shows a simplified banking business system, which consists of six segments, beginning and ending with the customer:

1. A customer gives the bank an instruction (for example, by writing a cheque) or requests a service (for example, by applying for a mortgage).

2. The bank receives and if necessary verifies the instruction or request, and initiates some kind of action.

3. The transaction is processed in the appropriate bank department.

4. The customer's account and the bank's books are changed to reflect the transaction, or some other record is created (for example, a mortgage loan account) or updated.

5. The fact that the transaction has been processed or the service provided is communicated to the relevant bank departments (such as the

customer's branch) and records (such as the management information system).

6. The customer is told that the transaction is complete.

In paper-based banking, this flow could be traced through the whole cycle simply by following the cheques, vouchers, ledger items and so on as they moved the information (which is what is being processed, the paper simply acting as a vehicle) from place to place.

Although the flows were very elaborate, and seldom exactly the same in any two banks, at heart something very simple was going on: debits and credits were being posted to customer accounts, or some other record of value was being created or altered. All the other complex systems in deposit banking revolve around this essentially straightforward record-keeping function at its core. The bulk of the work of banking involves getting the information needed to change the records to this core function, and communicating the resulting information back out to those who need to know.

This basic pattern of bank work is transformed by technology in four stages (Figure 2.11):

- *Stage A* occurs when the core record-keeping function, the third and fourth parts of the business system, moves from paper to a computer system. This stage affects the 'back office', whose work customers never see.

- *Stage B* is when bank staff can initiate transactions, and make follow-up enquiries, electronically – that is, through a computerised link with the core processing function, automated in Stage A. This stage automates the 'front office' – where customers meet bank staff.

- *Stage C* is when the customer can communicate directly with the core processing function, partly or wholly bypassing the second and fifth segments of the business system and the front office.

- *Stage D*, the final stage of transformation, occurs when all the piecemeal automation which happened in the preceding stages is integrated into a fully electronic business system, which can provide detailed information and analysis to both the bank and its customers.

These four stages generally occur in the same sequence in every business system, although the pace of transformation will vary greatly. The sequence is determined by two factors: the complexity of the work and the capability of the technology. These stages are now analysed in more detail.

Fig 2.11 The four stages of automation

Stage A: 'back office' automation

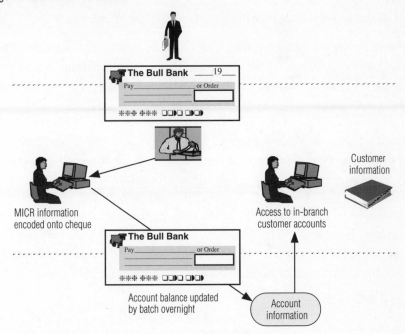

Stage B: 'front office' automation

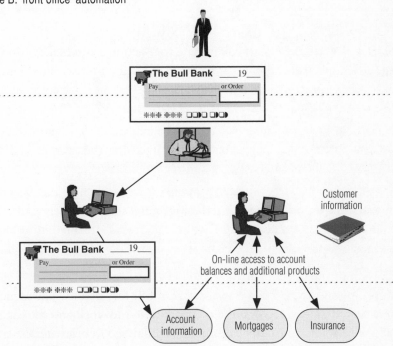

Fig 2.11 continued

Stage C: bringing customers on-line

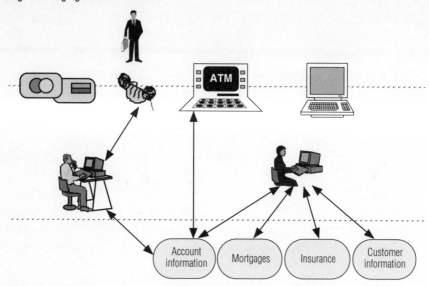

Stage D: an integrated system

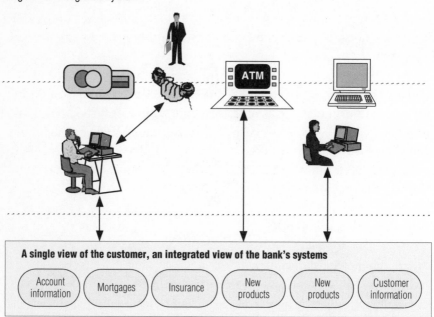

Stage A, 'back office' automation

This is basically the conversion of record-keeping from paper to electronic form – a task the computer was ideally suited to from its earliest days.

When bank ledgers were put onto even the slowest and crudest batch-entry systems, the initial gains in productivity and accuracy were tremendous, and easily realised. Previously, in the thousands of bank branches across the country, current accounts had to be updated manually every business day. This could not be done during banking hours, which traditionally were very limited as a result. Updating and balancing every branch ledger by hand, and sending the totals to head office for consolidation into the bank's general ledger, was the single most labour-intensive aspect of retail banking.

The 'back office' automation mainframe-computer technology of the 1960s enabled customer accounts to be maintained and updated centrally, eliminating branch ledgers and the work associated with them. This mainframe was in the bank's central clearing department, with direct input from reader-sorter machines using MICR technology to generate accounting entries automatically. Cheques paid in over branch counters were encoded in the branch before the cheques were dispatched to the central clearing department. Because of Stage A 'back office' automation, the boom in the number of current accounts and transactions during the 1970s was accommodated with a manageable growth in staff numbers. Eliminating ledgers freed staff for counter services, machine room processing, and 'middle office' functions such as opening accounts, controlling credit and processing customers' enquiries.

To customers, Stage A 'back office' automation was invisible, and had virtually no impact on the way they did business with their branch. Moreover, it had no fundamental impact on competition. All the large banks adopted similar mainframes and batch-processing systems at roughly the same time during the 1960s. They continued to add products and functions to the core 'back office' automation technology right through the 1980s. Recently, the renewal or replacement of these systems has become a major technology issue in the Big Four banks, but the initial Stage A automation of the industry is still in place.

Stage B, 'front office' automation

During the 1970s it became possible to transmit data cost-effectively between input/output terminals and mainframes. This gave branch staff the ability to access current accounts on-line, initially for balance enquiries, and to access the accounts of customers at other branches. For example, NatWest installed BOLP (branch on-line processing) terminals in the branch machine rooms in the early 1970s. Later, video display terminals in the branches were used to maintain and update customer accounts in the bank's central computer. While these investments allowed on-line access, accounts were still updated by overnight batch processing.

To implement Stage B 'front office' automation, banks had to build or acquire access to proprietary data networks, because Post Office networks were technically limited, and expensive. These data networks linked their data centres with the thousands of terminals in their branches throughout the UK. Given the scale and geographic reach of the Big Four, expensive investments in telecommunications networks are a continuing requirement for Stage B automation.

Generally, the Other Retail banks and the building societies have been able to adopt on-line processing and enquiry at less cost than the Big Four. This is because most of them automated their core systems later than the Big Four, after much Stage B technology, especially in telecommunications and on-line terminals, had become available. So processing was distributed and on-line from the start, and Stages A and B were folded into the original technology design. Banks like Abbey National, and the building societies, had in addition a far simpler task than the Big Four, because they never had extensive product lines to automate in the first place. Although they now offer a broader range of products and services, their businesses are still simpler than those of the Big Four, which is an advantage to them in adopting Stage B technology.

Stage B undoubtedly improves service to customers, by speeding up information and increasing their control over their accounts. Yet its economic and competitive effects are limited. Indeed, in some ways it simply restores to the branches the access they used to have to paper ledgers. Accessing an account directly through a terminal is more efficient than looking up stale information in a ledger or computer printout, but banks still need staff to do it. Similarly, setting up or changing accounts, direct debits and standing orders through a terminal eliminates the need for a flow of paper, but someone still has to enter the data. In short, Stage B automation allows incremental efficiencies, which are important, but does not greatly reduce staff. While the information tasks become more efficient, the banks still need people to talk to customers arriving in branches in a seemingly random way.

Stage C, bringing customers on-line

Stage C, on the other hand, does have profound economic and competitive consequences. In Stage C all six parts of the business system are handled electronically. Customers have direct access to their accounts in the core processing and accounting function – for example, through a push-button telephone banking account or through an ATM. Once customers can initiate their own enquiries electronically, the second and fifth parts of the business system become obsolete. If all customers of a product line use direct electronic access, the staff previously involved in these functions are no longer needed, or can be transferred to value-added functions, such as sales or marketing. This revolutionises the economics of that line of business – but only if *all* the business shifts into the more efficient electronic channel. More typically, the electronic channel captures some of the volume, but not all, so that parallel 'human' channels survive for a long time. So telephone banking is unlikely to make bank branches redundant in the near future. Unlike Stages A and B, Stage C requires customers to change their behaviour. As a result, there are very few mature examples at Stage C (and none in retail banking), although it is spreading into ever more product lines.

The well-educated, the young and the affluent tend to like Stage C technology, often preferring it to traditional banking for both business and personal needs. Customers feel they are getting better service when they can process their own transactions or enquiries; they enjoy the sense of control over their accounts. The ATM (automated teller machine) is a step towards Stage C automation. It is widely popular, partly because it eliminates the need to queue up to talk to bank tellers. However, the ATM is a hybrid: part direct access to the bank's core systems, but also requiring the dispersal and collection of paper (for example, to process deposits), which continues to be labour-intensive. Another hybrid is telephone banking using service centres open for 24 hours a day, but manned rather than electronic. True Stage C technologies, such as automated telephone banking, also make users independent of the branch and of banking hours, opening the door to world-wide, 24-hour banking.

Bringing customers on-line should be very beneficial to banks as well as to customers, by eliminating paper and labour and improving customer service. Moreover, expanding volume through Stage C technology is relatively cheap. In Stages A and B, volume or market share can be increased only by adding staff, which directly increases variable costs. However, in true Stage C automation, extra customer transactions tend to use excess capacity, so that variable costs can approach zero, at least in the short term. Even in the longer term, variable costs are kept low because the cost of adding extra communications and processing capacity is much less than that of hiring trained staff. (Incidentally, new capacity is usually cheaper to buy than the original – thanks to price/performance improvements of 20–30% a year in computers.) Even though Stage C automation is complicated to put in place, because customers need to be educated about the new systems and a whole range of terminals and other communications devices is required, the end is likely to justify the difficulties encountered.

These benefits may in practice be outweighed by a big disadvantage, from the banks' point of view, in Stage C technology. Ultimately, bringing customers on-line transfers control of the business system from the bank to the customer. Banks lose power because the technology is now in the hands of customers whose acceptance of it is critical to its success, and who will increasingly dictate how they want to use it, and thus how it will evolve. For example, once customers have been given access to their accounts through a cash management system on a PC, now common for business customers, they will decide how best to use it. Ultimately, customers will not accept limitations that are intended to lock all their business into one bank. This may be less of an issue in UK retail banking, at least at present, because customers are already tied more closely to one bank and simply use their PCs to manage their accounts more efficiently. Experience with PC treasury management systems in large institutions, however, suggests that such customers take control almost from the start.

When customers exercise closer control over their accounts, a bank's ability to make free use of customers' deposit money quickly evaporates, often with devastating consequences for the profitability of a line of business. While this is especially true of wholesale business, the more sophisticated retail customer can also use Stage C services to practise good cash management. Leaving substantial balances in interest-free or low-interest current accounts, the traditional keystone of clearing bank profits, was not surprising before customers had instant access to account information, and the ability to make transfers. Today it is only common for those with insufficient cash to invest elsewhere, a strong aversion to new technology or insufficient time or interest to manage their finances better. And banks cannot expect to recover in fees what they have lost through free balances. When the customers are providing all or most of the labour themselves, it is difficult to impose transaction charges, although in the US banks have had some success imposing ATM charges.

It may be possible to charge for Stage C transactions in the small business and mid-corporate sectors, because at least 75% of the English market is in the hands of four banks with shared interests. But in the personal, large corporate and institutional markets, banks will have difficulty in maintaining charges over time. A more subtle disadvantage of bringing customers on-line is that the branch loses direct face-to-face contact with the customer.

As described earlier, as a line of business becomes highly automated, with high capacity and high fixed costs, competitors seek to fill the capacity they have already paid for, and price wars loom. This also allows in new competitors, since the technology is usually modular and non-proprietary. The profits of all providers may then evaporate. Of course, not all businesses will follow the pattern of US international funds transfer. But in the UK, giving corporate customers direct access to BACS has driven down wholesale transaction pricing, which has caused the banks to limit Stage C access to CHAPS.

Stage D, an integrated system

The final stage is to link, not necessarily physically but at least virtually, all the incompatible and fragmented hardware and software accumulated over the years in the first three stages, to provide a complete picture of a customer's relationship with the bank. There is a general belief that this information is of great competitive value. However, Stage D is still over the horizon for most banks and for most lines of business. And its economic and competitive consequences can be as dire as those of Stage C automation.

Because of the history of automation described above, most banks have automated *ad hoc* without an integrating or organising principle, creating 'islands of automation'. The banks maintain and support a wide range of systems of varying age and quality, many of which are incapable of taking advantage even of the economies promised by Stage C, where the customer does the work, let alone of tracking processing volumes or revenues by customer or market segment. Stage D means one of two things: a more or less total 'retrofit' of existing automation around a coherent architecture of compatible hardware and software standards, or the installation of a whole banking system designed from the start to produce customer and management information, to limit maintenance, and to permit expansion. Either approach represents a very costly and very difficult endeavour. If it can be done, will it pay for itself? Stage D ambitions in the Big Four banks have already provided many cautionary tales.

As progress through the four stages of automation moves value and power into customers' hands, are the retail banks doomed to an upward spiral of technology investment inextricably linked to a downward spiral in profits? Not necessarily.

The IT investment cycle

What we have described in the previous section is the process by which technology transforms the operations of a bank. Its effect on the bank's profitability is based on fundamental principles of economics (Figure 2.12). Investments in technology displace labour and replace it with relatively high-fixed-cost/high-capacity IT factories. The incentive to initiate IT investments is often provided by the market; a current or potential player sees an opportunity to get ahead of its competitors or to prevent them getting ahead, and based on simple investment-return criteria decides to proceed with automation. As technology provides increased productivity and enables additional value to be provided to the customer through improved service or product features, all competitors are likely to follow a similar pattern of investment in order to stay in the market. As a result of these investments, competitors realise that they have a larger fixed-cost base to cover and significant spare capacity, and their propensity to lower their prices increases. A price war is then not very far away. Players who believe they can outlast a price competition have an incentive to initiate it, so that they capture the share of weaker players and then return to their high margins. Competitive intensity is not likely to decrease until the industry has been through a consolidation process and has seen its profitability eroded sufficiently to make any further price reductions unaffordable to all competitors. Margins can then increase again, but so can investments in technology to gain competitive advantage. The cycle starts again.

While this simplified description helps in understanding the underlying drivers of technology investment and its economic results, it does not always explain what is observed in the market – there seems to be a delay between investments and adverse profit impact. There are several factors external to the cycle that affect its progress; these can be described as *accelerators* and *decelerators*.

Accelerators

The main accelerating factors that UK banking has been experiencing in the last couple of decades are deregulation and advances in technology. Chap-

Fig 2.12 How IT transforms banking economics

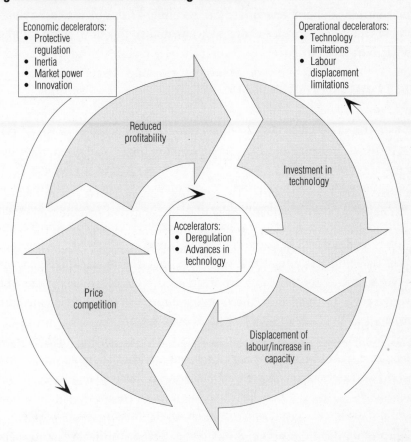

ter 1 described how the removal of barriers to competition between different types of institutions has facilitated the blurring of lines between them
and has encouraged the pursuit of increasingly similar target markets with
increasingly similar offerings. This process creates an incentive to invest
more in technology in order to gain cost efficiencies or to add product features that will enable competitive advantage to be gained, whether this is
sustainable in the long term or not. Deregulation also often enables market
activities that were previously constrained and thus creates new markets
that require additional investment to be served. This can also kick-start an
IT investment cycle, although the expansion of the market reduces the
competitive pressures in the short to medium term.

Advances in technology can also accelerate the process by making possible competitive activity that was previously impossible. The benefits of targeted marketing, for example, have been understood for some time, but

computing and data warehousing technology was not sufficiently powerful to make it possible and economic until recently. The same is true of product developments, like derivative instruments or linked accounts. Once these activities or products are made possible, investment in such a technology is likely to become a prerequisite for competing successfully.

Decelerators

Just as technology advances can accelerate the process, their absence can slow it down. Industries using a mature technology reach an equilibrium when technology cannot provide competitive advantage any longer. Profitability then settles at a required return of investment level until a new innovation is introduced. Technology in banking may contain such examples in specific lines of business that have reached a high level of systems intensity. As described in the next section, however, when one technology reaches its limits, it is often the case that another one starts evolving, as the relative incentive for investing in an untried technology increases. The slowing power of this factor, therefore, is limited to the short or medium term, until a new technology cycle takes off.

Another factor that can slow the process is a constraint on the reduction of labour, for example as a result of social government policy or union power. This can lead to competitors' incurring collectively higher costs and being unable to use the benefits of technology to compete on price. This however cannot be a sustainable situation. If incumbents invest in IT without displacing labour, their costs wili rise to the point that will lead them into losses and eventually force them out. As the products or services available to consumers start being affected, social or political pressure will eventually force a move away from the restrictive laws or practices, or the economy as a whole will come under pressure. Should incumbents choose to avoid investing in IT altogether, they would become highly vulnerable to new entrants offering better customer service with no existing labour forces.

While these factors tend to slow down the investment in IT or its effect on labour, there are other factors that can slow down the development of competitive intensity and price wars. One such factor is regulation or restrictive practices that protect incumbents from competition. The case of the Clearing House in the UK is an example of how a few players can exert an effective joint monopoly over a sector of the economy. As this case has shown, however, the tenure of such restrictive practices is limited, as consumers in today's information-rich society begin to understand the opportunity costs they are having to incur and press for the removal of constraints – with the effects observed in the UK since the mid 1980s.

Another decelerating factor, however, can replace restrictive practice as the effective constraint when the regulatory framework is liberalised: customer inertia. This factor is much more relevant in consumer markets. Consumers have less access to information on the options available to them than do company employees whose job it is to procure banking services. Also, consumers often feel a sense of loyalty to a provider or brand that has served them satisfactorily for a long period of time, frequently since school; they would need to invest a considerable amount of effort in investigating alternatives and they often perceive a significant amount of risk in switching. Furthermore, even if emotional loyalty is not an issue, the costs involved in switching providers can often be significant to individuals, whilst they might appear minimal to corporations. Indeed, whilst inertia has not been a significant feature of wholesale banking in the UK, it is very high among consumers. Only 1% of bank account holders switch providers in any year, allowing some to say that Britons are more likely to get a divorce than to change their bank. Inertia, however, like the other factors we have reviewed, can only be a decelerator; it cannot stop the process altogether. Inertia can be reinforced by the bank, whether in the form of switching barriers, e.g., the inefficient process of changing standing orders, or in the form of brand power and marketing muscle. The latter can prove a powerful decelerator as banks increase their market power through consolidation. The effects of inertia, however, are unlikely to be sustainable in the long term. We saw in Chapter 1 that, despite inertia, the Big Four have in fact been losing share rapidly. Admittedly this share may be in new markets or specific areas, but no product line can remain immune to switching. Eventually the competitive value propositions become too attractive to resist, switching becomes easier, and the cycle accelerates.

Although the decelerators we have mentioned can but slow the change process, they are nevertheless very important for banks to understand. Time is vital to banks in order to overcome organisational and operational barriers that might prevent them from competing successfully. Knowing how long they have before they come under increasing pressure can enable banks to develop an effective strategy to tackle market challenges.

A final decelerating factor is innovation itself. This is probably the most important factor to understand because banks can influence it directly. Innovation, when generating new products or product features rather than process improvements, can add value to a bank's customers, thus enabling a premium to be charged for products and services and limiting the effects of competitive price initiatives. Such innovation can also have more sustainable effects than other factors, especially if the organisational culture is geared towards continuous product innovation. However, research has shown that there are very few cases of incumbents successfully using innovation to defend their positions in the market. This poses a major challenge for banks: how to use innovation to prevent their competitive positions from being eroded by the IT investment cycle. This challenge is reviewed in the next section.

THE CHALLENGE FOR BANKS

Attackers and defenders

The challenge facing the banks is how to avoid simply automating the paper-based techniques and processes on which they have built their success and to redesign these processes from scratch to take advantage of the capabilities of the new technology. Technological evolution has been described by Richard Foster (in *Innovation: The Attacker's Advantage*, Summit Books, Simon & Schuster, 1986) as an S-curve: slow progress during infancy is followed by an explosion of growth and finally by maturity and decline. As Figure 2.13 shows, the curve plots performance, in terms of either cost-efficiency or increased effectiveness, on the vertical axis and the amount invested over time on the horizontal axis.

In infancy, the gradient of the performance curve is shallow, because progress is slow and expensive and take-up is slow, but in successful technologies the gradient then gets steeper, as progress becomes rapid and increasingly cheap, for a period. Then the curve flattens again as the technology inevitably runs up against the inherent limits to its efficiency. From that point onwards gains in performance get smaller in proportion to the extra effort invested, until at some point further investment in the technology becomes fruitless.

S-curves usually come in pairs, with the diminishing returns from the established technology providing much of the incentive for attempting the risky and expensive leap into the new infant technology. This is precisely where the banking industry finds itself, in the difficult and dangerous gap

Fig 2.13 S-curve attackers and defenders

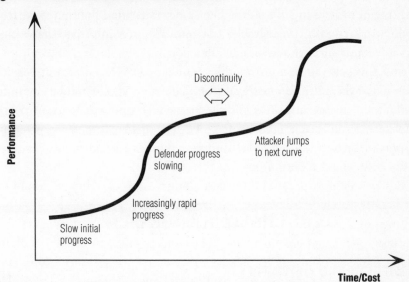

From Richard N Foster, *Innovation* with permission of International Creative Management Inc. and Macmillan General Books.

between the S-curves that Foster terms a 'discontinuity'.

As Foster notes, 'the leaders in the current technology rarely survive to become the leaders in the new technology […] this leaders-to-losers story has been played out not just by companies but by whole industries'. The reason is that leading firms have to manage simultaneously both the current technology and the move to the new technology. These firms, which Foster calls defenders, rarely attempt to bridge the discontinuity between the curves in a wholehearted way, preferring to trust to the continuing evolution of the *status quo*. For them, the new technology does not require the redefinition or reinvention of their industry; rather, it represents at most a way of doing what they have always done, more efficiently. Usually, the conservatism of their customers and their predominant position in the market allow them to enjoy good profits from the established technology until after it has become too late to make the jump to the new one.

In contrast, the firms that Foster calls attackers have no comparable stake in the *status quo*, and therefore are able to focus exclusively on using the emerging technology to take advantage of discontinuity. Because of this, they can come out of unexpected segments and niches, and become strong competitors quite quickly. For example, American Express, which for generations had been an American version of Thomas Cook, developed into one of the most powerful financial firms in the world by focusing on payment cards, an emerging technology-intensive business in which it was a pioneer. In UK banking, attackers include firms, like Abbey National, that emerged from niche markets with considerably more strategic freedom to reshape high-street banking through technology than possessed by the Big Four.

Foster points out that during discontinuity, *while few attackers actually succeed, even fewer defenders survive.* The only way defenders beat the odds is by counterattacking, using the new technology to leapfrog the attackers. Successful innovators from both camps become the new market leaders, only to find themselves on the defensive during the next wave of innovation and discontinuity.

Foster's S-curves are useful for describing the forces of innovation in traditional research-and-development environments. They are useful also in setting out a paradigm of attackers and defenders in which attackers (albeit a few only) win and defenders lose. The concept relies on the law of diminishing returns for its validity. Taking paper-based processes of 1960s banking, we all know that these do have limited scale economies – a bank clerk can only process 200–300 cheques an hour into manual books of account.

Clearly any paper-based processes will be outflanked by technology – a bank clerk can now process up to 3,000 cheques per hour – the high volume reader-sorter can cope with millions of MICR encoded cheques a day. Again, the 19th century joint stock banks invested in technology and survived as both attackers and defenders. In the process, a number of smaller private banks, who could not offer such services, disappeared.

Foster's work does not give weight to the potential escape offered by financial muscle – Microsoft caught up and probably passed Netscape, an attacker, with financial muscle. The Big Four banks have such muscle.

Research done by James Utterback (*Mastering the Dynamics of Innovation*, HBS Press, 1994) has shed more light on why incumbents are less likely to succeed in periods of major innovation, but also sets out the bases on which defenders can 'out-innovate' attackers (Figure 2.14). According to Utterback, innovation begins with radical product changes that, after a period of uncertainty and continued development at product and process level, crystallise into a 'dominant design'. Once that dominant design has been established, innovation becomes predominantly focused on process rather than product, and results in highly structured organisations that can extract maximum efficiencies from the improved process. That is until the next S-curve takes off.

Utterback found that these highly structured organisations that succeed

Fig 2.14 Three stages of innovation

The innovation process

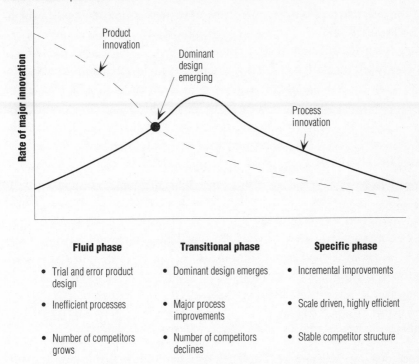

in process innovation periods generally fail to do so in product discontinuities. Leaders in mature industries create major barriers to change by excessively focusing on efficiency within dominant formats, whilst attackers usually begin with alternative technologies that lead to new formats and innovations. As a result, leaders in mature industries are vulnerable because they fail to recognise threats posed by new technologies and to adapt quickly enough once the threat becomes obvious. Leaders, according to Utterback's research, have successfully defended themselves in two instances: where the innovation did not expand the market and was limited to process; and where the individual firm developed independent structures that were both adaptive to change and became, themselves, attackers.

While Utterback's research did not cover the financial services industry, his findings can, suitably modified, shed light on the sector. There are few examples of pure technological product innovations in banking similar to the invention of the incandescent lamp or the miniaturisation of the Winchester disk drive. It is also more difficult to separate product and process innovations. While the tiered interest account was clearly a product innovation when TSB launched it, it could quite readily have been copied in a process based on clerks calculating interest manually, which is how Merrill Lynch launched the Cash Management Account. It is equally difficult to separate channel innovation from process innovation; so, for example, the launch of First Direct has been viewed as innovative, but should it be viewed any differently to telephone calls placed to a branch? The services available in both cases are largely the same.

Turning to the concept of dominant design, Utterback's thoughts on the concept of dominance need to be adjusted; because of the impact of the decelerators on the technology investment cycle, the rapid switch of market power from defenders to attackers may be less marked in financial services. Dominance may need to be measured in terms of share of market related to the potential to sustain 'better than market' margins; this could be measured in terms of share of wallet.

Using these adjusted concepts, we suggest that the following factors contribute to dominant design:

- technical innovations, e.g., MICR encoding of cheques, magnetic stripe on plastic cards, ATM card reader
- account concepts made possible by computer code, e.g., tiered interest rate accounts, automatically linked accounts, dual purpose accounts (debit and credit card), pre-approved loans
- infrastructures, e.g., London Clearing House, Visa authorisation centres, Switch EFTPOS (electronic funds transfer at point of sale) switching centre, BACS and CHAPS
- service concepts, e.g., cash management workstation, automated statement reconciliation.

Taking these concepts together and adjusting the 'dominance' definition, we can explain why it is, for example, that Barclaycard has a disproportionate share of the UK revolving credit market (around 40%) and continues to earn good margins. In this case we need to understand the contributions of innovations such as the Visa infrastructure, the revolving credit account concept, the magnetic stripe plastic card, low cost EFTPOS terminals, Profiles loyalty points, high reliability credit scoring, mass volume processing of payments and statements. Barclaycard's continued 'dominance' depends on whether dominance in revolving credit will be enough after the role of the credit card as a payment device is threatened by the debit card and the smart card. A further question, as we look through this case example, is the role of branding as part of the dominant design; in the early days, Barclaycard was the generic concept behind a Visa card in the UK. That brand dominance remains, with recent research showing that Barclaycard was the only recognised brand in financial services in the UK.

Going back to the concept of accelerators and decelerators, we see great potential for defenders, like Barclaycard, to exploit innovation, to reinforce decelerators and to sustain dominant market positions. Clearly this should not be an invitation to be complacent; the challenge is to exploit the decelerators and not to rely on them. To do this, the current dominant players may need to behave like attackers – Barclaycard certainly does.

Once they know where they find themselves, banks can decide to push ahead with process improvement, as discussed in Chapter 8, or to attempt the leap onto another curve, as discussed in Chapter 9. In order to use this insight, however, banks first need to understand their current position in the industry evolution process.

Using the S-curves

The critical question for bank management is this: where on the S-curve are the relevant information technologies that are currently transforming different lines of business, and how quickly are they moving?

The pace of progress up the S-curve is extremely rapid and shows no sign of slowing, if we take systems power as a measure of performance (Figure 2.15). Systems power means the combination of rapid *decreases* in the price of data-processing capacity and *increases* in annual systems expenditures. Data-processing capacity that cost a pound in 1980 could be had for less than 2.5 pence by 1996. Price performance, in other words, improved forty-fold in sixteen years, a rate far in excess of any of the technologies of the first and second industrial revolutions. Because IT spending by UK banks increased close to ten-fold over the same period, the industry experienced an increase in systems power of almost 400 times.

As computing power becomes radically cheaper, more powerful and more flexible, the range of work that can be automated and the volume of information that can be handled cost-effectively expands dramatically. So

Fig 2.15 Technology and overcapacity

How systems capacity has changed over time – Illustrative

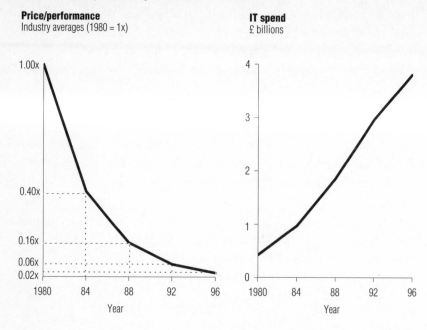

Price/performance
Industry averages (1980 = 1x)

IT spend
£ billions

Systems capacity
(1980 = 1x)

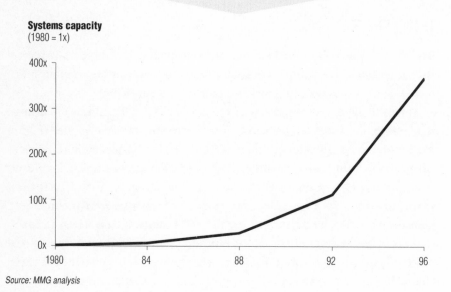

Source: MMG analysis

Fig 2.16 Systems intensity* by major consumer product area

1996   Percent

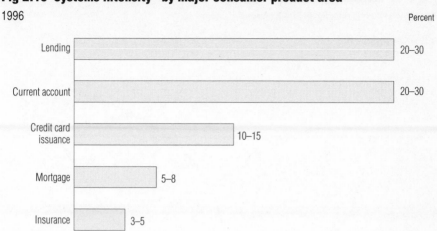

* IT spend as percentage of total operating expense
Source: MMG analysis

far, in spite of this high systems-power in the banking industry as a whole, individual lines of business with high systems intensity – that is, highly automated – are few (Figure 2.16).

An automation S-curve plotting the percentage of work performed electronically in the large US banks shows that funds transfer, described in the earlier example, has reached one of the highest system intensity profiles in the industry (Figure 2.17). Despite the considerable investments made to date in automating cheque processing or credit cards, these remain relatively labour-intensive, high-variable-cost businesses. In other words, they are still in their infancy on the S-curve, and banks are in the early discontinuity stage between paper-based and electronic business systems. We assume that the expansion of systems power and the forces of competition will probably pull more and more banking functions across the divide. If so, activities such as sales, marketing, credit decisions and customer service, which now take up a lot of human effort, will also become technology-intensive activities, characterised by high fixed costs and enormous capacity. This is not to imply that all bank businesses will inevitably run into a profitability crisis, as funds transfer has. However, it does suggest how challenging it will be to manage successfully through the discontinuity between paper-based and electronic banking.

All technological revolutions over the last 200 years or so have favoured attackers over defenders, and consumers over producers, and have created

Fig 2.17 Automation S-curve

Selected US banking examples – Illustrative

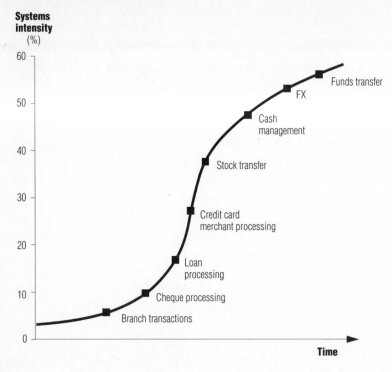

value for some while destroying profits for others. The new electronic technology may well be on the side of the attackers. But defenders do survive and make profits. In the transformation of banking, some will fail but some will prosper.

Adam Smith, or the emergence of specialists

We have stated above that banking is following other industries, which, from the start of the industrial revolution, have had their economics fundamentally altered by new technology. A concept formulated at that time – Adam Smith's concept of the division of labour – also helps us to understand the likely future development of banking.

Technology tends to divide the work in a business system into discrete functions. Organisations that have specialised skills and abilities in one type of function may enjoy a competitive advantage in that part of the business system. This may become apparent when over-capacity (from economies of scale) combines with deteriorating profitability (from pricing pressures) in the industry. This situation is starting to appear in banking, as we have seen. At this point, management must put high-spending, high-technology businesses under increasing scrutiny when these businesses make their bids for scarce corporate investment resources. Eventually the bank may decide that it is not economic to handle all segments of a transaction itself, when it can buy a service which is better and cheaper for parts of the process, improving the price and quality of the whole.

Instead of competing across all service and product areas, banks and other specialist providers, or shared utilities, emerge in segments of the business system where they enjoy advantages. (In bringing customers on-line, for example, connecting customers to the core functions of the bank involves interface devices and data communications, but banks do not design and manufacture the devices and they are not PTTs or value-added networks.) This process, which has become widespread in business systems for credit card and ATM transactions, and even core processing in US banking, can be described as 'competitive disaggregation'.

Disaggregation means that separate vendors, buyers and utilities develop in each business system. Sometimes they come from within the banking industry (several US banks specialise in switching ATM transactions, for example). Sometimes they come from the data processing or communications industries (e.g., EDS – the world's largest outsourcing company; ISSC – IBM's outsourcing subsidiary; ADP – the world's largest computer bureau). Sometimes a new utility is set up by a group of users (as the Depository Trust Company was set up by New York banks and securities firms). This process is well established in US banking, and is accelerating. The clarity of specialised roles and functions in an electronic business system helps the process along, but it is propelled mainly by the tight economics of an industry where profits are no longer protected by regulation. US banks can no longer afford to do a broad range of things at which they are not particularly efficient.

UK banking: becoming a specialist again

The UK is lagging behind in this process, but, as we have seen, the current competitive pressures on UK banks are generally similar to the pressures which began attacking profits in the US banking industry in the wake of the increased competitive intensity that emerged in the early 1980s. Because of this, UK banks will become increasingly selective about what businesses to be in, and what to make, buy or share, during the late 1990s and beyond.

This is not to say that the US pattern will be repeated here – the industry structures vary too much for that – but the same fundamental forces are at work. Industry structure can modify them, but not negate them.

Until about 75 years ago, the UK banking industry was very disaggregated. The clearing banks did one thing well – collecting lendable funds at little cost. Other institutions specialised in other services: discount houses, accepting houses and issuing houses dealt with corporate finance, foreign banks with international banking, building societies with mortgages, and so on. Later in the twentieth century, the London clearing banks expanded into almost every line of business and market in UK and foreign banking, while remaining at heart domestic branch banks. Robust profits from consumer lending through the branches allowed the banks to carry on in these new businesses, even though the skills needed to manage them were in many cases very different from those that underpinned the banks' traditional activities.

The end of the era of consistently high product profitability will bring disaggregation – along different lines – back to the industry. It will force the Big Four to focus their resources where they can be sufficiently cost-effective, or add enough value, to make returns acceptable to their shareholders. In practice it is very hard to disaggregate businesses such as those of the Big Four. The long process of amalgamation and expansion which produced these banks has left them with huge shared-cost structures, especially in their branch networks and the data processing and communications infrastructure that supports them. Nonetheless, while some banks may continue to extract value across a wide range of products by retaining control of the retail customer relationships and channels, economic reality will increasingly put pressure on them to focus their operations. For some, outsourcing has provided and will continue to provide a model for maintaining a broad customer franchise while achieving cost efficiency (although this will often require major organisational changes – beyond the narrowly defined areas being outsourced – to make it possible to manage external suppliers effectively, a skill still rarely found at financial institutions). For others, shedding non-core lines of business may be the only route to sustained returns on capital or even to survival.

PART

HOW LINES OF BUSINESS ARE BEING TRANSFORMED

Walter Bagehot's classic commentary on banking, *Lombard Street* (1873, reprint Orion Editions, 1991), describes changes in 19th century banking not unlike those the industry has been experiencing since 1980. This assertion might seem odd, since Bagehot does not even use the word 'technology' and is usually cited in connection with the emergence of modern central banking. Bagehot, however, recognised that he was living through a revolution in the structure of banking.

In Bagehot's day, banking was being transformed by key technologies, such as the railways and telegraph, from local franchises that operated on the basis of personal knowledge and specialised judgement into a national industry based on capital, scale and the industrial organisation of labour under professional management. At that time, many in the City, including the Bank of England and the private banks who owned the Clearing House, thought banks that were organised along these new lines were inherently unsound. Bagehot, however, prophesied that it was the private banks which had no future and, within a generation of the publication of *Lombard Street*, UK banking was well on its way to being dominated by a handful of very large joint stock banks intensely focused on a 'simple business' of taking deposits, clearing payments, and extending overdrafts on good security. By advancing the cheap deposits they raised in their branches to the smaller, highly specialised institutions of the City, the clearing banks, as they came to be called, could turn their efficiency at gathering interest-free or low-cost deposits into profit at minimum direct counter-party risk. This system, in broad outline, persisted for about a century after the publication of *Lombard Street* until the restructuring that began in the 1980s.

Today the industry looks very different than it did in 1979. Banks, building societies and other providers offer broadly similar products. Small, specialised, City institutions have largely disappeared or been marginalised as the Big Four have expanded (*de novo* and through acquisition) into virtually every form of direct risk intermediation – from issuing and underwriting securities to trading everything from foreign exchange to exotic derivatives and options for their own account. Branch networks have become less deposit-gathering machines than channels to market insurance and other non-traditional products. Branches, in turn, are being bypassed by a growing segment of customers who accept or actively prefer electronic delivery of services via ATM, telephone, PC or plastic card. The payment system itself, the key Big Four oligopoly when deposit money was synonymous with the paper cheque, has ceased to be a closed shop and the bank-run portion of it – now run by a relatively democratic club called the Association for Payment Clearing Services (APACS) – is shrinking in importance relative to payment cards, a business system increasingly penetrated by new, focused competitors.

Were Bagehot alive today, it is doubtful that any of this would have in the least surprised him. Just as the railways, telegraph and introduction of large-scale paper processing led to an entirely new industry structure a century ago, electronic data processing and communications are leading to a new industry structure for the next century. New winners and losers will emerge from this transformation, but the basic functions for which banks and financial markets were created – essentially risk intermediation and the storage and transmission of economic value – will remain.

The key feature of electronic technologies is that they make information concerning money and markets cheap, widely accessible and instant. This is a direct challenge to all institutional intermediaries – be they banks, brokers or exchanges – whose value lies in access to information. Banks, still wedded to the cost structures of the paper-based information era, face the most direct threat since it seems that technology cannot lower these costs at anything like the pace with which it erodes their market positions in their traditional deposit taking, value transmission and credit extension businesses. Broadly speaking, technology lowers the barriers to entry and creates the potential for new entrants – who can take a 'greenfield' approach – to compete with immense cost advantages, focusing on the lines of business where they can create a competitive advantage and overcome any brand awareness disadvantage they may have. The enormous shift from household deposit assets into fund providers, and retail transaction and lending volumes into credit card issuers, is testament to this phenomenon.

Chapter 2 reviewed the process by which lines of business are transformed by technology and the importance of understanding where in the evolutionary process each business finds itself. The fact that new entrants tend to focus on individual lines makes it even more imperative for every bank to understand these lines of business deeply, whether it continues to provide a wide range of them or it chooses to 'disaggregate' itself. Chapters 3–7 describe the main lines of business, the major developments in each, the role of IT and the inherent management challenges.

PAYMENT SYSTEMS (I): THE MOVE AWAY FROM PAPER

This chapter starts with a description of the mechanics and economics of the current account, because the cost of handling payments through these accounts has been a major spur to automation. The chapter then describes how technology is affecting, but not yet displacing, the more traditional ways of making payments: cash, cheques, and bank giro payments. The newer electronic pre-authorised payments such as standing orders, direct debits and customer credits are gaining ground rapidly, however, thanks to the technology of the automated clearing system BACS, described in the final section of the chapter.

THE CURRENT ACCOUNT

The current account is at the core of commercial banking, and a means by which many additional products can be sold. Current accounts, directly or indirectly (through the other products sold on top of current accounts), produce more than half of banks' profits and typically account for nearly two-thirds of all retail banking costs.

The traditional current account is changing rapidly and is the subject of intense competition in the personal sector. Interest is now paid on many current accounts, and credit limits and different types of cards are designed to attract specific types of customer. Advertising is extensively used to create an image of the current account 'product' and of the institution offering it.

The mechanics of the current account remain the same as they always have been, however. Customers can use their current accounts for three purposes: to make a payment (or receive cash), to store or receive deposit money, and to borrow money through an overdraft facility.

Payment, commonly referred to as transmission, was traditionally made by use of a cheque. Standing orders, direct debits, and the more recent

EFTPOS (electronic funds transfer at point of sale) are simply electronic cheque substitutes as far as the payment function of current accounts is concerned. Payment functions have been moving steadily away from paper-based processes to electronic means, with non-paper payments increasing from 10% of non-cash money payments in 1975 to 61% in 1996. Cheques, however, remain the largest single means of making current account trans-actions, especially between businesses.

Deposits held on current accounts offer safety and the convenience of total liquidity. They can be converted into cash instantly with the use of a cheque at bank counters or through an ATM. The trend towards paying interest on current accounts has blurred the distinction between current accounts and deposit accounts somewhat; but the defining feature of a deposit on a current account has traditionally been that it can be used for making payments without notice, whereas most interest-bearing accounts, such as bank deposit accounts and building society share accounts, required notice of withdrawal. Paying interest on current accounts, and linking cur-rent accounts to high interest savings accounts and other services, has required changes to core accounting systems, and is a relatively recent development which is still proceeding.

Credit can be acquired by simply making a payment or encashment that overdraws a current account. The amount borrowed can be reduced or repaid at any time by making a deposit to the account. Borrowing is always subject to the bank manager's discretion, but it is extremely flexible, and represents in effect a revolving line of credit. If the loan is adequately secured, the bank manager will often permit a virtually perpetual overdraft. Much of British industry and commerce has traditionally been financed through overdrafts. Indeed, the original clearing bank business system could be described as turning the interest-free balances in mainly personal current accounts into risk-free secured overdrafts on mainly commercial or indus-trial current accounts, with the minimum of formalities and paperwork.

These three elements of the payments system consisted entirely of cash and cheques until the late 1960s. Today, they have been substantially trans-formed by technology (Figure 3.1), as described later in this chapter and the next. IT has enabled the banks to create a wide range of ways to make payments, draw out cash and check on balances. Unfortunately from the banks' point of view, in spite of technology, they have not been able to entirely eliminate any of their traditional paper-based, person-to-person services.

Fig 3.1 UK non-cash payments volume
1987–96

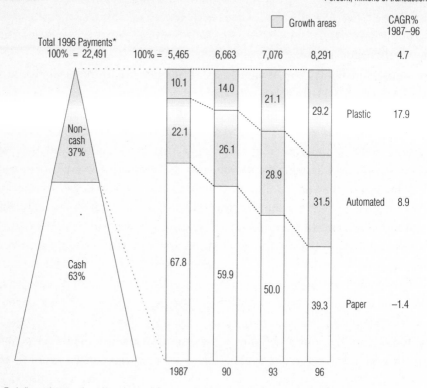

Percent, millions of transactions

□ Growth areas

CAGR%
1987–96

4.7

Plastic 17.9

Automated 8.9

Paper −1.4

* Excluding cash transactions of less than £1, PO order book payments (volume = 958 million in 1996), and cash acquisitions (Volume = 2,248 in 1996)

Source: APACS, MMG analysis

To understand the economics of the current account, we must look separately at personal customers on the one hand, and small business and mid-corporate customers on the other.

Personal accounts: the loss of free balances

Because of the ownership of the clearing mechanism mentioned earlier, before 1975 the London and Scottish clearing banks had a virtual monopoly on current accounts. In that year the Central Trustee Savings Bank (TSB) and the Co-operative Bank were admitted to the London clearing system, followed by the Girobank in 1983. Of these 'new clearers', only TSB had a retail base comparable to the big clearing banks.

Competition for current accounts began in earnest when Abbey National, then the second largest building society, introduced the first interest-bearing chequebook accounts through the clearing services of the Co-operative Bank. By 1989, seventeen building societies offered some kind of chequebook account. Abbey National remained an innovator; for example, in March 1988 it introduced Abbeylink, an interest-bearing current account linked to a high interest cheque account, with tiered interest. Abbey National took up direct membership of the clearing system in June 1988, and became a bank in 1989. Since then, Abbey National has continued its campaign, for example by advertising comparisons with high street bank charges and interest rates on current account overdrafts in early 1994; by cutting its overdraft rate in half in mid-1994; and, more recently, by introducing a new account with a wide range of services, low charges, and tiered interest-rate levels.

The Building Society Act of 1986 proved to be the trigger for the strong increase of competition for current accounts in the personal sector. Nationwide Anglia's Flex Account (1987) attracted over a million depositors and the Big Four banks were forced to start paying interest on current accounts. Lloyds, the first to do so, launched its Classic account in January 1989, closely followed by Midland, Barclays and NatWest. The proportion of interest-bearing current accounts has increased from zero in 1988 to 76% in 1996.

This loss of free current account balances is a significant economic problem for UK commercial banks. The clearing banks compare the cost of attracting and administering the deposits in their current accounts to the cost of raising similar deposits in the sterling money market. Their current account costs, excluding interest, are equivalent to interest rates of 5% or more. With interest on current accounts ranging from 0.25% to 3%, the all-in cost of these deposits can easily exceed prevailing base interest rates. They start to look expensive when base rates fall below about 6%.

Some of this cost could be recouped by charging personal customers more for current account services, but the scope for this seems limited, particularly when banks like Abbey National attack this income source. Traditionally, the personal sector has enjoyed 'free banking', meaning either that customers are not charged for transactions, or that the bank gives them an allowance for the value of balances maintained, which is used to reduce bank charges, provided the account is not overdrawn. Before interest was paid on current accounts, free transactions were largely viewed as payment in kind (in place of interest) made to customers for the use of their money. Banks still undercharge personal customers for transactions, but there is considerable customer resistance to realistic bank charges.

Another approach to recouping the cost of current accounts is to design a system that ensures that the bank gets paid for its overall account service. For example, fees for and interest on overdrafts may be set at a level that offsets both transaction costs and the value of 'lost' free balances swept into high interest accounts. Systems that control current accounts on this basis have to be able to link different accounts and services, and calculate interest on deposits of different amounts and time periods. The bigger building societies have been able to do this for some time. Midland was the first of the Big Four to do so.

However, few institutions look to these current accounts for profits, given the intense competition for customers in the personal sector, which is now a mature market. Rather, they hope to use the current account relationship as a springboard from which to launch the sale of other financial services, especially insurance and investments. We return to this subject in Chapter 7.

Business customers: profitable but branch-dependent

The intense competition that characterises the personal sector has not yet spread to the banks' business customers. Current accounts in the business sector are a virtual monopoly of the Big Four. Only the Big Four have the dense branch networks that small and mid-corporate businesses need for account servicing. Such customers want a branch close at hand because they make frequent use of it to pay in their cash and process their cheques, to arrange overdrafts, and to access other business services. This is especially true of high-street retailers, although the biggest of them are bypassing the branches by using the Big Four's bullion centres. Figure 3.2 shows the importance of business transactions in total sterling-payments volumes.

Current accounts are much more profitable in this sector than in either the personal or larger corporate sectors – but have in the past led to significant loan losses for the banks. Unlike personal customers, business accounts are subject to specific transaction charges, usually according to a fixed tariff in the case of the small and mid-corporate firms (larger firms can negotiate discounts). The small business also needs an overdraft facility, for which it typically pays 3% over the rate paid by larger firms.

Because these customers are heavily dependent on their branches, and

Fig 3.2 UK sterling transaction volumes*

1996   Millions of transactions

Primary payment method for every major payer/ payee combination

Paper (e.g. cheques)

Payer \ Payee	P	B	BfC	Total
P_R	–	463	–	463
P_S	53	1,373	494	1,920
B	261	1,105	74	1,440
Total	314	2,941	568	3,823

Plastic

Payer \ Payee	P	B	BfC	Total
P_R	–	19	–	19
P_S	–	2,399	1,680	4,079
B	–	5	–	5
Total	–	2,423	1,680	4,103

Automated (e.g. BACS)

Payer \ Payee	P	B	BfC	Total
P_R	–	1,487	–	1,487
P_S	–	–	–	–
B	815	311	–	1,126
Total	815	1,798	–	2,613

Cash > £1

Payer \ Payee	P	B	BfC	Total
P_R	–	1,251	–	1,251
P_S	118	11,722	–	11,840
B	366	743	–	1,109
Total	484	13,716	–	14,200

Consolidated

Payer \ Payee	P	B	BfC	Total
P_R	–	3,220	–	3,220
P_S	171	15,494	2,174	17,839
B	1,442	2,164	74	3,680
Total	1,613	20,878	2,248	24,739

P   = Person
P_R = Person – Regular
P_S = Person – Spontaneous
B   = Business/Other
BfC = Bank for Cash

* Excluding cash transactions of less than £1 and PO order book payments

Source: APACS, MMG analysis

because no bank outside the Big Four has a comparable network, the Big Four can maintain or even increase prices for transmission and overdrafts, as was the trend in the early 1990s, and thus protect profit margins. However, following significant media pressure, the Big Four have eased off on prices to small businesses since 1994, despite the fact that these businesses were a source of massive loan losses in the last economic cycle.

The need for an extensive branch network thus represents an effective barrier to entry for other competitors who might have designs on these customers. These barriers are not cheap. Most of the costs of running branch banking arise out of the current account – £5.3 billion out of £7.5 billion for the Big Four, or over 70% of these costs (Figure 3.3). Well over half these costs arise from providing services to businesses. As long as branches remain indispensable to smaller businesses, the Big Four's most profitable market segment is locked into them – but tied to the most expensive part of their infrastructure.

Any attempt to reduce banks' costs by cutting and reshaping their networks needs to take this into account. For example, it would be difficult to design separate strategies for delivering banking services to personal customers, on the one hand, and business customers, on the other. In theory, personal customers could use a 'branchless' bank, along the lines of Midland's First Direct. But in practice, for smaller companies the personal and professional affairs of the principals are often intertwined. Company overdrafts may be secured by personal assets, and personal creditworthiness depends in many cases on the cash flow of a small business.

Automating overdrafts

Rather than radically pruning branch networks, banks might find more value in automating functions such as credit control. Overdrafts remain the single most important form of credit for small and mid-corporate businesses, and an important form of flexible funding for larger firms as well. In the personal sector, too, the overdraft is a major source of credit, despite banks' attempts to direct consumer borrowing to credit cards and fixed-term loans.

Unfortunately, administering overdrafts is time-consuming and therefore expensive. Before banking became a mass-market business, bank managers knew their customers personally, which allowed them to make rapid and reliable decisions on whether to pay cheques or call in overdrafts. This sort of credit control is now impossible in the personal sector, except for

Fig 3.3 Location and breakdown of retail costs for a typical Big Four bank

1996   Percent

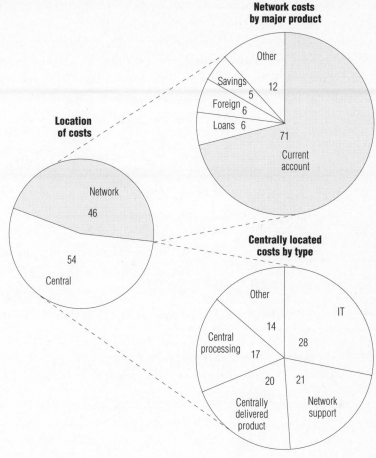

Source: MMG analysis

the wealthiest customers or for banks in the premium service sector. It is also impossible in the business sector: there are too many firms, and their financing needs are too varied and complex. Local discretion cost the banks dearly, and their approach has been to remove it from the branch and focus it in a few highly skilled centres, an approach made difficult by the 'my level is my discretionary power' culture prevalent among bank managers.

In mass-market banks where overdraft management has not been automated, monitoring even authorised overdrafts requires bank staff to review printouts each day showing the name of the account holder and the sum borrowed, and to have access to customers' files and recent account history. Frequently, the same £25 overdraft is reviewed every day until it clears. Most customers overdraw within authorised limits, but investigating unauthorised overdrafts is even more labour-intensive. It may, for example, involve making contact with the customer, or in extreme cases, bouncing his or her cheques and perhaps calling in the overdraft as well. Such decisions can be taken only by the bank manager, or by senior lending clerks – in other words, by the bank's most expensive staff. This means that they have less time to spend on product marketing and other value-added functions.

The challenge for banks is to use technology to administer today's vast number of overdrafts as efficiently and safely as yesterday's manager was able to do. Many banks have invested significant amounts recently to that effect. Centralising and streamlining the lending process and automating credit scoring are some of the solutions being pursued. However, more sophisticated methods and analysis tools for the management of debt or potential debt are required if costs are to be controlled without 'throwing out the baby with the bath-water', as poor debt situations frequently reverse themselves down the road.

THE DECLINING ROLE OF CASH

Most economically active adults today have a bank account, but still use cash for most of their payments. It accounts for nearly all payments of under a pound, not surprisingly, and for two-thirds of payments over a pound. But cash is on the decline: between 1981 and 1996, cash fell from 92% to 63% of payments over £1. And this is an absolute decline that is continuing rapidly: the number of cash transactions has fallen by more than 1 billion since 1990.

When we look at the pattern of payments, it is helpful to distinguish between regular payments, like mortgages and bills that arrive and are paid by post, and spontaneous payments, e.g., for shopping. Cash dominates spontaneous payments, accounting for 77% of transaction volumes. But its importance is on the wane: non-cash transactions increased from 4% of spontaneous payments in 1976 to 23% in 1996.

At first, it was cheques that displaced cash for both spontaneous and regular payments. They increased their share of payments from 5% to 11%

between 1976 and 1990, before declining to 9% in 1996. Non-paper payments increased from 2% to more than 20% over the same period, attacking cash, cheques and bank giro credits.

Of these non-paper payment methods, standing orders and direct debits have made big inroads on the use of cash and cheques for regular payments. Spontaneous cash and cheques payments are being attacked by plastic card payments, which have increased from less than 60 million in 1975 to 2.4 billion in 1996.

The most important reason for the decline of cash has been the move away from the traditional weekly pay packet towards a direct deposit into a bank account. Both banks and employers have been pushing this since the 1960s. In 1996, 71% of UK households had their pay deposited directly into an account, up from 26% in 1976.

This displacement of cash by cheques and established electronic means will soon have gone as far as it can. Currently, cash is used for some ten billion small daily transactions a year. Perhaps three billion of these may be candidates for automated payment. Then, banks will still be left handling large amounts of cash, a task which has obvious implications for the future of the high-street branch. Fewer and fewer individuals now make deposits at bank counters, but small businesses and shops will remain dependent on branches as long as we still use cash to shop. The banks are exploring ways to overcome this barrier to cost reduction, and electronic purse smart card initiatives, such as Mondex, are seen by many as a potential solution. As discussed in Chapter 4, however, these have yet to prove their effectiveness.

CHEQUES: NOW IN DECLINE

In 1996, 3.2 billion cheques were written in the UK, of which 63% were personal cheques, or about eight cheques per month for each 'banked' household. As with cash, it is interesting to distinguish between regular and spontaneous payment patterns. The average household used two cheques per month to pay regular bills, five for shopping or other spontaneous payments and one in bank branches to get cash.

Since 1980, households have been paying more bills at home and making increased use of electronic cheque substitutes such as standing orders and direct debits, although the use of cheques in-store has not been declining as steeply. The decline in cheque payments is underway, because of the increasing use of debit cards and other electronic payment systems, and this trend is accelerating. But cheques retain a major share of spontaneous transactions, making the infrastructure that supports their use a primary target of banks' cost reduction efforts.

The cheque guarantee card: bolstering cheque use

Cheque guarantee cards make cheques almost universally acceptable. Uniform cards for all UK and Irish clearing banks (except Barclays and TSB) have been issued since 1969. A cheque written for any amount up to the value specified on a valid card will be honoured if the number of the card is written on the back of the cheque. Banks developed the cheque guarantee scheme to counter the appeal of credit cards. Although it did not prevent credit cards from becoming a standard bank product, the cheque guarantee card soon became a universal feature of current accounts.

The cheque guarantee card is not an electronic product. It simply identifies the customer as being covered by the scheme. However, because of fraud, the card is expensive to administer. As the number of bank accounts rose, so too did fraud losses – losses related to all card types rose from some £5 million in 1979 to about £166 million in 1991, of which £29 million were attributable to cheque guarantee cards alone (Figure 3.4). These losses have led to the card being completely redesigned, in 1984 and 1988, in an attempt to produce a more secure system using holograms. Another technology, called 'watermark', consists of a fourth recording channel on the conventional magnetic strip; this carries 'hard data' which cannot be erased or copied, and which adds only a few pence to the price of the card. Some issuers now include a photograph on the card, although customer resistance has been high, driven by a distaste for ID cards. Fraud losses attributable to cheque guarantee cards in 1996 dropped to less than £13 million, partly as a result of enhanced risk management and security by banks.

The banks held the cheque guarantee limit at £50 from 1977 to 1988. In that year, consumer groups lobbied to have the limit raised. After the Office of Fair Trading decided to investigate the scheme, the banks were allowed to offer customers three tiers of guarantee card, at £50, £100 and £250 per cheque. In spite of their fear of fraud, and their big investment in paperless debit card systems, several of the banks have used this structure aggressively in their marketing.

Fig 3.4 Annual fraud losses of UK card issuers

1990–6   £ millions

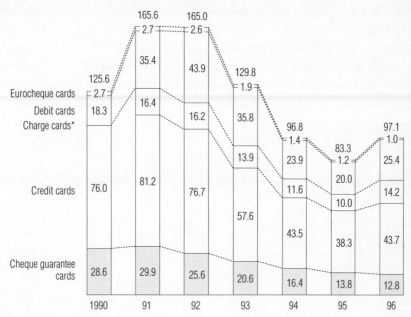

	1990	91	92	93	94	95	96
	165.6	165.0		129.8	96.8	83.3	97.1
Eurocheque cards	2.7	2.7	2.6	1.9	1.4	1.2	1.0
Debit cards	18.3	35.4	43.9				
Charge cards*		16.4	16.2	35.8	23.9	20.0	25.4
			13.9	11.6			14.2
Credit cards	76.0	81.2	76.7	57.6	43.5	10.0	43.7
						38.3	
Cheque guarantee cards	28.6	29.9	25.6	20.6	16.4	13.8	12.8

* In 1990 included in credit cards

Source: APACS, MMG analysis

The cheque guarantee card is now a feature of daily life, and is not likely to be easily displaced, particularly as most issuers have integrated their cheque guarantee, ATM and debit card products on to the same card. Membership in the standard cheque guarantee card scheme has expanded to 65 financial institutions, with close to 50 million domestic cards issued, or more than two for each banked household. With the card functioning also as a cash card and a debit card, banks do not have to issue separate cards for these functions. But the banks are still supporting different payment methods, each with very different cost structures – of which the card itself is a very small part.

Business-to-business cheques: strongly entrenched

In 1996 roughly half of all payments between businesses, by volume, were still made by cheque. Over a billion business-generated cheques still pass through the general clearing each year, the majority of which are repetitive payments to other businesses – to suppliers of goods and services, and to public utilities. These would seem to be prime candidates for automation, especially as corporate treasuries can have an electronic interface with BACS and CHAPS. But business payments are the least automated sector of the payments system.

The main reason for this is that cheques help the paying company to control cash flow, and it is the payer who normally selects the payment method. Just because technology allows payment to be speeded up does not mean that there are good business reasons for doing so. By using cheques, a company can partly finance itself by delaying payments to vendors and suppliers. Companies are unlikely to surrender this flexibility and move to pre-authorised electronic payments, except for small payments to individuals.

Inroads by purchasing cards – plastic cards used for business-to-business payments – may change this situation. These enable businesses to remove paper from many payments by eliminating the need both for cheques and for individual paper invoices, since the card statement acts as a collective invoice. But progress has still been slow, partly due to problems with recognition of the card statement as a valid invoice from the VAT authorities' perspective. Card issuers are now introducing a new line-item detail (LID) option for their statements that has the backing of HM Customs & Excise, so there are increasing hopes that purchasing cards may finally take off. Since business-to-business payments remain the final stronghold of cheques, such a development would be of great significance for the process of increasing the automation of payment systems.

How cheques are cleared

Three companies handle clearing in the UK:

- BACS Limited, which operates the bulk electronic debit and credit clearing (Figure 3.5)
- The CHAPS Clearing Company Limited, which operates the high-value real-time gross settlement (RTGS), both paper and electronic (Figure 3.6)
- The Cheque and Credit Clearing Company Limited, which operates the bulk paper clearings in London and Edinburgh (Figure 3.7).

Fig 3.5 BACS

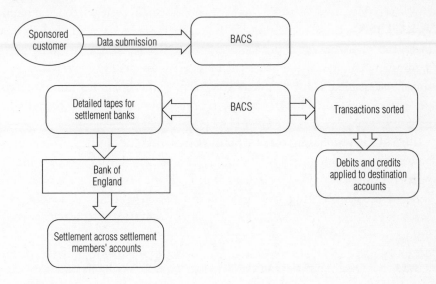

Day 1
- A sponsored customer submits data to BACS by magnetic tape, diskette or direct telecommunications link (BACSTEL)
- Each submission to BACS consists of a number of credit items matched by one debit item for the total (or vice versa)

Day 2
- BACS sorts payment data according to the bank branches to which they are addressed and prepares detailed tapes for those banks

Day 3
- The debits and credits sorted from the payment data are applied to the destination accounts
- The tapes created on the second day are posted to the settlement accounts during the morning of the third day, and interbank settlement is initiated

Fig 3.6 CHAPS

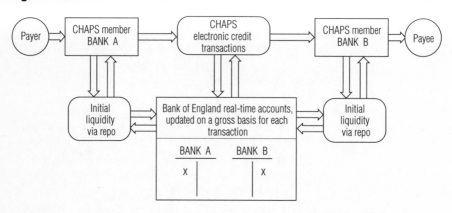

08:00   • Repo with Bank of England of eligible securities to provide intra-day liquidity in real-time gross settlement (RTGS) account

08:30   • Real-time customer payments begin; all payment final once made, but cannot be made unless the paying bank has a positive balance on its account

15:30   • Real-time customer payments end

17:00   • Repayment of repo from RTGS account

Fig 3.7 Cheque and credit clearing

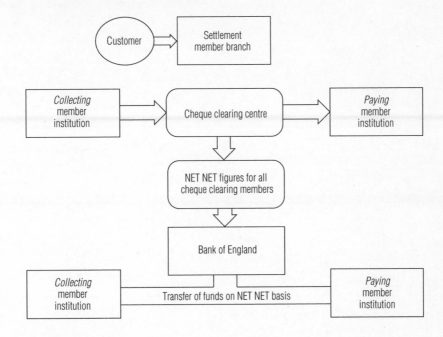

Day 1
- Cheques paid into branches of the member institutions are sorted locally at each member's own cheque clearing centre

Day 2
- Those cheques paid in the previous day that are drawn on other member institutions are exchanged through the cheque clearing centre
- The processing in the cheque clearing has been highly automated for several years, using magnetic ink character recognition (MICR) techniques

Day 3
- During the morning net positions are agreed at the Clearing House and a series of debit and credit transactions are delivered to the Bank of England for posting to the settlement accounts

These companies operate under an umbrella body, APACS (the Association for Payment Clearing Services). APACS was formed in 1985 to implement the Child Report, which recommended that the Bankers' Clearing House pass its exclusive ownership and governance of the clearing system to self-governing clearing companies. Membership is open to any financial organisation that meets criteria based on volume and financial and technical capacity, and that agrees to be liable for any expenses incurred from adding a new participant to the clearing system. Figure 3.8 shows the mem-

Fig 3.8 Membership of APACS

1997

APACS Members	BACS	CHAPS	Cheque & credit
Abbey National	6/87	–	6/88
Bank of England	F	F	F
Bank of Scotland	F	F	9/86
Barclays Bank	F	F	F
Citibank	–	F	–
Clydesdale	F	F	12/96
Co-operative Bank	F	F	F
Coutts & Co	F	F	–
Crédit Lyonnais	–	5/94	–
Deutsche Bank	–	5/94	–
Girobank	F	F	F
Halifax	6/87	–	–
Lloyds Bank	F	F	F
Midland Bank	F	F	F
National Westminster Bank	F	F	F
Nationwide Building Society	6/89	–	6/91
Northern Bank	1/89	–	–
Northern Rock	6/97	–	–
Royal Bank of Scotland	F	F	F
Standard Chartered Bank	–	F	–
TSB Bank	F	F	F
Yorkshire Bank	6/87	–	–
Number of members (APACS =22)	18	16	13

F = founder member

Source: APACS

bership of APACS in 1997, and Figure 3.9 summarises membership and ownership of all payment clearing services. Membership in any one clearing service confers full membership of APACS. For the purposes of retail banking, the relevant clearing companies are BACS and the Cheque and Credit Clearing Company.

For the banks, clearing cheques is the most expensive and risky way to make payments. Despite recent changes in legislation, most cheques still begin and end in a bank branch, and are handled many times on their journey, in a system that is wholly owned and paid for by the banks.

In the UK, payment takes three days from the time the cheque is deposited by the payee. Once deposited, a cheque follows one of three streams, depending on whether it is: a) drawn on the payee's branch; b) drawn on another branch of the payee's bank; or c) drawn on another bank.

A *cheque drawn on the payee's branch* is paid there, goes no further, and is not recorded as a cheque cleared. About 560 million such cheques were used in 1996, mostly to draw cash.

Fig 3.9 Payment clearing services

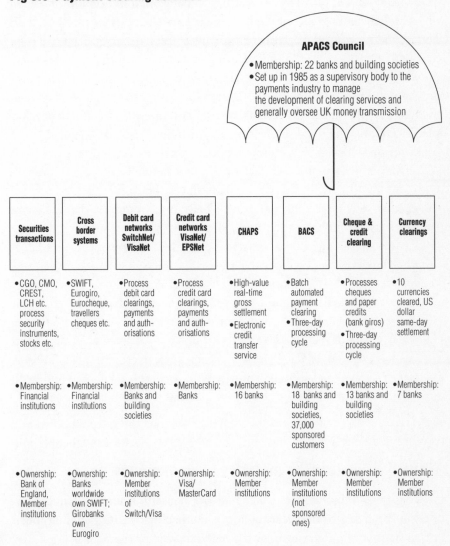

APACS Council
- Membership: 22 banks and building societies
- Set up in 1985 as a supervisory body to the payments industry to manage the development of clearing services and generally oversee UK money transmission

Securities transactions	Cross border systems	Debit card networks SwitchNet/ VisaNet	Credit card networks VisaNet/ EPSNet	CHAPS	BACS	Cheque & credit clearing	Currency clearings
• CGO, CMO, CREST, LCH etc. process security instruments, stocks etc.	• SWIFT, Eurogiro, Eurocheque, travellers cheques etc.	• Process debit card clearings, payments and auth-orisations	• Process credit card clearings, payments and auth-orisations	• High-value real-time gross settlement • Electronic credit transfer service	• Batch automated payment clearing • Three-day processing cycle	• Processes cheques and paper credits (bank giros) • Three-day processing cycle	• 10 currencies cleared, US dollar same-day settlement
• Membership: Financial institutions	• Membership: Financial institutions	• Membership: Banks and building societies	• Membership: Banks	• Membership: 16 banks	• Membership: 18 banks and building societies, 37,000 sponsored customers	• Membership: 13 banks and building societies	• Membership: 7 banks
• Ownership: Bank of England, Member institutions	• Ownership: Banks worldwide own SWIFT; Girobanks own Eurogiro	• Ownership: Member institutions of Switch/Visa	• Ownership: Visa/ MasterCard	• Ownership: Member institutions	• Ownership: Member institutions (not sponsored ones)	• Ownership: Member institutions	• Ownership: Member institutions

A cheque drawn on another branch of the payee's bank is presented for payment at that branch – until recently physically but now increasingly electronically – via the bank's inter-branch clearing system. In 1980, when most current accounts were operated by the major clearers, nearly 40% of cheques were inter-branch; in 1996, only 15% were. These payments do not pass through the London Clearing House. Instead, they are encoded with MICR data and routed to the branches through highly automated central or regional clearing centres. Inter-branch clearing accounted for about 480 million of the 3.2 billion cheques cleared in 1996.

A cheque drawn on another bank has to be cleared in London (if drawn on a branch in England or Wales) or sent to clearings in Edinburgh or Belfast in the case of Scottish or Northern Ireland banks. Payments are encoded and sent to head office clearing departments at the end of the day on which they are deposited. The clearing departments sort the payments according to paying bank. Early the next day, they are exchanged between members at the Bankers' Clearing House, and inter-bank settlement takes place. The paying bank's clearing department sorts payments by the branches on which they are drawn, and sends them that evening for 'presentment', which can now be electronic rather than physical, at the branch. Only on day three will the payer's bank have to decide to pay or bounce the cheque. The payee and the payee's bank may not know that a cheque has been dishonoured by the payer's bank until the fourth day.

Cheques are handled on a variety of electronic equipment. Each branch has a machine room or equipment at the tellers' desks, where branch deposits are encoded with MICR data giving the amount of the cheque; branch transactions are keyed in here, and other routine functions dependent on 'front office' automation links to the mainframe are carried out. In the central clearing departments of the banks, reader-sorters – the workhorses of the industry – capture the MICR data, endorse the cheques, microfilm them, and sort them at a rate of 33 per second in bursts. With developing technology, branch machine rooms or even teller positions may have equipment that can both encode cheques and read the information on them, while image technology, as we discuss below, is making increasing inroads.

Simplifying clearing logistics to save money

Moving these billions of cheques and paper credit vouchers from thousands of branches to the clearing house and back to the branches has been for decades a formidable task. As the move from paper to electronics slows, reducing the expense of handling the large residual volume of cheques is growing in importance.

As we have seen in the preceding section, the cheques are handled several times as they are recorded and shipped to clearing centres, cleared, presented at the branches on which they were drawn, and stored there. The average clearing bank branch has about twenty staff members who together account for most costs. Most of these are junior clerks or tellers, involved in one aspect or another of handling cheques in the branch. To improve branch economics, banks have been seeking ways of using IT to reduce the physical movement of cheques and remove cheque-related work from the branches themselves, rather than to speed up the actual transactions.

Currently, banks are pinning their hopes on cheque truncation – that is, stopping the cheque as early in the clearing cycle as possible rather than transporting it physically round the system. In truncation, the MICR data is captured and electronically passed to the paying bank, while the cheque itself remains at the collecting bank. Since the 1970s the UK banks have recognised this as offering the best prospect for improving the efficiency of the paper clearing system. It is standard practice in many parts of Europe – e.g., Belgium, Germany and Denmark – but only became legal in the UK in November 1996. Until then, bank branches, not a computer file, were where customer accounts were required to be held and where cheques had to be presented.

The geographical link between the account and the branch has been getting increasingly tenuous since the introduction of mainframe computers, and especially since the advent of 'front office' automation and the bringing of customers on-line. However, the law of negotiable instruments made electronic presentment questionable and restricted development of the systems for clearing cheques to the technology of the 1960s and 1970s. In 1988 the Review Committee on Banking Service Law (the Jack Committee) recommended legislation to permit electronic presentation, but given the extensive precedent surrounding the laws of negotiable instruments, wholesale revision of the law governing cheques was not straightforward and for many years the banks concentrated on electronic cheque substitutes, like BACS, which have no such legal complications preventing their use, rather than cheque truncation systems.

Image processing technology may now be providing a solution. Image processing involves optically scanning a document and digitising the image so that it can be stored, transmitted and reproduced in electronic form.

This could clearly save on paper-handling and transportation costs, especially as electronic transmission costs fall. Midland, which is installing a new image processing system, is expecting to reduce its cheque processing costs by up to 45% by 1999, mainly by displacing manual labour. Technological advancement in image processing is decreasing the importance of economic scale to a point where, for the Big Four, minimum efficient scale is significantly below current volumes. The main attraction of image processing is to decrease the importance of economies of scale per branch or per processing centre. As a result of this advance, truncation of paper-based flows will gain momentum. Because of the decreasing importance of scale economies, the Big Four cannot expect to sustain cost advantage for long, as late adopters will enter at a lower point on the cost curve, even if these are functional outsourcers rather than other banks.

In image processing, the document's image is captured, but not all the information can be processed. For this, optical character recognition (OCR) is needed. OCR involves 'reading' the data from a document into electronic form, which makes it suitable for processing. OCR can be used for reading ordinary typefaces and for 'courtesy read' (reading handwriting). The accuracy of courtesy read at present is 95% for the very best machines. As hardware costs fall, the new technology is becoming more accessible at the level of a branch or processing centre, and can thus reduce encoding costs.

These flows are being curtailed by organisational changes, as well as by electronic innovation. Banks are increasingly aggressive in their efforts to remove the handling of cheques from their branches. The key to this has been the development of regional cheque-processing centres or hubs for bulk commercial deposits. While all the Big Four banks have set out on this path, Midland has been especially aggressive in seeking to move the labour of encoding cheques from branches to regional centres, and expects to cut £200 million a year from its costs. Because the accounts of big companies and institutions are maintained on centralised current account systems, electronic and paper presentments can bypass branches altogether. Bulk cheques from such organisations can be directed to regional centres, truncated (at least for inter-branch items), cleared, credited to accounts and stored without touching a branch office. Since banks in England and Wales have long since ceased returning cheques to customers, it does not matter where they are stored until they are destroyed, as long as the system knows where they are stored in case a copy is needed.

Toward paperless clearing

The story thus far is very typical of investments in the banking industry, both in retail and wholesale banking. The ultimate need is for an industry-wide utility function. However, the starting point is invariably that of a single firm taking actions to meet a customer need – e.g., create a paper cheque as a means of transferring value – followed by a sequence of steps to deliver some form of inter-institution working or even an industry utility. Invariably this second generation form represents little more than an automation of fairly arcane practices inherited from the original paper systems and the participating institutions. In cheque clearing this is clearly shown. In the UK, APACS and the London and Scottish clearing service go as far as an automated paper-clearing system can go. In the US, cheque clearing has not even reached this stage as there is no APACS equivalent. The most recent attempt to establish such an industry utility in the US, involving a small number of participants and technology providers, could not get past the vested interests of the players.

All the London and Scottish clearers know the limits of these paper-based systems and have an idea of what the answer might be. The key is to eliminate the paper, either completely by supporting the debit card, direct debit, direct credit and bank giro payments, or by stopping the movement of paper as close to the first point of entry to the system as possible, i.e., by truncation. Most banks now do this for their own cheques, for example by truncating own-branch cheques at the branch or at the clearing centre for all own-bank cheques. Some banks (NatWest and Midland are in the midst of pilots) are investing heavily in using image technology to courtesy-read amounts – replacing the work of the clerk running the voucher reader encoding the numbers – and to move the images.

Barclays has gone a stage further in building its new cheque clearing centre in Northampton, the first London clearing centre to be located outside London. This centre uses the latest high-speed imaging technology and has sufficient capacity to clear and truncate all cheques in the UK. Barclays now has significantly lowered its unit costs as a result of stepping away from the old paradigm. The key questions are whether the other banks can be persuaded to join – recent discussions have so far not been fruitful – and whether Barclays will be able to hold on to the cost advantage or whether competition and over-capacity will force this benefit across to the customers.

On the competitive front, EDS, the world's biggest third-party processor, has also built a similar facility – on a smaller scale but claimed to be even more cost-effective than that of Barclays – in conjunction with the Royal Bank of Scotland, which went live in June 1997. Like Barclays, EDS has not succeeded in persuading other banks to join.

These may be early shots in an upcoming competitive battle in which the customer will ultimately prove to be the winner, whether in the form of uniform same-day clearing across the country and across institutions – no more waiting for up to eight days for a cheque drawn on another bank to clear – or in the form of lower costs. These may also, however, be moves that are rendered redundant by the introduction of a single European currency, where clearing and payments systems that currently prevail in Europe obliterate the old ways and traditions of British joint stock company banking.

THE BANK GIRO: IN DECLINE

The UK clearing banks established a credit clearing called 'bank giro' in 1960. With a giro, the payer's account is debited (or cash is handed over the bank counter) and the credit – the giro form – moves one way through the clearing system to the payee's bank, specifying the account to be credited and the sum involved. A credit clearing thus involves only half the movement of paper required by a cheque clearing, and eliminates the risk that the cheque will bounce, and the need to return it if it does.

The payer must know the bank and account number of the payee. This information is easily included on a printed giro form for bills and other demands for payment, which makes giro suitable for at-home transactions. In Germany, Scandinavia and other continental European countries, giro systems (managed by post offices) serve both banked and un-banked households, which use giros to settle virtually all at-home payments. These postal giros (and continental bank-owned giros) hold and update all accounts centrally, making them true giros. It is an effective system for cutting down on the use of cheques and cash. The UK bank giro is not a true giro, because there is no centralised debiting and crediting of accounts (the UK Post Office set up a true giro system with National Girobank in 1968 but the service never really caught on in a cash- and cheque-using society) .

The UK bank giro uses the same infrastructure as the cheque clearings to exchange paper credit transfers between banks. Customers can consolidate many cheques and cash items into one bank giro credit transfer. Before the automated BACS clearing arrived, its main uses were the payment of standing orders and the crediting of salary payments.

The bank giro was a purely manual operation until 1984 when the addition of encoded information on all giro credit vouchers enabled them to be processed automatically. The code is machine-read by MICR techniques, sometimes in combination with optical character recognition. Like the cheque, giro credits operate on a three-day cycle, with items exchanged in the clearing house on the second day and credited to the beneficiary's account on the third.

Bank giro has been declining in volume and in relative importance throughout the 1980s and 1990s, mainly because of the success of BACS in absorbing these and similar applications. In 1996 it had a total volume of 419 million items, of which only about 40% passed between banks (bank giro forms are also used as deposit paying-in slips, which largely accounts for giro being used mainly in inter-branch transactions). In 1996 less than 1% of regular non-cash personal payments were in the form of giro, down from 5% in 1976.

PRE-AUTHORISED PAYMENTS: ELECTRONIC DEBITS AND CREDITS

Pre-authorised payments – standing orders, direct debits and customer credits – have been rapidly increasing in importance, as people who used to pay all bills by cheque moved first to standing orders for some payments and then to direct debits. These payments accounted for less than 20% of all regular payments in 1980, but had risen to 45% of regular payments by 1996 – a remarkably fast volume growth rate of over 12% a year. They already account for the majority of regular payments, having passed cheques in 1977 and cash in 1995 – a very impressive transformation.

Pre-authorised payments are now processed through the BACS electronic clearing system. Current accounts have to be computerised in Stage A, and most input is still by magnetic tape.

The standing order: little scope for expansion

The standing order first became widespread in the 1930s, and by the 1960s was the most widely used current account facility after the cheque. Today, the standing order is mature: volume growth averaged less than 2% between 1985 and 1990 and actually shrank on average by 2% per year between 1990 and 1996. It is being replaced by more flexible and technologically sophisticated processes, notably the direct debit.

A standing order is only suitable for obligations which do not vary in amount and date, since any changes must be communicated to the bank in writing and entered into its computer system. Mortgages are the classic application. Although most UK mortgages are floating rate, rates were not traditionally reset more than once or twice a year. A standing order for buying a major home appliance in instalments, or a regular insurance or savings scheme payment, also requires little reprogramming, but most household expenses are variable by nature, and the use of standing orders has little scope for expansion.

While convenient for the customer, who only has to set it up once by filling in a form and signing it, a standing order creates a considerable amount of work for the bank. It initiates the transaction and also has to process changes and cancellations (and correct the many errors that can arise). Standing orders also create work for the recipient – most often a building society, life assurance company, or finance company – which has to reconcile the credit, once received. For this reason too the standing order is likely to diminish in importance.

The direct debit: popular with banks

The drawbacks of the standing order led banks and their large BACS recipients to promote direct debits in their place. Direct debits are BACS transfers initiated by the payee, who in effect takes the money out of the payer's current account after the payer has signed a debit authority. Though customers must sign a mandate for every new authority or change to an existing one, the costs to the bank are much lower than for a standing order, partly because less information is required. To encourage the use of direct debits, banks charge those of their retail customers who are subject to bank charges substantially less for processing direct debits than for paying cheques. Most of the expense of direct debits is borne by the wholesale customers, who prepare the magnetic tapes and deliver them to their banks or transmit the debit claims via various electronic cash management services. Wholesale users are prepared to do this because they no longer have the headache of reconciling credit transfers (and cheques), and they are sure to obtain their payments on the due date (assuming of course that funds are available in the payer account). They can integrate the BACS service into their own back office and treasury automation.

Currently about 37,000 companies, as well as local authorities and financial institutions, input data directly into the BACS clearing through the sponsorship of the 18 settlement members. Most input is still by magnetic tape or diskette, though the latter is being phased out. BACS has provided a direct telecommunication link called BACSTEL since 1983 and it is constantly being upgraded. Many of the top one hundred UK companies, who account for the majority of BACS usage, use this Stage C automation to access the service.

There are two types of direct debits, fixed amount and variable amount. The fixed type is the same as a standing order from the point of view of bank customers. Variable direct debits are not so readily accepted, especially by older bank customers, because they are concerned about the possibility of billing errors, disputes and defective service or merchandise. Consumers want the same sort of protection and control they enjoyed when they received a bill or invoice in the mail before paying by cheque. Since it is very much in the interests of payees and their bankers to 'sell' the direct debit, arrangements have been developed in most cases to bill consumers first and allow them an interval to raise any objections before the transaction is processed. However, acceptance of the variable direct debit will depend on a combination of trust (not so much that mistakes won't occur, but that banks will make things right when they do) and habit on the part of the consumer. Promoting this trust has required effective co-operation between the providers of goods and services and their banks in marketing direct debit as a safe, cheap and convenient method of settling bills. On the whole, they have been remarkably successful, especially among the newly banked, who never formed the habit of using cheques to settle regular bills.

In 1972, a year after its formation, BACS Limited processed 98 million standing orders, and only 55 million direct debits. By 1980 direct debits, at 173 million, had surpassed standing orders, at 169 million, for the first time, and by 1996 direct debits stood at over 1.4 billion while standing orders were on a declining trend at around 210 million. Direct debits now account for well over half of BACS volume and are still growing faster than BACS as a whole, at over 10% a year.

This growth cannot be maintained indefinitely, since the average household has only a certain number of regular bills to pay. However, many regular transactions have yet to be converted from cheques and cash. To a large extent, BACS direct debits have been expanding both at the expense of cash (as the un-banked became banked) and at the expense of cheques (as the younger generation of the traditionally banked classes seeks to save time and effort). The banked population over 50 years of age remain committed to the cheque, which alone or in combination with the bank giro is still the single most popular way for them to settle regular bills at home. We expect that while BACS direct debits will gradually level off – indeed the pace has slowed since pre-1990 levels of over 19% – high growth will be sustained at least for the next few years.

The customer credit: the electronic pay packet

The BACS application which has grown fastest after direct debit is the customer credit. These transactions for the most part are salaries and wages transferred to employees' accounts by companies, and pensions and other benefits paid by employers, financial institutions and government bodies. Direct crediting of salaries was originally a Bank Giro application, but BACS soon absorbed it and expanded it rapidly. Customer credits have grown from 37 million a year in 1975 to 815 million a year in 1996, and continue to expand at about 8% a year.

Employers are keen to promote customer credits, because of the high administrative and security expenses arising from traditional weekly pay packets. Less than 15% of the working population is now paid in cash, and this percentage is being driven lower as more employees are paid monthly – over 60% in 1996 from 29% in 1976 – rather than daily, weekly, or fortnightly. Customer credits via BACS account for over 90% of monthly salaries and wages, and over 40% of weekly pay. Already over 16 million salaries and 6 million pensions go through BACS and weekly wages payments are running at over 4 million. Customer credits probably prevented the pay cheque from becoming important in the UK (only 9% of all employer payments were by cheque in 1996). Overall, the number of individual pay transactions over BACS now exceeds considerably the use of cash or pay cheques, though scope for further conversion still exists.

Customer credits directly encourage the use of bank services among the previously un-banked, many of whom open accounts expressly for the purpose of receiving their pay electronically. The government also strongly promotes current accounts for recipients of state benefits so that those too can be paid by BACS rather than by cash over post office counters.

THE UNDERLYING TECHNOLOGY: BANKERS' AUTOMATED CLEARING SERVICES (BACS)

When current accounts were first centralised on mainframe computers during the 1960s, the members of the Clearing House saw an opportunity to slow the growth of cheques by expanding the use of standing orders. By the mid-1960s, the clearing banks had millions of standing orders on their computers, but to pay them each bank was printing out hundreds of thousands of paper giro credits (which were largely invented for this purpose) each day for exchange at the Clearing House. The receiving banks had to re-enter the data in their own computer in order to credit the beneficiary's account.

The volume and cost pressures resulting from these highly labour-intensive transactions led the members of the Bankers' Clearing House to set up the world's first Automated Clearing House (ACH). In 1968 the clearing banks established a shared-data processing company, the Inter-Bank Computer Bureau, to exchange composite tapes of debits and credits. This became a limited company owned by the Clearing House banks in 1971 under the title Bankers' Automated Clearing Services Limited (BACS). Until 1985, when it became one of the original three clearing companies under APACS membership rules, BACS was partly financed by the Bank of England, the Scottish clearers, TSB and the Co-operative Bank, all of whom had direct access to its services, but it remained wholly owned and managed by the six London clearers. BACS now has 18 full settlement members, the largest of any APACS clearing company. It processed nearly 2.5 billion electronic debits and credits in 1996, more than the volume of all cheques cleared in London. Volume has almost tripled since 1985, when BACS processed 835 million items, and its compound annual growth between the mid 1970s and 1996 has averaged 11% (although it has been slower recently). Retail customers have no direct contact with BACS, though they must give their bankers signed permission to set up the standing orders and debit authorities on which its use depends.

The technology of BACS has until quite recently been old, proven and simple, built around ICL mainframes from the late 1960s. Magnetic tape input still predominates. The system runs on a three-day cycle, like cheques, and the customer tapes can to an extent move through the same channels as the paper media which must be shipped to London for clearance. Some Stage C automation has been achieved by providing direct

BACSTEL telecommunications links to the largest corporate and institutional users, but at core BACS remains a Stage B batch processing system.

BACS has invested in a new generation of ICL mainframe automation to increase its capacity. There are, however, no plans to make BACS an on-line system or to shorten the clearing cycle. By remaining simple and easy to access by a wide range of banks, BACS increased the number of firms inputting directly by 25% a year between 1985 and 1990, and this number is still growing at 5 to 10%.

By far the largest growth has come from repetitive business-to-individual payments, particularly automated wage and salary payments but also including annuities and dividends, which lend themselves to batch processing. The 37,000 corporate users of BACS account for all its volume; yet they confine their BACS transactions to payment of staff salaries and wages. Few use BACS for corporate trade payments, which are normally made by cheques that travel with the associated documentation (both BACS and CHAPS are limited in their ability to transmit trade payment detail). The displacement of these cheques by BACS or CHAPS is of considerable interest to the banks, and to many of their more sophisticated customers. However, the system would have to be fundamentally upgraded to handle Electronic Data Interchange (EDI – see the following chapter) between corporate trading partners. This would almost certainly make BACS more expensive, and undermine its great virtue as a cheap and simple substitute for the biggest categories of cheques, which are business-to-individual and individual-to-business.

The key to the success of BACS is that companies and banks have worked together to encourage people to accept standing orders, direct debits and credit transfers as the normal and preferred means of paying bills and receiving payments. Such co-operation has been a hallmark of the successful introduction of new technology into British banking.

PAYMENT SYSTEMS (II): TOWARDS A CASHLESS WORLD?

Many sceptics fear that attempts to produce Pan-European or even national cashless payment systems are not worth the resources the banks are putting into them. Others, more optimistic, believe that the future lies with these high-tech substitutes for paper and cash. We examine three main electronic payment systems in this chapter: EFTPOS debit cards and electronic purse smart cards, which primarily automate spontaneous payments by individuals to companies, and electronic data interchange (EDI), which automates business-to-business transactions.

The technology for all three exists. Debit cards are widely used already; electronic purse cards are the subject of many pilot projects; and EDI is used extensively in several industries. The issues for the banks are familiar: should they co-operate or compete in developing standards for the new technologies? And will increased value for customers translate into bigger profits for the banks?

DEBIT CARDS AND ELECTRONIC FUNDS TRANSFER AT POINT OF SALE (EFTPOS)

APACS believes that debit cards will absorb most of the growth in retail payments in the next five to ten years, in spite of early problems with the system.

APACS tried to create a national debit card system, EFTPOS UK, but had to abandon it at the beginning of 1990. EFTPOS UK was the last of the co-operative efforts of the clearing banks to use technology and common standards to increase payments efficiency in retail banking. It collapsed because the participating banks had ceased to be a cartel with common interests after the Child Report was implemented. By 1989 the banks were competing to introduce rival debit cards, notably 'Switch' and 'Visa Delta', and their products developed further and faster than EFTPOS UK (which emphasised standards, integration and security). The joint approach was no longer adding value to the member banks funding it. EFTPOS UK was, in its inaugural service test, a technical success, but it was simply overtaken by events. Now the Switch and Visa Delta EFTPOS schemes have substituted for EFTPOS UK, even though they provide a dual approach to technical standards and operating procedures.

Debit card competition: Visa Delta and Switch

During the 1980s most EFTPOS schemes in the UK were off-line services operated by banks in conjunction with credit card companies, with terminals located in high-street retail outlets and petrol stations (both of which are highly concentrated and nationwide businesses in the UK). Data was captured for later transmission to a processing centre and the store terminals themselves accepted a wide range of credit cards, charge cards and some debit cards. PISCES was by far the largest of these off-line systems.

Visa Delta

The first large on-line system was Barclays PDQ, which had 5,000 terminals in 1988. In June 1987, Barclays had launched the first multifunction bank card, Barclays Connect, which was a cheque guarantee card with a limit of £50, an ATM card and a debit card. It could also be used like a normal Visa card, with paper sales slips, in the hundreds of thousands of retail outlets which accepted Visa but lacked EFTPOS terminals.

In forging the way for the acceptance of debit cards, Barclays Connect was nearly sacrificed in a marketing and public relations disaster. Barclays promulgated an 'honour all cards' rule, whereby all retailers had to accept Visa as both a credit and debit card, even though many did not want to accept credit cards. More important, they insisted that retailers pay the same commissions for debit card transactions as they did for normal Visa sales. Faced with united opposition by major retail chains, Barclays backed down and accepted their position that since the debit card was a direct substitute for the cheque, bank charges for debit card transactions should be the same as for cheque deposits. This proved to be a key precedent for all debit cards, settling the terms on which merchants would co-operate with banks to expand debit card usage. (The transaction fee that Visa eventually settled on at 17.5p was subsequently brought down by competitive forces to 10.5p.) Barclays had to accept that retailers might honour the Visa debit card but not the credit card, and the Visa Delta brand was created to enable that distinction.

The scheme has recovered strongly from these problems. Lloyds had joined in with the launch of its own Visa product, the Classic Card, in the spring of 1988. The card had all the features of Barclays Connect but also was linked to a personal overdraft facility and full protection under the Consumer Credit Act provisions for credit cards. Before this, Lloyds had only been a member of Access. The participation of two of the Big Four in the Visa Delta scheme ensured its continued vitality. By 1996 it had 16.2 million cards in issue, largely from Lloyds, Barclays and TSB, was accepted at 480,000 outlets, largely on the back of the Visa credit card franchise, and was used in 1996 for 587 million payments in the UK, a turnover of more than £17 billion.

Switch

Shortly after Barclays and Lloyds launched the Visa Delta scheme, Midland, NatWest and the Royal Bank of Scotland launched, in October 1988, Switch, which was the first all-electronic debit card system with no credit card connection. The card has the same ATM and cheque guarantee features as the Visa Delta cards and can be linked with an international electronic point-of-sale scheme at the discretion of the bank.

Switch avoided many of the pitfalls of the Visa-linked scheme. As it was not tied to any one bank, it offered a more neutral entry point for other financial services players than the Barclays and Lloyds schemes. Indeed, Switch followed the EFTPOS UK standards and is open to any other bank or building society that wishes to offer payment transmission services to its members and can meet these standards. A low cost option (Stasis), set up by Midland Bank and Britannia Building Society in the early 1990s, made it easy even for small building societies to join, which helped Switch membership to grow rapidly and contributed to the acceptance and distribution of the card. Although Stasis ceased to exist in June 1996, Midland continued to facilitate access for small players through Midland ISIS (Interbank Switch Issuer Service). Switch also worked at establishing an equal and mutually beneficial partnership with the large retail chains through a low flat fixed rate and a Switch Card Users' Group (SCUG), aimed at encouraging use of the card.

With active membership of two of the Big Four and tremendous growth to date, Switch claims to be synonymous with debit cards in the UK. By

1996, it had 16.3 million cardholders and 280,000 outlets. It has signed up many top national retailers and most of the major petrol companies. Vast national chains like WHSmith, the newsagent, Boots the chemist and, most important, supermarkets like Sainsbury's, Tesco and Asda have joined the system. Even retailers that traditionally did not accept cards other than their own, like Marks & Spencer, broke with their rules and now accept Switch. This wide availability, and an effective advertising campaign, resulted in 684 million Switch transactions in 1996, producing an annual turnover of nearly £20 billion. By the end of the century Switch expects these numbers to have increased to 1.5 billion and £35 billion per annum respectively.

Currently, seven full and fourteen associate members issue Switch cards. Bank of Scotland, Clydesdale, Yorkshire Bank and Halifax have joined Midland, NatWest and Royal Bank of Scotland as full members of Switch, while Britannia and many other regional building societies and banks have become card-issuing associates. Full members manage and control the scheme and can issue cards and acquire transactions. Associate members can also issue cards and use the infrastructure of a full member to authorise and clear their transactions. In addition to the issuing members, Switch also has merchant-acquiring-only members, a status that had not been planned, but that Switch had to accept. Barclays and Lloyds, having introduced and built the Visa Delta franchise, insisted on keeping their own Visa-based debit cards, but realised that, as Switch grew its cardholder base, they were increasingly at a disadvantage on the merchant acquisition side: the Visa Delta franchise could be provided to retailers by any merchant acquiring bank, as the Visa franchise – available from all merchant acquiring banks – automatically carried Delta with it, but Switch was only available from the Switch issuers. The Switch banks insisted that only banks prepared to issue Switch cards could join, and the matter ended up with the Office of Fair Trading – a far cry from the clearing bank co-operation that existed at the start of the EFTPOS UK scheme. Barclays and Lloyds did eventually join Switch, in 1991 and 1994 respectively, while retaining their Visa Delta products.

Widespread debit card acceptance

Debit cards have taken off in the UK. They accounted for over 192 million payments or 6% of spontaneous non-cash payments in 1990, their first full year of operation, subsequently rising to 35%, or 1.3 billion in 1996. Although over a short period and unlikely to be sustained over the long run, this shows an extremely impressive CAGR of 37% in the period 1990–6. Indeed, on current trends, debit card use is forecast to rise dramatically, reaching more than 3 billion transactions by the year 2000. Within this, over 70% is likely to arise from payments which would previously have been made by cheque. Substitutions from cash and credit cards are expected to represent 20% and 9% of debit card purchases respectively. We believe debit cards will continue to penetrate the UK consumer banking market successfully and may well have an impact on in-store cash and cheques comparable to the impact of BACS on at-home transactions. This removal of paper from spontaneous payments, along the same trend observed for regular ones, is another illustration of the increasing systems intensity in the retail payments business.

International debit cards

On an international scale, debit cards are following the path that credit cards have taken. In continental Europe, the creation of international debit card schemes is particularly important for banks which have for decades been issuing mostly debit rather than credit cards, consistent with credit and other regulatory constraints. Eurocard, a part of MasterCard, and Eurocheque have introduced a joint European electronic debit card (EDC) scheme bearing a separate logo. MasterCard has also launched an international debit card called Maestro, linked to the EDC scheme but marketed separately with its own logo, as European banks wanted to retain control of a European debit card scheme. The arrival of these schemes was particularly significant for Switch in the UK, since the lack of international acceptance was a disadvantage versus Visa Delta. It currently appears that Switch cards are adopting the Maestro logo, while leaving the EDC logo for the Eurocheque card – the card that started life as only a cheque guarantee card for the Eurocheque scheme but is now becoming a European multifunction card. EDC/Maestro are routed through the European Payment System Service (EPSS) network on-line to the issuing bank of authorisation. Debiting and crediting can occur simultaneously the day after the transaction. Technology is yet again, at least at a European level, providing customers with enhanced services while taking banks further along the path of increased systems intensity and the ensuing dangers of overcapacity.

Advantages for consumers and merchants

Debit cards are in effect another feature added to the already familiar ATM and cheque guarantee cards that almost every current account holder already has, and so access to debit cards is easier than to credit cards. Debit cards offer clear advantages over cheques: they are easier and faster to use at the shop counter, remove the limits associated with cheque guarantee cards, and provide a complete record of transactions. They also clear no faster than cheques: in the case of Switch the transactions are electronically gathered overnight by the acquirer, sent to the issuer on the second day and settled on the third. So the benefits for cheque users are manifest. Furthermore, debit cards may attract certain users of credit cards, as many UK consumers tend to use credit cards as payment cards, rather than for borrowing, but often have to pay an annual fee for them. With debit cards, banks can offer consumers the 'plastic money' convenience of a credit card, without charging a fee – although the benefit of an interest-free period is also removed and annual fees are increasingly being eliminated for credit cards.

Merchants have proved relatively receptive too. The trend to debit cards is being encouraged by banks offering discounted processing charges. Switch banks charged five pence for a debit card transaction against a typical charge of twenty-five pence for a cheque, although disputes arose when banks doubled Switch processing charges to ten pence. Visa Delta has been faced with a similar problem from a higher base charge. But processing charges are still relatively low compared with other payment systems, so this problem is unlikely to stunt the growth of debit cards. And retailers who have resisted credit cards, due to their high charges, see debit cards as a way to provide customers with the ability to use their bank cards without giving in to credit cards.

Furthermore, debit cards eliminate the expense and security risk that stores run when handling large amounts of cash; the emergence of the 'cashback' facility on Switch transactions (where the customer debits his or her account for more than the price of goods bought and receives the difference in cash from the retailer) in fact removes cash from the stores. Debit cards also create value when merchants link their EFTPOS to their accounting and inventory control mechanisms and assemble data on their customers and their buying habits. Finally, debit cards, when used as a replacement for cheques, can help automate and thus speed up the checkout process, cut back office staff, reduce the time needed for end-of-day processing and thereby increase opening hours. It is easy to see the attractions that debit cards hold for shops and other traders.

The banks' perspective on debit cards

The economic effects for the banks of this emerging success are unclear. The debit card enables them to claim that they are adding convenience to customers' accounts, but it offers little scope for adding proprietary features or value-added extras, as it is in effect an electronic cheque. Some net benefit to the banks as a group is likely, however. On the positive side, it is certain to increase the use of deposit money at the expense of cash, generating transaction fees from merchants for millions of payments that otherwise would be made with cash (although the payment of interest on current accounts somewhat offsets this advantage). Although competition between banks can be expected to drive fees down, such fees will in many cases represent new revenue to the banks.

More important perhaps, debit cards are far cheaper to process than cheques, so substituting debit card transactions for cheques may enable banks to reduce operating costs too. Among other advantages, Switch transactions bypass the branch network, minimising time-consuming and costly clerical work. We estimate that a debit card transaction costs less than five pence while a cheque transaction may cost as much as thirty pence, including all labour costs, i.e., execution, exceptions and returned items.

Expansion of EFTPOS, however, implies what may be very expensive Stage C automation. Full transformation of in-store into EFTPOS transactions requires linking the consumer's current account with the multitude of retail outlets. The owner of the account must be positively identified, the transaction authorised, and settled through terminals (the Hot Card File of Switch) and data networks that are secure, reliable and extensive. The extra expense that this entails for software, telecommunications, data centre capacity and support may well equal the expected benefits. At the very least, it increases the level of fixed cost in the current account business, which can ill afford it at the consumer level, and creates parallel cost structures to the other payment systems over a long, indeed indefinite, transition period.

In the Switch data communications network (SwitchNet) the problem is alleviated by a design enabling new members to integrate their current IT equipment without the need for significant investment or re-programming.

Furthermore, SwitchNet's current capacity is expected to be sufficient beyond 2000. Following this, the modular nature of the system may make upgrading straightforward and at least relatively cheap. Also, variable costs are at least slightly defrayed in the Switch system by the establishment of a 'floor' below which the transaction requires no authorisation.

On balance, however, the bulky fixed cost structure together with the competition from the many new providers of current accounts, and hence debit cards, points the way to overcapacity problems.

Other winners and losers from debit cards

With tens of thousands of terminals being installed by large retail chains, vendors and companies providing support and maintenance benefit from debit cards. In some cases banks will provide EFTPOS access services to merchants under contract, but this business could be dominated by independent vendors and data processing companies.

Operations like Midland ISIS which provide EFTPOS gateways to smaller financial institutions will also benefit. All retail competitors will have to be able to access the system, as debit cards emerge as yet another payment channel which all banks will have to support.

Credit cards, on the other hand, may face some dangers by the success of debit cards. Since merchants can now charge less for non-credit-card sales, they may favour debit cards to divert transactions from Visa and Access cards. This may give them leverage to drive the credit card discount even lower. Some consumers may turn away from credit cards too, to avoid the fees and potentially expensive debt that credit cards are associated with. Indeed, debit card growth is partly coming from a transition of credit card users, although this phenomenon may not necessarily be all bad news for credit cards; most switchers are likely to be cardholders who do not use revolving credit, the major source of credit card profitability. In fact, some banks actively use debit cards as an alternative to credit cards when wanting to offer the facility of a payment card to a customer that is likely to be a high credit risk or to use a credit card only for a few transactions that will be repaid every month. To the extent, however, that such a beneficial segmentation can not be ensured, credit cards can lose out from the growth of debit cards.

The transition to debit cards is very well advanced. The same is not yet true for the second cashless payment system we describe: stored-value smart cards.

STORED-VALUE SMART CARDS

Smart cards are a sophisticated payment system in the form of a plastic card with an integrated circuit to store key information about the holder. Memory capacity can be over 30 times greater than that of traditional cards, so that accounting and other data can be stored as well. First developed in France in 1974, smart cards have since attained various levels of sophistication, ranging from a simple prepaid card similar to a phone card, to portable electronic devices that may feature a keyboard and a liquid crystal display. The technology of smart cards allows a huge expansion of the uses to which plastic cards can be put, the most significant difference coming from the ability to store on a card value that can be spent and reloaded easily and reliably.

Even before mass marketing, smart cards have gripped the imagination. There has been a number of interesting applications, for services ranging from medical records and school dinners to gas meters, followed by a host of schemes from supermarkets. Such projects tend to be tied either to particular products or particular places and simply function as prepayment or consumer loyalty schemes. In the UK there are relatively few smart cards in circulation, many issued by BSkyB or used in digital mobile phones. BT has adopted smart cards as its new generation of phonecards. A few other applications have actually been implemented, such as the Thomas Cook Travel Card and the Shell Smart card, and many have been piloted, including bus passes in London, British Gas' Quantum prepayment system, and Loreta, a scheme introduced by PHH, the fleet management firm.

One of the most significant aspects of the stored-value smart card is that it enables customers and merchants to effectively circumvent banks in many transactions. For example, in Manchester, where a project was established to introduce smart cards to its rail links, the transport authority signed a deal with one of Manchester's supermarket chains. Each store will have a card reader, and store customers will be able to use their smart cards, initially purchased from the transport authority, to buy groceries. The cards can then be recharged at newsagents and bus stations. It is apparent that many, indeed most, of these applications do not necessarily involve banks. This is precisely why banks should take note.

Smart cards in banking: arrival of the electronic purse?

Smart card technology, in general, has many applications in banking. The one used internationally more than any other, albeit not yet in the UK, is the application in the reduction of the fraud problems associated with plastic payment systems. As we saw in Chapter 3, fraud cost the banks an estimated £166 million in 1991, and, although it had halved to £83 million in 1995, it rose again in 1996, reaching £97 million. Indeed, Cartes Bancaires, the country-wide network operated jointly by all French banks, has adopted the smart card for precisely this purpose. The cards are implanted with a microchip capable of storing more information than a conventional magnetic stripe card. Accordingly they can carry information about cardholders and their accounts, almost eliminating fraud. The large memory of smart cards (16 Kilobytes and up), their logic and their read-write capability imply that the card can hold information about any biometric (physical) feature of the cardholder and has the logic to enable it to make a judgement on the basis of this information. Furthermore, because the cardholder's identification profile is stored within the card and not in a central accessible database, the cardholder can feel confident that his or her privacy is being preserved. Another security feature is that the user has to key in a PIN number when using the card. The fraud problem is now of such dimensions in magnetic stripe cards that banks are gradually coming to accept the inevitability of smart cards for just this reason – although the reliability of smart card security features has been put in doubt by research proving they can be defeated.

The smart card has further advantages over magnetic stripe cards. Because its memory is so much greater, transactions can be made off-line in remote places, or where communications facilities are overcrowded. The information can be stored and then later referred to central databases at the first available on-line period.

The application, however, that could provide the most important smart-card-generated innovation in banking is the electronic purse. A fixed amount of money is held in the card at any given time and may be used as cash for all types of payment. Money is deducted each time the card is used with a reader or automatic machine, with no need for on-line verification. The recipient's bank may simply enter into the account the total amounts received each day without unbundling the individual payments.

As described in Chapter 3, cash remains the major payment method for small value in-store transactions, largely because of the high transaction costs – in the form of processing costs for banks, fees for merchants, and payment inefficiency for consumers – that cheques, credit cards and debit cards involve. It is these small value payments that the electronic purse can target more effectively than earlier payment systems, because of the efficient process it enables. The electronic purse really represents a complex Stage C development which effectively eliminates the middle stages of the business system. Transaction costs are thus significantly reduced: recently published studies indicate that the relative cost per transaction of the new forms of electronic banking and traditional branch banking may differ by a factor of 1:10. This allows banks to charge lower fees to merchants, thus giving them an incentive to promote the use of the electronic purse. Consumers will be attracted by the relative ease of use compared to debit and credit cards that require a complex process of validation and authorisation for every transaction. And compared to cash, the electronic purse will also offer consumers easier use, by eliminating the need for multiple notes and change, while it can be used to retrieve 'cash' from one's account at remote terminals, such as at-home PCs.

The British banks are involved in developing two competing types of electronic purse at the time of writing. Mondex, in which MasterCard recently acquired a majority holding, is supported by NatWest, Midland, Bank of Scotland and British Telecom; VisaCash is supported by Barclays, Lloyds TSB, Abbey National and Royal Bank of Scotland.

One Mondex card can hold up to five different currencies, and remember the last twelve transactions on it. The Visa system appears to be more in line with Continental systems, which is an advantage. The two systems are using different standards, so, for both to succeed as currently tested, retailers would have to install two different payment systems, which would be very costly.

Mondex trials are more advanced than VisaCash in the UK. The Mondex system has been tested in Swindon, where more than a thousand retailers and nearly half a million members of the public have been involved. Users of the card tested there can download 'cash' on to their cards at a cash point, telephone booth or at home if they are linked to the system. It is also possible to move money from one card to another by using a device like a pocket calculator. Purchases are made through a terminal. Mondex trials have now been extended in the UK and several international projects are under way, while VisaCash has also announced UK trials, following a successful test at the 1996 summer Olympics in Atlanta.

Despite the advances of technology that have made smart cards possible, and although trials have taken place, as we saw, the electronic purse has not yet penetrated as far as many had predicted. Its acceptance by users will depend primarily on acceptance by retailers. But the latter will require significant investment in smart card readers, since the UK, unlike countries such as France, has not installed this infrastructure. The slow progress of the electronic purse may be revealing a reluctance by banks to invest in smart card technology, both on the consumer and on the retailer side.

Do banks want smart cards?

What will the market do? The answer will depend on whether consumers, retailers and banks feel that smart cards have advantages that outweigh those of other payment systems. As usual, the young will be more ready than older people to accept them (although in the Swindon trials elderly people and the disabled liked them because they are easier to handle than small coins). Point-of-sale availability will be a key factor. Retailers will be looking for reduced costs and increased revenues, and value-added services such as cheque guarantee. But most fundamental of all to the success of smart cards is the banks' willingness to push the product.

From the banks' viewpoint, significant benefits are associated with smart cards. As we saw, electronic purse cards can reduce significantly the costs incurred currently by banks for other payment systems, while they can provide a new source of revenue and reduce costs further if they replace cash. Smart card technology also appeals to banks as a substitute for magnetic stripe credit and debit cards, as it is more durable (surface scratches do not damage it), it does not necessarily need expensive on-line verification, and, most importantly, it reduces fraud and the need for other expensive anti-fraud measures.

Such benefits will have to be substantial to compensate for the cost of smart cards. Card readers, the conversion of existing point of sale terminals and central processing involve a significant initial investment; whether these will be compatible with existing hardware is clearly crucial to this calculation. The development costs associated with the card for Cartes Bancaires were estimated at over FFr1 billion. And the initial expense of the card itself, were it to be used for credit and debit cards, is put at three times the price of a magnetic stripe card. For the moment at least, although technology costs and costs of conversion are falling, many argue that the costs remain prohibitive.

Edging towards smart cards

The paradox is evident. The time is approaching when smart cards will take off in the UK, as the technology is becoming cheap enough to encourage banks to use them to replace conventional bank cards. But unless banks (or other users) put in large orders, volume will be insufficient to create economies and thereby cut the price. The key is volume growth sufficient to bring production costs down. This is likely to come either through the bold initiative of individual players perceiving an advantage to being a first mover, or through collaborative initiatives that ensure cost sharing and volume growth. It is difficult to tell when UK banks will push smart cards more aggressively. The sale of Mondex to MasterCard could provide a trigger. Because of the large installed base of EFTPOS readers, there will need to be some other impetus; the potential advent of a single currency in 1999, where in phase I retailers will have to support two currencies, may be just the time. Should this not happen or not be sufficient, the year 2000 could be the turning point. Current EFTPOS technology may not be able to cope with the famous 'millennium bug'. Should new equipment need to be installed, it will almost certainly be smart-card-compatible.

The transition to smart cards may be smoothed in a number of ways. Smart cards may come into their own where readers can be installed for the first time, say, in small shops and taxis. The PDQ IV smart card system introduced by Barclays Merchant Services allows small retailers to accept and verify credit and debit cards without EFTPOS equipment. The scheme encourages them to replace conventional manual imprinters with a smart card reader. When credit and debit cards are used to pay for goods or services, transaction data (card issuer, customer details and value of transaction) are captured automatically at the terminal and then recorded on the retailer's smart card. At the end of the day, the smart cards are removed from the terminal and taken or sent to a collection point, which could be the firm's office or a bank branch. Here a special reader scans the card, extracts the day's transaction data and enters it into the bank's computer system. Such automation bypasses many of the middle steps in the business system and minimises the manual work of banks.

In order to be truly useful in banking, the smart card must of course be international. By 1992 the smart card was being used extensively in continental Europe (mostly in France) and Japan. In the US the principal users were government agencies, but widespread usage in the near future was forecast. However, before the card can become truly viable in Britain and substitute for other means of payment, and certainly before it can become international, universal standards must once again be agreed upon, particularly the biometric ID standard. Perhaps the experience of the debit card has taught the industry that such hurdles will be more rapidly overcome if institutions, instead of competing, co-operate in setting standards for the new technology.

Whatever the course that banks take to adopt smart cards, we have little doubt that they will sooner or later join the other payment systems to provide consumers with more and enhanced services. But what they will also be doing is increasing the payment systems capacity, providing consumers with more direct control of their finances and generally taking banks down the same road as all the technological advances we have described. The outcome is therefore unlikely to be increased profits for the banking industry. But banks can, once again, not afford to ignore this new technology. And those banks that manage their investments most effectively will be the ones that stand to win.

Smart cards on the Internet

The Internet has caused the biggest boom in electronic business since the invention of the telephone. Both customer and vendor could benefit greatly from home shopping and home banking, but both are worried about the risks associated with credit card payment over the Internet. Hackers can intercept messages, change origin, destination and text, and thus obtain credit card information.

This is where the smart card comes into its own, as it can provide the ability to control the secure communication of transaction information between customer and supplier. This can be achieved by using the smart card to hold encryption keys or as a stored-value card.

In the former case, the customer's card contains the necessary keys to encrypt information into a message that is sent to the supplier, whose smart card decrypts the message and retrieves the information. There are two main schemes for encryption and decryption: single key and public key. With single key cryptography, a common secret key is used both for encryption and decryption. This requires that the two communicating parties exchange the key by some other secure means and can then use the key, for example, to authenticate information. Public key cryptography uses a pair of keys, one that is public and one private and secret. The owner would have a personal key pair: the public key is used by other people to send encrypted messages to the owner, while the private key is employed by the owner to decrypt messages received. Public key cryptography can be used to implement digital signatures, the owner's private key being used to sign documents, while the public key is used by the recipients to verify the signature. Public key cryptography implementations are considerably slower than most single key systems owing to their complex algorithms. They are generally used to establish a secure communication session and a means for exchanging private keys which are then used for, say, on-the-fly data encryption.

With stored-value cards, such as Mondex, the transactor can complete a transaction through a smart card reader attached to the telephone or built into a personal computer. Such transactions also need some form of electronic signature verification. Again, launch of such a programme will depend on the installed base of readers being large enough. The key that unlocks this rollout could come from the telecom or pay-TV companies.

In order to establish a credible system for digital cash transfers or credit card transactions over the Internet, an agreed standard will be required. Considerable effort is being put into creating the necessary standards to protect customers and merchants alike from abuse.

ELECTRONIC DATA INTERCHANGE (EDI) AND ELECTRONIC COMMERCE

Debit cards and smart cards will mainly affect transactions between individuals and businesses. As we saw in Chapter 3, business-to-business transactions pose a different challenge due to their complex accounting and other requirements, and purchasing cards are providing an alternative to cheques in this sector. Purchasing cards, however, automate only part of the end-to-end process, as they basically replace the cheque with a more efficient payment medium. Notwithstanding their importance, a major technological breakthrough for business-to-business payments is most likely to come from the spread of electronic data interchange (EDI), that transmits both payments and supporting documentation between companies, and from the development of electronic commerce over the Internet, which allows smaller firms to use EDI without the major investment required until now for getting access to proprietary networks. This could prove to be a major technological innovation with significant implications for banks.

EDI technology, opportunities and challenges

As a data communications technology, EDI is fairly simple. Data to be sent is represented in a format agreed upon by both trading partners so that both companies' computers can understand it. For example, a purchase order should always have the customer number, date, order number, etc. in the same place and in the same coding scheme (e.g., ASCII). EDI transmissions are usually sent via a value-added network (VAN) with which both parties have service agreements, although high volume users may opt to use their own private network for data transmission. The VAN provides a 'mail box', storing transmissions until the recipient is ready to process them, and ensures the reliability and security of the network. The main value-added-network providers in the UK are GE Information Services (GEIS), AT&T, IBM, and British Telecom. These companies have been providing their services via proprietary networks, but are now building Internet-based solutions along their proprietary software in order to tap the emerging new market potential.

EDI has promised, and in many cases provided, significant benefits to businesses. It eliminates the need for several manual activities, thus tackling the vast white-collar bureaucracy in manufacturing and distribution that deals with the process from request for bids and designs through to payments and after-sales service and can account for up to 10% of the cost of a product. EDI enables companies to reduce paper-handling delays, and can reduce the average cost of processing a form by a factor of ten.

EDI has made great progress in certain concentrated industries, like chemicals and automobiles. Its spread, however, has been hampered by the lack of common networks and universally-followed message standards that would allow, for example, a plastics firm to do business electronically with a car manufacturer on a one-off basis. While EDI was growing at 50% p.a. in the late eighties, it later slowed down to a growth rate of 10%, and has reached only about 20% of its potential coverage. In the absence of formal access arrangements between networks, most companies have had to restrict themselves to having access to the participants of one network only, while other companies have had to support several networks, leading to very high costs and complexity. The lack of common message standards has been a further complication. National standards, such as Tradacoms used in the UK, and several industry-specific, or even company-specific, standards are deeply entrenched. Much of the early work on standardisation was built into the ANSI X12 standard, though this contains little in the way of direct financial transactions. The European standards work, culminating in the UN-sponsored EDIFACT standards, has produced standards that are gaining increasing acceptance. Among these are such key documents as the remittance advice and, significantly, banking instructions, such as payment instructions and debit and credit orders. But progress in having any standard universally accepted and used has been very slow.

The electronic commerce revolution

The growth of the Internet could prove to be the catalyst for the resolution of the obstacles that EDI has been facing and the emergence of a dominant design in electronic commerce. By 'electronic commerce' we mean the completion, in whole or in part, of the arrangements between sellers and buyers for the sale, procurement or barter of goods and services over a public or private telecommunications network in which digital communications replace or supplement face-to-face, paper-based and voice interactions.

Until now the necessary link to a proprietary network and the ensuing high costs meant that the number of EDI users was kept low and usage was generally limited to communications between large corporations and their suppliers or distributors. In this environment, the lack of common standards was, of course, a problem, as it increased costs and constrained growth, but there was no sufficient momentum being built up for a common standard to emerge. As wide access to EDI over the Internet becomes a reality, it is likely that the dynamics will change, and several initiatives are already underway to create simplified EDI standards that will enable Internet-based Web forms – which can be used with a simple Web browser, like Netscape – to be translated into EDI messages and vice versa.

The key assumption behind this expectation, supported by the evidence to hand, is that the cluster of technologies embodied in the Internet/ Intranet phenomenon and its related developments (e.g., the World Wide Web) represent an emerging common carrier for information and interaction towards which proprietary data exchange standards and networks will converge. Such a development has far-reaching value-generating potential for commerce as a whole, way beyond any benefits that EDI has provided to date.

Electronic commerce is bringing about a fundamental shift in the cost and efficiency of information logistics that can be compared to the change in the cost of physical logistics from the nineteenth century to date. In that case, the cost of moving goods fell steeply in real terms (both cash and time) as the capability in terms of volume and speed, as well as range, increased by orders of magnitude. Furthermore, the value generated was not only the reduction in cost; cheaper transportation led to increased trade and to a dramatic improvement in market efficiency. Similarly, electronic commerce today has the potential to free-up enormous economic value, which will be the combination of the value of direct information interaction, the value of continuous price discovery, the value of risk reduction and, of course, the value of integrated logistics – i.e., electronic procurement, which brings benefits such as integration with information management systems (e.g., SAP), improved physical logistics (just-in-time delivery, proof of delivery, etc.), reduction or elimination of paper flows and manual processing, reduction of manual order/invoice/payment matching, increased payment efficiency, and overall reduction in working capital.

By some estimates, the total value generated by electronic commerce could represent 40–90% of the final cost of goods sold, dependent on item values, in business-to-business commerce. Yet this prospect is not necessarily good news for the current players. As with the physical logistics revolution, this transformation in information logistics is, to use the terminology of Foster's S-curves, a discontinuity, that gives attackers an advantage and makes survival a challenge for all players involved. Banks are not immune from this threat.

Implications for banks

Banks have been participating in the evolution of EDI by providing mostly proprietary 'financial EDI' services to their customers, enabling them to send payment orders and other messages to their bank electronically. They have done this by linking the EDI service (carrying the transaction data) to a BACS service (carrying the payments data and a key to identify the EDI message). In this way the EDI transactor can be assured that payment will only be released at the appointed time and that payment will be guaranteed to work to BACS schedules. Some of the Big Four banks have been setting up agreements with software companies to develop integrated solutions so that even small businesses can link their accounting applications with the financial EDI service and payment orders can be issued automatically. The agreements between Barclays and Pegasus Software and between Midland and Sage are prime examples of this. The use of automated bank reconciliation procedures completes the circle for high-volume transactors, where bank statement data and payment instructions can be recorded automatically. For payees who do not have EDI links, the banks are using a service provided by Royal Mail, called EDIPOST, which makes it possible to have an EDI message containing the remittance advice printed and then mailed to the relevant payee.

EDI is raising issues for banks similar to the ones raised by the other payment systems we have reviewed. On the one hand, it could eliminate the vast majority of UK business-to-business cheques and the costs associated with processing them. On the other hand, these costs are largely fixed, and supporting EDI is creating additional infrastructural costs without necessarily creating additional revenues.

Bankers say that an efficient customer is a good customer, and that electronic commerce will give them new opportunities to create value-added electronic banking services, but the more realistic among them sense a cul-de-sac. There are many similarities between this situation and the one that US banks faced in the 1980s in the US dollar clearing example we discussed in Chapter 2. In that case, as in the case of EDI and electronic commerce, banks found themselves having to invest in new technology to stay in the game but generated efficiencies and overcapacity that ended up destroying their profits. Automation of the process turned them into commodity providers competing aggressively for marginal customers. The similarities can only worry banks.

EDI and the electronic commerce revolution are presenting some further, potentially more dangerous, challenges for banks. By bringing buyers and sellers and their technological infrastructures together, they are raising the possibility that banks could be cut out altogether from many payments, through the emergence of electronic bills of exchange (after all, there were negotiable bills of exchange financing wholesale trade for centuries before there were commercial banks). In such a scenario, banks might see electronic commerce being dominated by global technology companies like IBM and Microsoft, which could establish exchange systems that made banks redundant. Of course, regulatory constraints restricting the set of institutions that may act as payment transmitters are likely to provide some protection for banks. Similarly, customer perception is likely to favour banks as reliable financial intermediaries for commerce. Evidence of this is

that whilst there has been significant take-up of the EDI services for transactions, the willingness to use EDI for payments without the active participation of a bank has been low. Research conducted by NatWest in late
1993 suggested that this was because customers did not trust the EDI supplier to make payment at the stipulated date and time. The consequence of
this is that banks have been able to make important inroads into the financial EDI market.

Regulation and perception, however, probably would not protect banks
from another significant threat presented by electronic commerce. EDI has
shown that electronic communications facilitate just-in-time production
and with it a major reduction of stocks of finished goods, work in progress
and parts. Furthermore, electronic linkage of payment instructions to the
purchasing process reduces the risk of settlement delays. As a result, business requirements for working capital, which mostly arise from the timing
gaps between suppliers paying to produce things and their getting paid by
their customers, could be significantly reduced. This is the heart of the corporate overdraft business.

It is the notion of 'assured payment' that may hold the key for banks to
become more involved in commerce, as they once were in a world of merchant banking and 'real bills banking'. In this back-to-the-future world the
banks could reintegrate themselves in the real transactions flow by managing the financial risks borne by suppliers at the time transactions are executed, rather than through the now traditional provision of 'working
capital' finance. This would have the effect of reducing the cost of borrowing, especially for small businesses, as the financial risk assessment
would be based on the credit-worthiness of the business' customers at payment time and not by a snapshot of the smallness of the business.

CREDIT CARDS: A HYBRID PRODUCT

Credit cards combine payment functions and credit functions, as does a current account, but, through the use of worldwide networks for approving and processing transactions, they can be used almost anywhere. They are not a complete payment system, as they do not on their own complete a transfer of funds from the payer to the payee. What they do is to create an obligation that is later settled with another payment. As a result, they can be maintained independently of the banking system. Because cards share a largely electronic infrastructure, the business is influenced considerably by economies of scale. It provides consumers with a service that traditional bank payment and credit mechanisms do not, and the banks can share in this by charging cardholders interest on outstanding balances and in some cases annual fees for their cards, and receiving discounts from merchants who accept the cards. In considering scale economies, however, the picture is not totally clear, as it is possible to operate profitably at three different scale points; consider the low entry cost for a small PC/server-based application package, the potential to share costs through an industry utility (e.g., FDR) and the scale of Barclaycard.

The future shape of the UK bank credit card business is unclear. The market for issuing cards seems to have great growth possibilities, but will it be the UK clearing banks that benefit, or the many new entrants that have come onto the scene recently? Transaction processing activities will probably be dominated by one or two big-scale companies, a trend that is already apparent.

WHAT IS A CREDIT CARD?

Credit cards are hybrids: part payment, part credit facility in function; part paper, part electronics in technology. Bank credit cards are not part of the payment system. They convert and consolidate in-store transactions, which would otherwise have been payments, into receivables. The merchant can discount these receivables with the banks for cash, the consumer can delay paying the credit card bill or convert it into an instalment loan, and banks can play the role of discounter, processor, lender or all three. The credit card bill can be paid by cheque, standing order, direct debit or cash and giro credit, all in-home payments. Credit cards do not displace in-store payments, they just consolidate many such payments into one bill. They can, however, facilitate in-home purchases, when used for mail, phone or Internet shopping.

Credit cards have no necessary connection with banking and are not intrinsically a banking service. The product is really a deferred payment or instalment credit account, which any type of commercial or financial institution can maintain for a consumer. The card itself simply serves to identify the holder of the account. This does not require much technology in its simplest form of running an imprinter over a paper voucher.

There are three types of card providing some form of credit (Figure 5.1).

Store cards (or retailer cards) are issued by an individual store or a retail chain. They are the oldest type, since embossed cards or charge plates linked to credit accounts have been used by retailers for about a century. Store cards are an extension of this old sales and marketing tool. In addition to being able to defer payment generally without having to pay an annual fee, store cardholders have the option of paying as little as 5% of their outstanding balance each month, though interest is charged at rates generally well above the cost of other consumer credit. Since these cards are tied to one retailer (or retailing group), they have limited value to consumers as a payment method or as a source of credit. A recent Mintel survey suggested that although customers pay their bills promptly, thus not generating revenue for the retailers, stores value their cards as a marketing tool to encourage the shopper to visit the store and buy more items. Another, probably more important, reason for offering store cards is the fact that these provide retailers with valuable information on their customers, such as contact details, lifestyle attributes and shopping patterns. Such information enables retailers to target their marketing campaigns.

Fig 5.1 Number of plastic payment cards in issue*

1989–96

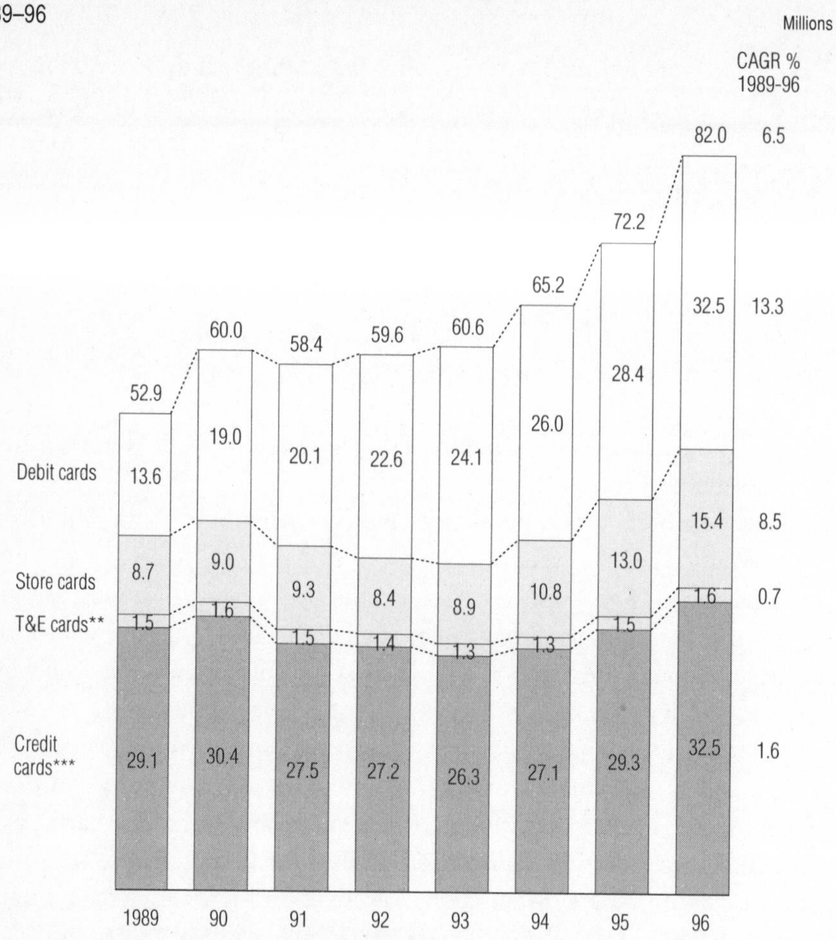

Millions

CAGR %
1989-96

	1989	90	91	92	93	94	95	96	CAGR % 1989-96
Total	52.9	60.0	58.4	59.6	60.6	65.2	72.2	82.0	6.5
Debit cards	13.6	19.0	20.1	22.6	24.1	26.0	28.4	32.5	13.3
Store cards	8.7	9.0	9.3	8.4	8.9	10.8	13.0	15.4	8.5
T&E cards**	1.5	1.6	1.5	1.4	1.3	1.3	1.5	1.6	0.7
Credit cards***	29.1	30.4	27.5	27.2	26.3	27.1	29.3	32.5	1.6

* Excludes ATM/cheque-guarantee-only cards and Eurocheque cards
** American Express and Diners Club
*** Includes all 'gold' Visa and MasterCard. Prior to 1991 number of cards issued by building societies is estimated
Note: The drop in issued credit cards from 1990 to 1991 reflects the widespread introduction of annual fees and the cleaning-up of many inactive accounts by issuers

Source: APACS, BBA, MMG analysis

T&E (travel and entertainment) cards (or charge cards), such as Diners Club and American Express, were the first cards to offer customers wider acceptance than traditional store cards. A broad national and international network of merchants who would accept the card as a form of payment was developed. The T&E card did not provide instalment credit. Its value to consumers lies in its broad acceptance worldwide, and in the services it offers to cardholders. Its value to merchants lies in the fact that a relatively affluent group of consumers are encouraged to use their products and services. There are only about 1.6 million T&E cards in the UK, approximately 80% issued by American Express and 20% by Diners Club. This number was shrinking between 1990 and 1994 as credit and debit cards were eating into the share of T&E cards. Their number is now growing again and, although it is still a small part of the plastic card market and T&E cards are accepted at only 40% as many outlets as bank credit cards, they maintain their significance for some profitable segments. Many banks have sought to tap these segments with 'gold' cards, which in some cases are charge rather than credit cards (i.e., like T&E cards, they do not provide instalment credit) and carry benefits similar to the traditional T&E cards.

Credit cards, as instalment credit cards that are not issued by a specific retailer are simply referred to, in effect divorce both payment and consumer credit from geographical restrictions: a merchant anywhere in the world can depend on the card company for payment, rather than on the cheque of a stranger; the card issuer can generate loans based on the card anywhere with minimal processing and no physical presence. The credit card effectively combines the advantages customers get from store cards (deferred payment and easy if expensive credit) with that provided by T&E cards (wide acceptance), creating a very attractive product.

In the remainder of this chapter we focus on this last type of card, which is generally issued by banks and clearly dominates the market for cards with a credit function.

THE CREDIT CARD BUSINESS SYSTEM

Credit cards were not designed to increase the efficiency of the payments system, displace labour, or otherwise improve the productivity and cost structure of the banking system. They in fact create additional work and expense, as well as more transactions. They represent a unique and complex business system, which allows banks to add value for both cardholders and merchants, and in turn gain new streams of revenue from both. The business system has five major segments (Figure 5.2):

1. Issuing cards, including credit checking and marketing.
2. Processing card accounts, including billing, collections and customer service.

Fig 5.2 Major players in credit card networks

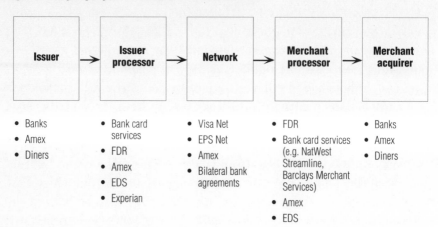

3. Running authorisation and transaction processing networks.

4. Processing merchant transactions.

5. Acquiring merchant accounts.

Each of these segments can be pursued by banks (or other institutions) relatively independently of the others. However, the segments themselves are highly interdependent. Cardholders can be attracted only if the cards are widely accepted by merchants, and merchants will sign up only if there are substantial numbers of cardholders. These needs are met by having a readily identifiable brand name and worldwide networks for authorisation and transaction switching, which hold the whole business system together. Bank of America invented the credit card, but its success depended on the emergence of global bank card associations to support common logos, standards and networks.

CREDIT CARDS IN THE UK: EUROPEAN LEADERS

Barclays Bank issued the first credit card in the UK in 1966 when it launched its Barclaycard as the British licensee of Bank of America's Bankamericard. Barclays operated from the beginning across the whole business system in the UK, owning its authorisation and transaction processing channels and having exclusive use of the Visa connection.

In 1972, the other UK clearing banks formed the Joint Credit Card

Company (JCCC) which created and supported the brand name Access for cards issued by its member banks as well as serving as transaction switch between participants and signing up and servicing all merchants for its members. Essentially it acted as a 'develop and share' utility. Access was affiliated with MasterCard and the continental Eurocard system. Barclaycard, Access and Trustcard, a Visa product issued and processed by TSB, accounted until the late 1980s for virtually all credit cards in the UK. During 1988 all four big clearing banks took up direct membership of both Visa and MasterCard ('dual issuance'). Barclays led, as usual, because it wanted to offer both MasterCard and Visa products. Most of its eligible current account customers had the Barclaycard, and most of its merchant base accepted Access as well; consequently it wanted to process both.

The UK was the first market outside the US and Canada to be penetrated by credit cards, and is by far the most mature credit card market in Europe (Figure 5.3). In 1996 there were 26 million credit card accounts in the UK and roughly 33 million cards in issue. About 42% of the adult population holds at least one credit card, the highest penetration in Europe, and there is a high degree of multiple card-holding, since there are 0.56 credit cards per person. However, the UK market is not nearly as saturated as the US, where there are just under two credit cards per inhabitant, which indicates that there may still be considerable room for growth in the UK. The number of cards in the UK decreased between 1990 and 1993, because of a limited degree of saturation, a revolt against fees, emerging competition and tightened risk control during the recession (Figure 5.4). The number of cards, however, is now growing rapidly again, propelled by the growing number of new entrants who are capturing existing and new cardholders, and it has now surpassed its 1990 peak, with the volume of transactions up more than 40% since then.

It is the relatively affluent 40- to 49-year-olds who are most likely to have a credit card. More than half of them have at least one card. Ownership is also more common in South East England and East Anglia. Cardholders made around one billion purchases in 1996, up from 150 million in 1980. It is estimated that credit cards account for 17% of all non-cash consumer transactions in the UK, with a turnover of around £50 billion. The proportion is higher for spontaneous payments, at 26% in 1996. Cards are accepted at more than 500,000 retail outlets in the UK, double the number of ten years ago. It appears, then, that the credit card is a success in the UK.

Fig 5.3 Credit and debit card penetration in Europe

1996 estimate

Number of cards per thousand people

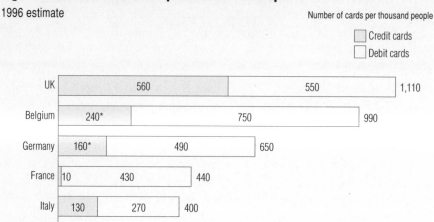

* Most cards that qualify as 'credit cards' in these countries are in fact 'delayed debit' or charge cards

Source: BBA, Bank for International Settlements, MMG analysis

Fig 5.4 Credit card holding in the UK

Percent of adults holding at least one card, 1989–96

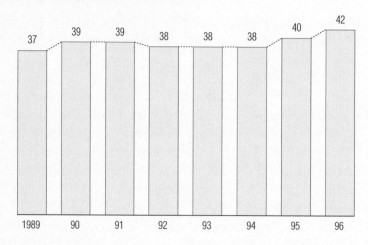

Source: APACS

HIGH PROFITABILITY BUT INCREASING COMPETITION

In fact, the UK credit card business has shown high profitability recently but faces a challenging future. Although transaction volumes continue to increase, and people are now using their cards more as a source of credit (Figure 5.5), competition is increasing rapidly. And, based on high margins, left over from a long period of high interest rates, many banks have added features that could prove very costly when margins start shrinking. For example, the use of the direct debit option to clear balances before they collect interest charges is widespread. And in many cases interest is calculated on purchases from the billing date, not the date of purchase, leading to interest-free periods of up to 56 days. As people begin to use their cards more as methods of convenient payment with a free credit period and less as a source of interest-bearing credit – as they often do in the down phase of the economic cycle – the high rates of interest produce less and less income.

In fact, banks are currently reaping the rewards of the high charges they introduced in the late 1980s. At that time, when they realised that profits were contracting even as card ownership was expanding at a high rate, several major card-issuing banks changed their strategy from trying to expand card ownership to extracting more income from their existing business and controlling their costs, which had not been an issue until profits started to falter. Lloyds decided to impose an annual fee for credit cards. The results were little short of devastating in public relations terms, but only resulted in around 200,000 account closures, less than 5%. This break set the direction for the whole UK industry in the early 1990s.

Experience to date would indicate that customers are relatively indifferent to interest rates, but that fees deter new customers and drive away many existing cardholders. In the US the introduction of fees on cards was unpopular too, but the credit card provided value to customers that could not be obtained otherwise in the US system (a fragmented banking system with no cheque guarantee mechanism – the credit card was *de facto* the national payment system in the US – and no credit function in the current account). UK customers have real alternatives to credit cards: debit cards, guaranteed cheques and the traditional overdrafts (though more expensive in recent years, particularly if unauthorised). The major issuers have held on to the annual fees for the time being, but competition has intensified and an increasing number of cards are being offered with no annual fee, especially by new entrants trying to capture market share.

To boost card ownership, the big banks have been launching new cards at a fast rate, using many of the tactics developed in the US credit card market for marketing and stimulating card use. Barclays introduced a MasterCard with a low introductory interest rate and large credit limit, in addition to Barclaycard 'Profiles', a loyalty card scheme that offers rewards to customers who accumulate points by using the card. NatWest has offered a card which earns airline bonus miles on a similar basis. Lower priced credit

Fig 5.5 Consumer credit composition and credit card interest generation
1990–6

£ billions

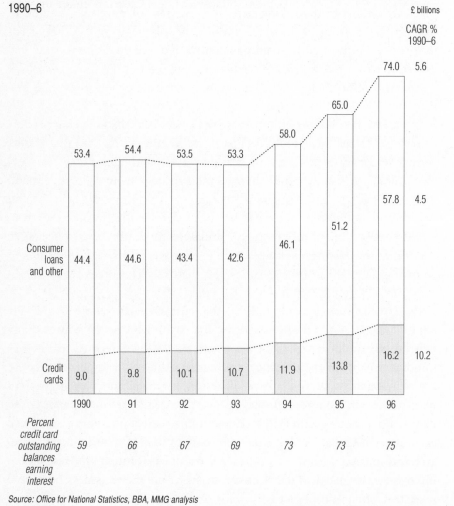

CAGR %
1990–6

Source: Office for National Statistics, BBA, MMG analysis

cards are being offered to customers who open accounts with Midland's branchless bank, First Direct. Affinity cards, i.e., cards that carry the brand of an association, group, charity, or other institution with which certain people feel related and which benefits in some way by the card (e.g., by receiving a percentage of the transaction value) are on offer from several smaller banks and building societies, the larger of which have been in the credit card business since their deregulation in 1986. We now also see banks aligning with big-name franchise holders, for example, NatWest's 1997 launch of an Executive Club card with British Airways.

T&E cards seem to be following the same trend. American Express started a rewards programme for cardholders, offering members points towards air travel or hotel accommodation. Diners Club has linked up with British Airways to offer a similar scheme. Such promotional schemes generally have proved successful at raising transactions. Whilst big-spending customers get the most real value from these schemes, they do serve to lock in customers and to consolidate payments that might otherwise have been split among many cards.

Although the English and Scottish clearers and TSB accounted for 93% of the market in 1988, many new entrants have now arrived, notably aggressive players from the US market. Currently there are more than eighty varieties of Visa and MasterCard on offer in the UK. Many new players are small; but short-term profits are not necessarily critical, because in many cases they see the credit card as a way to build up a list of customers to whom they can market other services or products.

Some of the entrants bring substantial financial and marketing clout. In 1993 Vauxhall launched the British version of the GM card. The card, either Visa or MasterCard at the customer's option, aimed to compete on both price – a low interest rate and no fee – and through added benefits from frequent use. The principal benefit was points collected towards a new car but Vauxhall also signed up corporate partners to entitle the holder to other benefits. Not to be outdone, Barclaycard linked up its Profiles loyalty scheme to Ford, and is now a leading buyer of Ford cars in the UK. British Telecom has also considered a combined credit and phone card and British Gas has now entered the market. Even football clubs are entering the league. Manchester United is using its database for developing financial services, starting with the credit card before venturing into insurance, life policies and even the travel sector. The basis for entering the credit card market is often not a banking infrastructure but information powered by technology. The impressive success of manufacturer-branded credit cards, like GM's, in the US may be a cause for alarm for UK banks, although the real threat in the UK may come from different types of entrants.

Among new entrants, Chase Manhattan was the first to introduce a credit card with interest rates lower than those of the Big Four. Save and Prosper, the retail money management subsidiary of the merchant bankers Robert Flemings, has also launched low interest cards, with an APR (annual percentage rate) a full 7% below the market norm. Capital One, a major card issuer in the US, entered the market with a card offering an APR of 8% for the first year, compared with 22% from Barclaycard. Large building societies like Nationwide and Bradford & Bingley also have aggressive programmes, competing on rate.

Many new issuers remain niche players. For example, Save and Prosper has deliberately restricted the eligibility of its low-interest-rate card in order to attract borrowers. Similarly, MBNA, one of the largest credit card lenders in the US, has established an operation and issues cards in the UK. In the US it has tended to focus on specific vocational groups. In the long run such entrants may have a significant effect on the industry. However, mass marketing is not their intention, and at the moment it does not appear that their contributions will significantly change the market structure.

The Big Four are beginning to respond to the competition from these new entrants by trying to sell cards to people other than their own customers. Given their nationwide market and heavy investment in branch networks, the Big Four other than Barclays have been highly reluctant to separate credit cards from the branch relationship, and indeed had no reason to do so until very recently. However, as happened in the US fifteen or so years ago, the credit card is increasingly becoming divorced from the current account; more consumers are beginning to shop around for credit cards, and more financial institutions are marketing them independently of other banking services, sometimes by direct mail. The major banks are joining this trend, adopting affinity programmes that target lists such as National Trust members and contributors to popular charities rather than their own depositors. The Bank of Scotland is the most active affinity card issuer of the major banks, although Midland and Royal Bank of Scotland are also active in this field, and from the smaller new entrants MBNA and Beneficial Bank have long lists of affinity arrangements.

A new type of loyalty card arrived on the market in mid-1996. For the previous two years the supermarket chain Tesco had issued loyalty cards, known as Club Cards, to 20% of the adult population of the UK. It then went a step further by producing a proprietary payment card in association initially with NatWest and then with the Royal Bank of Scotland. The card-holder transfers a set sum into the Club Card Account each week or month. When the card is used for purchases, the card is debited and loyalty points are calculated. The customer can get 'cashback' of up to £100 per day at the store and withdraw up to £250 from bank ATMs. Rates of interest for deposits and borrowings are slightly more attractive than most similar products available at UK banks and building societies. Gross interest is cal-culated daily and credited monthly at 5% p.a.

Beyond the objective of creating loyalty among customers, Tesco has launched this card to deter customers from using credit and debit cards, and thus to reduce its merchant processing fees. Another advantage to the store is the information it gains on shopping habits, and the ability to tar-get suitable customers with special offers. For its part, the Royal Bank of Scotland now has many outlets and marketing opportunities in Tesco supermarkets. Such initiatives enable banks to move their presence from the high street, with its high costs and decreasing appeal to customers, to shopping malls and retail parks. Abbey National's link-up with Safeway has similar objectives, while such schemes exist also in Germany for the Metro Group and in South Africa for ABSA/Pick'n'Pay. It is still not clear if so-called 'mutually beneficial' partnerships could actually challenge the retail banks' traditional franchise, turning them into low margin wholesalers of payments and funds, in a development that would extend beyond simply credit cards. We look at this issue in more detail in Chapter 6.

UK banks claim to be less concerned with competition than their coun-terparts in the US, because they have stronger relationships with their cus-tomers, who as a result are less likely to go elsewhere for credit cards. Even if new credit card issuers, however, do not enjoy the same success as in the US, they could still shake up the market and significantly affect market share. Many believe the casualties in a credit card war would be smaller existing issuers, such as some building societies, which can neither exploit economies of scale nor offer a sophisticated package of discounts. On the other hand, the smaller issuers argue that those who focus on niche mar-kets will not be in direct competition with big cheap issuers, and that the brunt of the competition will fall on the market leaders.

While the longer-term participants and eventual winners in a credit card issuance war are not yet obvious, the grounds on which it would be fought are more apparent. Fees and interest charges, customer service and market-ing benefits are all areas of rivalry. Given the difficulty of spending one's way to real value through promotional schemes, fees and rates are really the most important areas. The UK market has seen major changes, both in the levels and in the range of these charges since 1990 (Figure 5.6). The prolif-eration of low-rate, no-fee cards offering a variety of benefits implies a degree of over-capacity which can only drive down prices and profitability.

Fig 5.6 Cardholder charges
1990–7

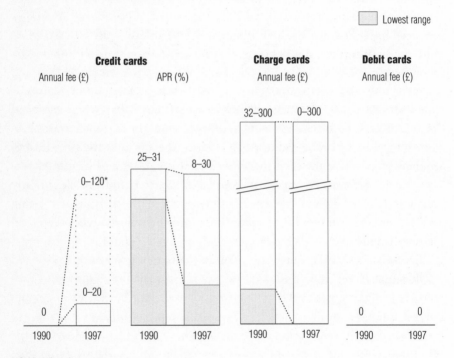

* Gold credit cards

Source: BBA, Moneyfacts Publications, American Express

ISSUER PROCESSING: THE CHALLENGE OF LOW-COST PROCESSORS

Until the mid-1980s issuer processing in the UK was a simple duopoly controlling 100% of the market. The JCCC (later renamed Signet when it was sold by the participating banks) serviced all nine Access issuers and Barclays serviced all Visa cards. Since 1988, dual issuance and the emergence of new competitors, particularly the arrival of the American third party processors, has complicated the picture. The American processor First Data Resources (FDR) entered the market in the late 1980s, quickly obtaining over one million accounts from eleven clients, including Midland Bank.

FDR provided services that the UK processors lacked, at very low prices – for example, choice of card design, variable interest rates, tiered debit and credit interest rates, choice of statement date, rebates on annual turnover, 'pay ahead' and 'skip payment' options, over-limit and late payment fees. It was also fundamentally more efficient, with on-line applications processing and collections features. FDR also offered the ability to analyse the cardholder base that marketing beyond the current account customer increasingly required, especially since there was at the time no UK equivalent of TRW for credit-worthiness information, and consumer privacy protections are stronger than in the US. Since banks can obtain only very limited 'black' data (like court judgements and defaults) from existing credit bureaux, the ability to track and predict credit quality from card activity is vital.

The success of FDR illustrates the competitive importance of advanced technology. In the late 1980s the main rivals to FDR were Signet and Barclays. Although Signet was moving to update its technology, it was highly labour-intensive and employed more staff to process 11 million cards and support 310,000 merchant outlets in the UK than FDR did to support 33 million accounts and 700,000 merchants in the US. We estimate that processing costs in Signet were at least twice US levels, and that Barclays is scarcely more efficient. In consequence, after phasing out Signet's role as sole merchant-acquiring organisation for Access, the Signet banks sold the remaining processing business to FDR in 1991.

This sale has changed the face of the credit card processing business in the UK, and perhaps in Europe, because card processing has the potential to become a pan-European business dominated by capable low-cost third-party providers like FDR and relative newcomer Experian (formerly TRW and CCN). This process is proving slow, but in 1996 FDR signed up Hypo Bank in Germany, its first client outside the UK, and has since also entered the Spanish market.

MERCHANT ACQUISITION AND PROCESSING

Until the late 1980s, the UK merchant acquisition market was also a duopoly: JCCC/Signet signed up merchants for the Access card and processed their transactions, and Barclays did the same for all Visa merchants. Each card had about the same merchant base (323,000 for Access and 315,000 for Visa in 1988), but since there were more Visa card transactions, Barclays' revenues were somewhat higher (£206 million compared with £181 million for Signet in 1988), even though Barclays had a lower average value and discount rate.

In 1988, along with dual issuance, dual acquisition arrived (when a merchant acquirer signs up a merchant for both Visa and MasterCard) and the market for acquiring merchants opened up to serious competition for the first time. By 1990 Signet had stopped acquiring merchants to concentrate on cardholder processing because its bank owners, starting with Lloyds, wanted to approach merchants directly, in order to tap into steady revenues on the merchant side. Subsequently, NatWest, Midland and the Royal Bank of Scotland all competed for merchant accounts, though they sub-contracted to Signet for the actual processing (Figure 5.7). The chief impact of this competition has been to allow merchants to negotiate down the discounts charged by banks, which fell from an average of 2.3% in 1986 to 1.5% in 1996.

In this context, and as in the issuer processing side, the FDR purchase of Signet heralded the emergence of a dominant low-cost producer, making competition on cost an inevitable feature of this side of the business as well.

THE OUTLOOK FOR CREDIT CARDS: GROWTH FOR SOME

Although the number of credit cards in issue declined in the early 1990s, as we saw, it has now picked up again, and the credit card issuing business in the UK has substantial growth possibilities. Less than 50% of adults own

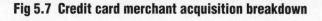

Fig 5.7 Credit card merchant acquisition breakdown
1988–96

Percent

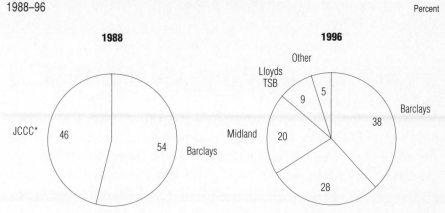

* Joint Credit Card Company

Source: MMG analysis

credit cards, far below the penetration in the US, where card issuance is still growing. The consumer revolt against fees, which contributed to the limited downturn, may well have rid the issuing banks of convenience users (who can easily cut up their cards) rather than borrowers, especially those with substantial balances to pay off. Furthermore, card ownership may continue to expand even if debit cards and higher limits on cheque guarantee cards dampen the growth in transactions somewhat in the short term. The US experience shows that a great deal of extra value for customers can be built around a credit card account, setting it apart from essentially single-purpose payments products. As we saw, card accounts can be linked to airline miles, retailer incentives, bonuses, charity contributions, and other attractive features. This allows credit cards to become a branded product; if their features and benefits are distinctive enough, many consumers will hold more than one, even from the same issuer.

The economics of specialisation will break up the card business system as it becomes more systems-dependent. For this reason, a shake-out on the issuing side is likely; the survivors will be those who can acquire the technology and skills to excel at new product development and direct marketing. This will be a challenge for the current market leaders. Since the UK credit card business started later than in the US and was kept linked to the current account branch system for so long, the database and modelling technologies that power the most successful US cardholder businesses are not in place. As a result, the banks cannot segment and fine-sort their customer bases by card use and profitability. So they tend to employ across-the-board solutions to profitability pressures, such as standard fees. Furthermore, they often try to impose those fees without the ability to build value-added features into the card account. As a result, consumers, already armed with substitute cards and alternative payment mechanisms, have the ability to resist.

The entry of aggressive new players from the US, with robust infrastructures and well-developed marketing models, may be the catalyst for the downturn in margins on the issuing side, despite the growth in volumes. Current players are already responding with major technology investment programmes to improve their product launch and targeting capabilities. This is increasing their costs, but the benefits, as so often with major IT investments, remain, at least for now, unclear. The ability to identify those investments that will truly lead to a stronger competitive position and genuinely deliver increased shareholder value will be a key success factor in the coming years.

Processing, for both issuers and merchant acquirers, will be dominated by players who develop and share utilities, and who may issue 'private label' cards for smaller financial institutions. Currently it looks as though this segment of the business system is consolidating around FDR, but it is also attracting other companies who have the skills and the technology. The Big Four's branch networks give them an edge when it comes to acquiring merchants; this part of the business too will probably be concentrated in the hands of the most efficient competitors. Only Barclays has the scale and in-house capabilities to compete across the whole business system, but pressures for disaggregation and specialisation may cause even Barclays to concentrate on some functions and outsource others. Barclays' ability to match FDR in giving value to customers and processing transactions efficiently will be critical.

So it seems that the same forces are working in the credit card business as in other financial services examined in this book. Economic pressures are leading to specialisation, technology is challenging the economics of the established players, and competition is increasing at all stages. A future of increased consumer choice and value, rather than increased bank profits may well lie ahead for credit cards too.

THE CHANGING ROLE OF THE BRANCHES

When did you last see your bank manager?

The Big Four retail banks arrived at their current dominant position in UK banking essentially by controlling a vast and comprehensive deposit machine. They collected interest-free deposits and returned the funds to the commercial sector in the form of interest-bearing overdrafts and loans. To collect the deposits, a dense branch network was vital.

Today, with the advent of new electronic channels, such as the ATM, and the adaptation of old technologies, particularly the telephone, the traditional bank branch business system is changing. The standard processing services of bank branches are being replaced by new technologies, as we have seen in earlier chapters. Now too Stage C technologies – which give customers direct access to their accounts – are making available new ways of delivering financial services that supplement or bypass the traditional branch.

This chapter describes three of these new delivery channels. The first of these is the *ATM*, which has extended the hours in which customers have access to cash and a (somewhat limited) menu of other services traditionally provided over the branch counter, and is increasingly providing access to services away from a branch location. The second is *home banking*, which enables branch current account holders to carry out a wide variety of banking transactions at home or in the office, usually by telephone but sometimes with a computer screen. Home banking has only recently started to win broad acceptance. The third is really a packaging of telephone and ATM services, described as *branchless banking*. While far from pure Stage C technology, it is growing fast and bears watching as a potentially important alternative to the traditional bank branch.

ATMS: CASH ON DEMAND

ATMs are the first, and to date by far the most important, Stage C development in retail banking. To the banking public, they are the most visible and familiar aspect of electronic banking. Most ATMs currently in operation are essentially cash machines, but the functions of the ATM are now expanding. With some machines customers can now pay some bills, transfer funds between accounts, order cheque books and Eurocheques, request statements and deposits, and receive mini-statements. However, few machines can do all of these things; the majority remain early-generation cash dispensers. Future services may include drawing a loan (credit card advances are widely available), setting up savings plans, and applying for insurance and mortgages.

Reliability – critical to customers – is also improving. The early machines were prone to failure, but now ATMs average 35,000 transactions between failures. Nowadays, the problem lies not in the failure of the equipment, but in the ability of banks to keep machines adequately stocked with bank notes.

In the UK, transactions grew at a CAGR of over 35% before 1990 but have since inevitably slowed to around 8%. It is mainly younger, better educated and urban customers who use them, although ATMs have also been successful in servicing sparsely populated and remote areas, especially in Scotland.

In the UK, people made 1.6 billion withdrawals from ATMs in banks and building societies in 1996, more than four times the number of cheques they cashed in bank branches (Figure 6.1). In this way, ATMs have helped contain the rate of growth in cheques. They may have also enabled some spontaneous cheque purchases to be replaced by cash, but reliable statistics on this point are difficult to develop.

The decline in the use of cash that we discussed in Chapter 3 clearly has implications for the future of ATMs. Obviously, if cash declines in importance relative to electronic payments, and if debit cards are increasingly used in shops for cashback, people will make less use of ATMs. On the other hand, cash will still be used for small transactions; and the growing sophistication of ATMs may mean that people, especially the young who are more comfortable with technology, will use them for services over and above drawing out cash. These different pressures will probably largely offset each other: ATM withdrawals are forecast to rise by a slower growth rate than we have seen up to now.

Fig 6.1 Growth of ATM usage in the UK

Withdrawals volume, 1980–96

Billions of transactions

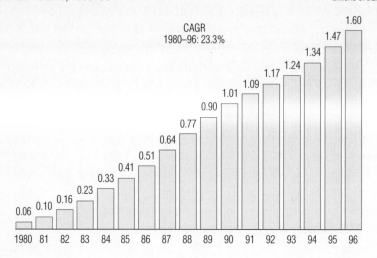

CAGR
1980–96: 23.3%

0.06 0.10 0.16 0.23 0.33 0.41 0.51 0.64 0.77 0.90 1.01 1.09 1.17 1.24 1.34 1.47 1.60

1980 81 82 83 84 85 86 87 88 89 90 91 92 93 94 95 96

Number of ATMs, 1980–96

Thousands

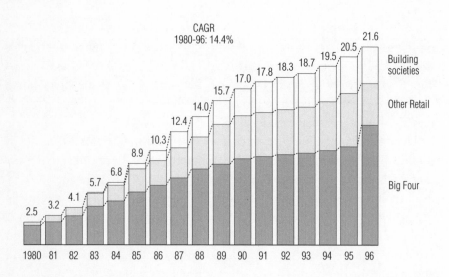

CAGR
1980-96: 14.4%

2.5 3.2 4.1 5.7 6.8 8.9 10.3 12.4 14.0 15.7 17.0 17.8 18.3 18.7 19.5 20.5 21.6

Building societies

Other Retail

Big Four

1980 81 82 83 84 85 86 87 88 89 90 91 92 93 94 95 96

Note: Abbey National included in Other Retail from 1989
1996 change in shares reflects partly mergers across groups

Source: APACS, BBA,MMG analysis

More ATMs than branches

The first UK ATM was installed by Barclays Bank at Enfield in 1968, over a year before Chemical Bank installed the first ATM in the United States. Despite this early start, the UK's ATM network density, which until recently was among the highest in Europe, is now relatively low, probably reflecting some saturation but also very high utilisation of the ATMs that are installed; usage of ATMs in the UK is significantly higher than in most other European countries (Figure 6.2).

All the Big Four banks now have more ATMs than branches (Table 6.1).

Fig 6.2 ATM network density and utilisation
1996 estimate

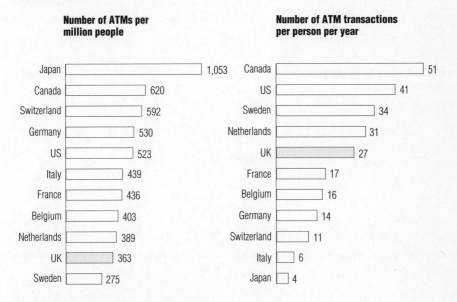

Number of ATMs per million people		Number of ATM transactions per person per year	
Japan	1,053	Canada	51
Canada	620	US	41
Switzerland	592	Sweden	34
Germany	530	Netherlands	31
US	523	UK	27
Italy	439	France	17
France	436	Belgium	16
Belgium	403	Germany	14
Netherlands	389	Switzerland	11
UK	363	Italy	6
Sweden	275	Japan	4

Source: Bank for International Settlements, MMG analysis

Table 6.1 Big-Four ATMs and branches, 1996

	ATMs	Branches
Lloyds TSB*	4,300	2,797
NatWest	3,137	1,920
Barclays	3,136	1,997
Midland	2,505	1,702

*Lloyds TSB is the sum of the Lloyds and the TSB networks
Source: BBA

The three Scottish clearing banks were early ATM users and all have large numbers of ATMs, the largest being the Royal Bank of Scotland Group with 1,171 ATMs across the UK in 1996. The building societies entered the ATM market late, with only 112 machines between them as late as the end of 1983, but this number had increased to 1,300 machines by 1986 and exceeded 4,000 in 1996.

Fig 6.3 ATM networks
1997

Network	Ownership structure*
• 'Four Banks'	• Bank of Scotland • Barclays • Lloyds • Royal Bank of Scotland
• Mint	• Midland • National Westminster • TSB
• Link	• Building societies • Abbey National • Bank of Scotland & other smaller retail banks

* Other institutions may have reciprocity agreements with each network, e.g., Clydesdale with MINT

The practice of sharing ATMs, by linking different banks' machines through an ATM network, has grown rapidly since 1983. UK banks, with their large nationwide branch networks, originally showed no interest in sharing except within a group. Today all the main banks and building societies in the UK are part of one of three shared networks (Figure 6.3). Two,

Mint and 'Four Banks', are dominated by the Big Four and the third, Link, by the building societies and Other Retail banks. This is the same degree of sharing that prevails in the US, where regional (NYCE, STAR) and national shared networks have become competitive forces in their own right, as have third-party switching services. However, the UK banks have kept sharing firmly under control through simply establishing reciprocity between their large nationwide proprietary networks, and do not stress their reciprocal relationships to their customer bases. Unlike the US, the shared networks of the Big Four have no common logo or identity. On the other hand, the banks widely publicise their increasingly extensive international hook-ups, mainly via the Visa and MasterCard (Eurocheque) networks.

Serving a much more fragmented industry, the building society shared network Link bears a certain resemblance to US developments in ATM-sharing and has forged links with its North American counterparts. Many small societies have only a handful of machines and need the network to provide a good ATM service to their depositors.

With more ATMs in place than branches, the UK banks' networks can be considered relatively mature. The opportunity for adding new installations lies mainly in placing machines away from banks – which is indeed what the banks are doing. They have doubled their installations at such sites as university campuses, airports, factories, industrial estates, hospitals, military bases, shopping centres, stores and London Underground stations. In 1996, 20% of all ATMs, or more than 4,000, were located away from branches, up from 15% in 1995 and less than 8% in 1990.

A necessary evil?

ATM technology has not yet reduced branch costs in a fundamental way. The costs of the ATM itself and its quite labour-intensive servicing are high. Even replacing a full-time teller with an ATM would not have much impact on costs. And as we have seen, no matter how many ATMs are in place, banks need branches and counter staff to handle commercial cash and cheque deposits, which have not been automated through ATMs. Nevertheless, ATMs are on average likely to be making a positive contribution. UK data indicate that the break-even level for a through-the-wall ATM is around 4,000 transactions a month, whereas average use in 1996 was around 6,000 transactions a month. (But there is a large dispersion around this mean, with some ATMs being 'loss-making' under such an assessment.)

The British banks have always had a realistic view of the benefits of ATMs. Until recently, they have not considered the ATM as an alternative to the branch, except in one early instance when Lloyds, with the smallest branch network of the Big Four, deployed over 1,200 machines by 1981 in its heavily promoted Cashlink programme (then the largest on-line ATM network in the world) while the other Big Four banks had only 1,300 machines between them. Instead, the first ATMs were intended to allow banks to close on Saturdays (a day when they had little real business except cashing personal cheques) while still enabling customers to draw cash. (Banks' opening hours were originally very limited, although they have expanded in recent years because of competitive pressures.)

ATMs are often seen as carrying a potential drawback to the banks. Automatic cash withdrawals, and the cashback facility, tend to diminish contact between banks and their customers. This in turn reduces the banks' opportunities to market other, more profitable, services to their customers. As a number of non-traditional banking products are increasingly important to the banks' bottom line (see the discussion in Chapter 7), the loss of such opportunities could be significant, provided banks could truly use the interaction with the client as a selling opportunity.

To date ATMs have been a necessary evil from the point of view of the major banks. They are expensive to own and operate and generate little additional revenue, while increasing the movement on retail current accounts. However, they add value greatly in terms of customers' ability to access their accounts, and have displaced hundreds of millions of cheque encashments at bank counters and in central processing areas. ATMs also represent an indispensable component of the move towards alternative delivery channels, including home banking, as we shall see in the next part of this chapter, and they are increasingly providing access away from a branch, thus potentially enabling further reductions in branch networks.

HOME BANKING: STAYING AWAY FROM THE BRANCH

Home banking is an 'add-on' to a current account held in a branch. It enables customers to carry out from home (or the office) most operations on their accounts by using a personal computer, or, more commonly, the telephone.

The Stage C technology required to bring banking services into the homes and offices of retail customers is not new. Efforts in this direction are more than a decade old, and most UK retail financial institutions continue to invest in these services at some level. Today there is a proliferation of home banking services offered by banks and building societies. For these competitors the concept of home banking has four basic attractions.

First, home banking can help to *convert regular payments to electronic by BACS*. It passes the work of initiating direct debits, for example, to the customer, thus eliminating the costly paperwork and pre-programming associated with pre-authorised transactions. It can further attack spontaneous at-home cheque payments that will not be handled through BACS.

A second advantage is that home banking can *reinforce efforts to divert routine enquiry and transaction services from the branches*, helping in the banks' efforts to transform them into retail outlets for higher value services such as insurance, investment and property transactions.

Third, home banking gives any financial institution the potential to *reach every household in the UK*. Through home banking, smaller banks and building societies may overcome their lack of geographic reach without making heavy investments in new branches.

Finally, home banking allows a virtually unlimited range of services to be *delivered to those customers who rarely enter a bank*. This is a large and important market segment, especially among younger and better educated customers. One survey by Midland indicated that 20% of retail customers had not visited their branch in the past month, 10% had not visited in the last year, 51% said they would rather visit their branch as little as possible and almost 50% had never met their bank manager. Most of these customers preferred to access their accounts via ATM. The combination of home banking and the ATM can provide this segment with full 'branchless banking' (discussed later) at far lower costs than traditional delivery channels.

From the customer's point of view, home banking would seem to offer considerable advantages in convenience, control and information, which conventional channels lack. On a more cautionary note the Consumer Association's *Which?* magazine has surveyed home banking channels and found relatively few cost advantages over regular current accounts, particularly if the customer is often overdrawn, and a striking lack of protection for consumers against systems problems. Despite this, growth has accelerated since the launch of competing telephone banking services. Today around four million accounts are accessible by telephone, up from half that two years ago.

Screen-based services: at last, the Internet!

Services based on personal computers (or videotext in the past, a system similar to teletext in look and concept but with interactive access) have represented until now the least popular form of home banking. Most of the banks' screen-based home-banking systems launched in the 1980s have either failed or are not actively promoted any longer. At the present time, we believe that PC-based services may make sense as a niche product offered by financial institutions with limited geographical reach. Citibank made its home banking service available in the UK in the hope of reaching a small affluent group of computer-literate customers. The most important UK niche player, and one of the few success stories in screen-based banking, has been the Bank of Scotland, which has 385 branches in total, with only 25 of these located in England. Given the far greater affluence of southern England, especially Greater London, and the high costs of acquiring and staffing more English branches, the Scottish banks as a group have been attracted by the potential of home banking (and small business banking).

In 1985, the Bank of Scotland launched Home and Office Banking Service (HOBS), aimed at both small businesses and personal customers. A screen-based service, it could be accessed either through a modem linking a PC to a telephone data line or through the then British Telecom videotext service Prestel, which provided a keyboard adapter linking the data line and a television set. Services offered to private subscribers included ordering cheque books, initiating payments – with a smart card option – and setting up and amending standing orders and direct debit authorities. HOBS allowed customers to pre-programme individual payments up to thirty days in advance, so that they could maximise cash flow and interest, a facility lacked by pre-authorised payments. For statements of account, they could view up to 600 transactions at once, covering a six-month period. Visa and MasterCard accounts could also be viewed. Later, HOBS was augmented by the addition of a cash distribution interface with users of ACT Financial Systems' Capital product, thereby providing brokers with cash management services and allowing them to offer a 'one-stop-shop' service for investment accounts. For clients this permits all banking transactions to be centralised, including investments.

Bank of Scotland specifically aimed HOBS at the corporate sector with the launch of Corporate HOBS. The service was augmented to provide same-day CHAPS high-value sterling transfers to accounts in the UK, domestic and international payments to third parties and a cheque reconciliation facility. Details of all these could be viewed on-line by accessing the bank's central computer via the PC, although information on balances and account transactions could be downloaded overnight to avoid on-line costs during the day. A special Corporate HOBS Investment Account would also pay interest on surplus funds. The MS-DOS based system included a smart card security system for same-day and international payment instructions, while a Windows version was launched in 1997.

The standard HOBS system proved quite attractive to small businesses or professional firms because PCs are widely available, and thus set-up costs are low. This group in fact constitutes the majority of users. However, the great virtue of HOBS was that it simultaneously straddled two delivery technologies (neither ideal) and two markets which overlapped considerably. For example, a business owner, chartered accountant or solicitor might have been a small business user when using the system from the PC at his or her firm, but a private user when accessing the same account from a television at home.

Given its lack of branches in England, where HOBS was mainly promoted, the Bank of Scotland maintains that it has acquired many current accounts which it otherwise could not hope to attract, and has managed to avoid expensive acquisitions or branch building in the English market. This has been the objective of many home banking experiments.

Competition emerged slowly. The Royal Bank of Scotland countered with RoyLine, a PC-based service which was targeted at the small and medium-sized firms which were probably HOBS' real customer base. Some of the Big Four compete in middle market PC electronic banking products.

In the UK the pioneer in home banking was the Nottingham Building Society, which was seeking to break out of its depressed regional market in the Midlands and into the lucrative mortgage market of the South East. Homelink allowed users to check the state of their savings accounts over videotext, automatically pay bills, transfer money to and from a cheque account and use a unique 'automatic loan facility', a complete screen-based mortgage lending service. Seven years after launching the service, half of the Nottingham's customer base was in the South. However, Homelink at its peak had only 5,500 users. Claiming that home banking had not captured the public's imagination, the Nottingham ended the service in 1991. Home banking, at least through this medium, did not allow the Nottingham to overcome its small size and lack of branches.

Videotext is now an outdated technology in the UK, where its launch, unlike the launch of Minitel in France, was generally a disappointment. The Prestel videotext service was launched by the Post Office in 1979 as an alternative interface to computer services, as PCs were still relatively rare in British households. The service was intended to be a mass market information delivery system and many financial institutions based their choice of technology for home banking on its anticipated success. However, UK consumers had to buy or rent an adapter to use Prestel and few did so, in part because of high charges from British Telecom. In 1996 Prestel, which was spun-off by BT in 1994, decided to move away from its proprietary system to become an Internet service provider.

The growth of PC ownership in the UK is now finally taking off. Currently only 5% of British households have a PC with a modem, but this number is expected to reach 40% by the turn of the century or shortly thereafter. As a result, some banks are now reconsidering retail screen-based systems. TSB was the first British institution to offer real-time access to an account over the Internet, via CompuServe, allowing also the payment of bills and the setting-up of standing orders. Barclays has joined up with Microsoft and Visa International to develop a system running on Microsoft's Money software package and offering immediate transfer of funds between accounts, payment of bills, amendment of standing order and direct debit instructions, checking of balances and transactions, and ordering of cheque books and statements. The other major banks are slowly following and, despite the failures to date, screen-based banking looks set to become a viable, albeit niche, distribution channel in the short to medium term. The growth of the Internet is a major factor in this development.

The Internet has produced the biggest boom in electronic business since the invention of the telephone. Currently most UK banks are on the Internet, but, with the exception of TSB, as discussed above, they are using the services for marketing and advertising purposes only. Barclaycard attempted to use the Internet in a pioneering way, by creating the 'BarclaySquare' site where cardholders could use their cards to shop from high-street retailers, but this initiative did not generate any significant interest, selling only a very small number of items in its first year and being rated by a survey as one of the 'least exciting experiences on the Internet'. The most advanced European Bank in using the Internet for full banking purposes is the Bank of Ireland. Customers can now conduct direct banking and insurance business with Premier Banking and Premier Direct Insurance Services, the 'direct' arm of this bank.

In the USA hundreds of banks are on the Internet, with their number growing exponentially, and they are far more technically advanced than anywhere else in the world. Some banks offer direct on-line facilities via the Internet. Studies there are showing that Internet banking offers significantly lower marginal costs per transaction, with a transaction costing less than 15¢ versus twice that much on proprietary PC banking, four times on telephone banking, and eight times for the normal branch transaction.

UK banks are still hesitating about using the Internet for full banking purposes, both because of its, still, relatively low penetration and, primarily, due to security considerations. A major breakthrough could come from smart cards. The security of the Internet is poor, but smart cards can, as we saw in Chapter 4, provide a solution to this problem, and go beyond by providing additional functionality, e.g., transforming one's PC into an ATM that downloads cash from a bank account to an electronic purse smart card.

Internet banking provides exciting prospects of end-to-end automation that could change the rules of the industry. We explore further the implications of such a discontinuity in Chapter 10.

Telephone banking: unclear objectives

The drawbacks of the PC (too few in the home) and the videotext services (too few subscribers) made the telephone the choice of most retail banks for offering home banking. Indeed, there is nothing new about customers telephoning banks to make an enquiry or give an instruction. Banks, however, have over the last ten years or so made several attempts at providing telephone banking as a special service to their branch customers, as a complement to the relationship with the branch. Some of these attempts have been relatively successful, but many have failed to take off, in view of unclear objectives on how this service should be promoted versus the branch network. Banks have realised that telephone banking along the branch network is creating additional costs with no visible savings from the fixed branch network infrastructure, while customer service benefits are not always clear in the short term. Banks have often taken, as a result, a 'half-baked' approach simply to counter competitive initiatives.

In their effort to minimise the costs created by telephone banking, banks have tried to implement computerised systems that minimise or eliminate the need for human operators and the related premises, equipment, etc. Efforts to transform the telephone into an electronic interface have not, however, proven easy, and today most telephone banking services are based on human operators.

There are two types of computerised telephone banking technology, and both have drawbacks for the user. In the first type, the customer relays messages to the computer by pressing the telephone keypad, first entering his or her account number and PIN. The computer responds using an autophone or synthetic voice, which provides instructions for pressing a series of keys to access services, and reads out the information requested or confirms transactions through the keypad. After each sequence, the synthetic voice tells the customer the options for proceeding. Though such systems are fairly convenient, the customer can be confused by the sequence of steps or instructions given by the computer. Customers who do not have touch-tone phones need to buy one or buy a portable electronic tone-pad that imitates the bleeps which are emitted from touch-tone phones.

The second type is a voice recognition unit, in which the caller speaks to the computer and listens for a response. The customer is required to say his or her account number and, in some cases, a password over the mouthpiece. The computer then compares the speech to a voiceprint on file before proceeding. If the speech is approved, the customer then continues to speak to the computer, giving instructions for account inquiry, transferring funds, and so forth. Most systems have a vocabulary of approximately 50 to 100 words. Customers may feel happier talking rather than relaying messages through pressing numbers, but computers handle voice-recognition considerably more slowly than keypad instructions. Also, tests show that the computer may have trouble distinguishing between such essential words as 'two' and 'to' or 'four' and 'for' or understanding instructions in noisy or echoing places. Another problem is that 20% of the time the computer fails to match an authentic user to the voiceprint. In addition, questions of privacy or confidentiality may arise when a user is required to voice instructions in open, public areas. Technology, in time, may well alleviate these problems, but voice recognition has not seen any significant successful implementations in the UK.

Telephone banking systems, several computerised, have been most actively developed by Other Retail Banks and building societies, which lack the extensive branch networks of the Big Four. The pioneer, albeit with a service based on human operators, was Girobank, in 1986. With no conventional branch network – using the 20,000 or so Post Offices – telephone banking appeared like a natural extension to the service of Girobank. Others followed soon after.

Before 1985 TSB had only 1,235 branches in England and Wales, but was a leader in branch automation with an on-line real-time retail banking system. For an additional investment of only £1 million TSB added an on-line, real-time telephone banking service called Speedlink, a keypad and autophone system developed by Autophon Ltd. using equipment from Periphonics Corporation in the US and an existing software package. Launched in 1987, within two years Speedlink had 230,000 subscribers, with approximately 1,500 new customers a week signing up. Several of these were small commercial users. The most widely used service provided by Speedlink provided balance enquiry and instant transfer between deposit and current accounts. It also allowed users to pre-program up to 31 BACS transfers and provided full details on the last six. Full statements by fax could also be called up for additional charges. Priced at only £2.50 a quarter, the service provided free transactions to accounts that were in credit. In essence, Speedlink was a mass market electronic cash management service which deliberately avoided big jumps in sophistication. Speedlink stopped being promoted in 1992 and a new service, PhoneBank, was launched in 1994. This is a much bigger-scale initiative with an upfront investment of more than £17 million, combining a human and a computer interface.

Some building societies have also been active in telephone banking. Nationwide launched a service called FlexAccount in 1987, which was basically an interest-bearing current account that could be accessed by telephone using the touch-tone approach. FlexAccount allowed a limited number of payments to be programmed up to a month in advance and provided details of the last six transactions, and full statements by mail on demand. FlexAccount attracted over 1.2 million depositors, 600,000 in its first seven months. Its appeal was strengthened by adding a high interest feature in conjunction with telephone access. FlexAccount is one of the few surviving computerised telephone banking services. Another one is Halifax's Maxim, an interest-bearing transaction account, launched in 1989 with a limited touch-tone and voice recognition telephone service.

Several other players have also provided telephone banking services, like Abbey National (human or computerised), Alliance & Leicester (human), Bank of Scotland (human), Clydesdale (human), Co-operative (human or computer), and Royal Bank of Scotland (human).

Of the Big Four, only Midland has not created a service to complement its branch network; its First Direct standalone operation is by far the most developed telephone/ branchless-banking service in the UK, but it does not serve Midland account holders. The other three all provide some telephone-based service, although their approaches differ.

NatWest has adopted a dual approach to home banking, recognising a relationship between the type of technology used and the scope of services offered. ActionLine is a 24-hour telephone banking service, the only computerised one (both voice recognition and touch-tone) by a Big Four bank, and is offered to all branch customers, serving routine needs such as balance inquiries or setting up bill payments. After a slow start in 1990, it has signed up more than a million of its 6.5 million customers. The second service, PrimeLine, was launched in 1991 and constitutes a 24-hour full banking service independent from the branch network but marketed to NatWest's existing premium customers. It uses human operators, based on a designated Personal Account Manager for every customer, and has not been made available to the mass market; it only has 40,000 customers, albeit this is three times the number two years ago.

Barclays introduced a human-interface telephone banking service, Barclaycall, in 1994, as a complement to customers' branch relationships. Its aim was to recruit 20,000 customers a month, and the system was backed by several hundred telephone staff, based in Coventry. It is offered to all the bank's 6 million customers and in mid-1997 400,000 had signed up. The service is available seven days a week but only 16 hours a day (8 hours on weekends) and offers a wide range of services.

Lloyds too has launched a human-interface telephone banking system, LloydsLine, based on branch accounts and available 14 hours a day. As with Barclaycall, the service is available to all branch customers and offers a wide range of services, including overdrafts. Following the merger with TSB, there has been discussion of adopting TSB's PhoneBank.

With all of these services, telephone banking has primarily been a service support concept rather than a marketing concept. Emphasis has been on serving existing customers with existing products. Success in this has been varied, hampered in some cases by technical difficulties in linking the telephone service to the branch accounting system. The one bank of the Big Four that took a different perspective was Midland. Its approach was to provide a distinct model for alternative distribution of banking services.

BRANCHLESS BANKING

The success of First Direct

The culmination of telephone banking is to use it as a replacement for the branch. All the services described previously are add-ons to ordinary current accounts and have often been limited defensive measures to challenges such as First Direct, rather than consistent strands of an explicit strategy. Only Midland Bank's subsidiary First Direct, launched at year-end 1989, is essentially a branchless bank. Transaction accounts and other services can be accessed exclusively by the telephone, 365 days a year and 24 hours a day. Customers talk to a human operator instead of speaking to a machine or pressing numbers on the keypad. When First Direct was launched, the only precedent of such a major standalone telephone operation in UK financial services was Direct Line in motor insurance (discussed in the next chapter). According to a survey that Midland commissioned to support its approach, 75% of consumers interested in telephone banking prefer to talk to people rather than interact directly with a computer via keypad.

First Direct offers all the banking services of a conventional bank, without the branch costs incurred by other banks. The lower costs of this branchless bank are to some extent passed on to customers through higher interest rates on savings accounts (e.g., 5.65% for a 60-day notice account versus 4.00–4.60% from the Big Four for a 90-day notice account), lower charges on First Direct credit cards (18.8% and no fee vs. 21.6–22.3% and £10–12 annual fee) and competitive facilities, including an automatic overdraft facility with no arrangement charges up to £250. While competitive pricing is obviously a selling point, it should be noted that not all First Direct products are the cheapest on the market; the main selling point is the convenience of a full-service 24-hour home bank.

Services provided include current and savings accounts, automated bill payment services, overdrafts, mortgages, debit and credit cards, insurance products, investments such as unit trusts and money market accounts, and even travel services. Cash withdrawals can be made at any Midland-affiliated ATM. Indeed, the very large network created by ATM reciprocity between Midland, NatWest, TSB and regional banks has probably been key in the acceptance of branchless banking. Deposits are made through the post or Midland branches. It can now realistically be claimed there are no visible gaps in the service of First Direct compared with a branch bank, although some of the services were not planned from the beginning, such as insurance, and accommodating them has proved more complicated than expected.

First Direct is based in Leeds and employs more than 3,000 staff, including banking representatives, able to handle 85% of requests at first point of contact, and product specialists (financial services advisors) trained to handle more complex offerings like mortgages, insurance, investments or foreign exchange. Representatives sit at workstations equipped to display customer profiles. Statements and other correspondence are sent in the post as normal but paperwork is generally kept to a minimum. Midland initially spent about £35 million on this project, for key call-centre technology, database tools and advertising. It has invested a lot more since to support the expansion of First Direct and has recently announced the creation of another call centre in Hamilton, Scotland, with capacity for 5,000 jobs.

First Direct has expanded its offering to PC-based banking, by launching a service to its customers following a trial in the summer of 1997. This service complements the telephone service and uses First Direct's own network, accessed with proprietary software via a local number, rather than the Internet.

First Direct had gained over 750,000 accounts by 1997. This base has been growing at a rate of 12,000 new customers every month and First Direct's forecasts predict more than one million customers by the year 2000. First Direct attracted twice the branch banking average of 25- to 44-year-olds (the most active bank customers for financial services); in addition, the household income of First Direct depositors has averaged £40,000, well above the clearing bank average. Indeed, one of the objectives of Midland in establishing the bank was to increase its market share among 'upscale' customers. Further, about three quarters of those customers were apparently recruited from competitors. First Direct research has indicated that the market potential for telephone banking services in the UK may be around 10% of the banking market, or about three million people, rising to 20% by the year 2000. As the market leader, First Direct expects to have a 20% share of this market by the end of the decade.

Customers like First Direct: according to an NOP survey conducted for First Direct in December 1996, 87% of First Direct customers are very or extremely satisfied with the service compared to 41% for Barclays and Lloyds and 52% for NatWest. First Direct says that one in three new customers join following a recommendation by existing customers: 94% of customers think First Direct is better than other banks and 87% have recommended it to a friend or colleague in the last 12 months.

In spite of the relative success of First Direct, attracting retail deposits for a branchless bank remains hard. This is due to lack of presence on the high street, inherent customer conservatism and a remaining, albeit unfounded, concern about security (many people do not like to put their savings into an institution they can't see). This problem makes the management of advertising crucially important and implies that the initial costs of setting up a network can be formidable. The investment at First Direct was significant. In the first year, £8 million was spent on support, added to £2.5 million in other start-up costs, generating rumours that up to £500 was spent on attracting each new account in the first year of operation. The expense of advertising obviously falls once the brand is established and word gets around, and, as we saw, First Direct is already reaping those rewards. Nevertheless, Midland has indicated that it made its investment not expecting a return for five years. It is claiming its investment has been a success, but competitors are divided on their assessment of the bottom line success of this experiment.

Introducing the staffless branch

The First Direct model of a full-service standalone branchless bank has not been replicated, but some banks have experimented with concepts aimed at reducing or eliminating their staffed branches, by providing staffless interfaces at their physical locations. Several banks and building societies are operating schemes developing the ATM concept to give customers a better interface and access to a wider range of financial services, thus eliminating the need for a staffed branch.

In 1993 Nationwide opened a Touchlink branch in Aylesbury as part of a pilot scheme. The branch was fully automated, with no counter staff, and two specially trained customer advisers at the enquiry desk, which was open during normal office hours. Outside these hours, customers could gain entry with their passbooks or cash cards. Nationwide's self-service branches now number 16 with a total of 51 self-service machines. Each branch offers customers a wide range of transaction options and a variety of services. The staffless branches are linked to Nationwide's network of 800 ATMs and are available 24 hours a day.

Another example of such an approach has been that of the Co-operative Bank. It has also taken the staffless branch route, with 'kiosks' that enable customers to withdraw and deposit cash 24 hours a day, 365 days a year, and provide a direct video link to the Armchair telephone banking service if the customer needs assistance. This service began in 1994, and by mid-1996 100,000 were estimated to have been introduced to it.

Supermarket banking: a variant of branchless banking

1996 saw the launch of supermarket banking initiatives by the major UK supermarkets, each with slightly different concepts. Supermarkets have played an important role in the evolution of technology in UK banking, through their support for increasing levels of automation in payments and their opposition to bank charging practices. For example, Sainsbury's opposition to credit card merchant charging levels, backed by a commit-ment not to accept credit cards, contributed importantly to the take-up of debit card payments. We now see 'cash-back' services changing the pattern of cash withdrawals away from ATMs, a service which incidentally helps supermarkets reduce the costs of handling cash.

Supermarket banking could be one of the most damaging attacks on the banks; the four major chains account for more than 50% of UK shopping volumes and each chain has more customers than any of the Big Four. To understand the threat we have contrasted the development in the US with that in the UK.

US experience: cost-effective banking

Stores sell 'shelf space' to banks conceptually much in the same way as they would to any producer of consumer goods. Therefore what stores are sell-ing is 'footfall', access to a group of customers browsing in the aisles. Branches retain bank branding and, more important, customer ownership is held by the bank. The model is to open a branch, either full-service (6 to 8 person) or mini (2 to 4 person), in the store. From the bank's point of view, this would make sense only if:

- The cost of delivery in a store was less than in a traditional branch.

- The transaction (sales) volume was high enough to justify the cost.
- The work volume performed displaced enough existing volume in the branch network to allow more expensive traditional branches to be closed or was completely due to new business that could not have been captured through the traditional branch network.

The theory of the case is that the combination of banking and shopping provides added convenience and 'one-stop' service to customers, i.e., a 'win-win' situation in that banks gain access to customers and customers stay loyal to supermarkets due to added convenience. Industry statistics suggest a typical customer visits a supermarket 2.3 times a week or nearly 120 times a year, which is attractive to banks where visits are much fewer.

It is not clear, however, that banks do win. Some institutions admit that most business generated is simple low-margin cheque cashing and transaction processing, rather than higher margin selling of financial products; the supermarket visit is frequently too rushed to allow the time.

What are the economics? Supermarket branches cost one quarter as much as a typical branch to set up ($250K versus $1 million), can be operated more efficiently, turning a profit in 12–18 months versus 3 years, and can be profitable at much lower deposit levels ($3 million versus $10 million). This is attractive in its own right, but competition is intense as the industry structure in the US is a relatively small number of large supermarket chains that tend to dominate specific geographies and supermarkets are now able to dictate terms. Despite this, growth has been impressive.

In 1971 there were about 55 supermarket branches; there were still under 200 by 1981; the late 1980s, however, saw about 100 new branches per year and now banks are announcing plans for 300 or more each per year. More than 14% of the 50,000 commercial bank offices are in supermarkets. About 4,400 full-service and 400 mini supermarket branches opened in 1996, up about 40% from 1995, and 10,000 such branches are expected by the year 2000. Nearly 50% of banks have at least 10% of their network made up of supermarket branches, and ten banks have at least 30% of their network as supermarket branches. The biggest individual players are Wells Fargo, with close to 1,000 supermarket branches, and Bank of America, with 750.

Early branches were simple cheque-cashing stations put up by small local banks, i.e., banks with presence in the same locality as the store and who had small retail networks of their own. This evolved in the 1980s to sales outlets for high-interest CDs (certificates of deposit) run mainly by Savings

& Loans institutions. The 1990s are seeing the introduction of full-service automated (ATMs, video-banking) locations for large retail banks. Bank of America announced recently it would close 30 of its California branches while opening 50 supermarket branches in the same geographical areas. Therefore, displacement may be occurring. Bank of America has also used this as a market entry strategy in the Midwest, where its entire retail network consists of supermarket branches.

How long before supermarkets realise that, as with all fast moving consumer goods, there is more profit to be made in own-label goods, i.e., in launching their own bank?

A few supermarkets are already launching their own-brand banks. In a reversal of this thinking, Wells Fargo is now renting space in some of its branches to drugstores.

What we learn from these activities is that there appears to be value in adding convenience to the customer. What is not clear is whether customer loyalty has grown and whether cross-selling has improved.

UK experience: battle of the franchises?

In the UK, the supermarket bank launches and early results point to a different world and a real challenge to the banks where there may not be a win-win situation. The model is of stores leveraging their brand and customer base to create new financial service providers, with bank partners merely used to provide access to payment system infrastructure. Branding is that of the supermarket, not the bank, and, more importantly, customer ownership is held by the supermarket.

Services are being made to fit the supermarket brands, e.g., Asda, the value for money supermarket, is looking to provide the UK's 'lowest-priced' banking service. The delivery model is generally one of direct (telephone and/or post) service delivery backed up, in some cases, by in-store 'offices' to discuss more complex products, such as Marks & Spencer's lending and retirement products. Some, however, like Safeway, are considering full-service in-store branches.

Each of the supermarkets has converted its loyalty cards to fit into the bank model, as a debit, credit or combined card. These loyalty cards are only a few years old and yet more people have these cards than credit cards. Tesco and Sainsbury each acquired 7 million loyalty card customers in just over a year. This is almost as many cardholders as Barclaycard, which took decades to acquire that many customers. Safeway has 5.5 million cards.

Current partnerships are Sainsbury/Bank of Scotland (55% Sainsbury, 45% BoS), Safeway/Abbey National, and Tesco/Royal Bank of Scotland, a replacement of the previous Tesco/NatWest association that broke down. Marks & Spencer offers financial products itself, but not transaction payment products. Tesco offers a debit card which has a deposit facility, paying a higher rate of interest, 5%, than comparable products, an overdraft facility, again priced better, at 9%, than comparable products, and cash withdrawals through bank ATMs. The switch from NatWest to the Royal Bank of Scotland may be a signal of Tesco's intent to extend its financial product line further. Safeway is offering an interest-bearing debit card, a credit card and free 24-hour telephone banking, as well as cash withdrawal through Abbey National's ATMs. The Safeway card can also be used to pay for goods and services at over 70,000 Visa Electron outlets. Safeway eventually plans to offer insurance, mortgages and other lending products. Sainsbury plans to offer a full range of banking services including current accounts, savings and insurance products and consumer credit and mortgages.

Sainsbury has announced a £10 million advertising campaign to launch its bank, the first new bank brand launch in the UK since First Direct, which also spent £10 million in advertising. Its goal is to create a new business entirely and give the bank its own identity, and it is planning to remove existing bank ATMs in favour of its own-brand ATMs once the bank is launched, thus cutting off banks not only from a revenue stream, but also from a set of existing and potential customers.

One of the driving forces in this evolution is customer attitude, which seems to belie the levels of customer inertia we referred to in Chapter 2. Segment-based marketing, coupled with strong brands that instil trust and understanding, could be the key; these are areas in which the supermarkets have a big advantage over banks. A 1996 MORI poll of over 1,000 adults showed that 32% would be happy to open a current account with their supermarket, and 21% would buy other financial products from the supermarket in addition to the current account, while 25% would bank with Marks & Spencer, 21% with BT and 20% with Virgin. (62% would trust Richard Branson with their money!)

This would appear to be a real challenge in convenience terms and in credibility terms. The question is whether defences can be built or whether it is better to join the party. In our experience, such a strategic partnership makes sense for banks if:

- It gives them access to a customer base they otherwise would be unable to acquire (the logic the Scottish banks are using to justify their tie-up with predominantly English supermarket chains: Sainsbury has just 9 stores in Scotland and Bank of Scotland has only 25 branches in England).

- It is a defensive move to prevent a competitor gaining advantage through such a tie-up. In other words, if it is inevitable that a bank will link with a supermarket, then it makes sense to be the bank that does it.

- They feel this is better than having to compete head-on with supermarkets for financial services clients, i.e., supermarket-branded banks will be hard to beat and so, if you can't beat them, you may as well join them.

It is difficult to project how far supermarket banking will progress and whether it will become a dominant model. We know from the Barclaycard story that brand power can be the key to building a dominant position; the supermarkets have that. We also know that control of the payments system is important; the supermarket banks may not evolve without access through the existing banks. Equally, supermarkets now dispense a significant share of cash withdrawals through 'cash back' and switch a large percentage of credit and debit card transactions through their own systems.

It is also difficult to assess the sustainability of current partnerships. The Tesco/NatWest partnership broke down, possibly under the pressure by Tesco to offer a much wider range of products than originally anticipated, in order to compete with Sainsbury's bank. This chapter in banking history has some way to run, with other large-customer franchise holders entering the fray.

While the US experience suggests that supermarket banking is little more than a new channel of reformatted branch-based banking, the UK indications point to a newly franchised direct-banking model. It is hard to deny the contribution of the supermarkets to the evolution of electronic banking. It is difficult to deny the customer growth numbers behind the card launches. We are inclined to speculate that the banks will be able to defend their position through their own customer franchises and through their role in credit provision. We also suspect that the regulator, the Bank of England, may level the playing field in favour of the banks; it seems somewhat unfair that Tesco can mine its shopping data to sell financial services and

NatWest is precluded from mining its credit card data to sell shopping services.

The economics of branchless banking

The economics of branchless banking are quite unique. The branch networks have historically had an inherent advantage in attracting cheap retail deposits. Therefore, making branchless banking viable demands that management devote sufficient efforts to promoting it to minimise this disadvantage; also, the advantages of low-cost transactions in a branchless bank must outweigh the cost of forgoing some of the profits from cheap retail deposits. From the customer's perspective, branchless banking is generally cheap: the telephone calls are usually either free or charged at local rates, and no subscription charges are normally applied. The convenience factors and, often, the more favourable interest rates provide significant tangible and intangible advantages. Furthermore, as retail deposits become more expensive to attract, current account charges in conventional banks may be inevitable. In that case, branchless banks like First Direct, with value-for-money transaction services, will find it easier to attract deposits. Branchless banking may well represent the predominant force behind a new S-curve in the banking industry.

THE MANAGEMENT CHALLENGE: DECIDING WHICH DELIVERY CHANNELS TO INVEST IN

ATMs are a double-edged sword for the banks. Many customers prefer using them to going to a bank, and a small but growing number are not owned by banks. The ATM therefore supports the drive to move routine services and transaction processing out of the branch, while undermining the aim of using the branch to sell other, more valuable, services.

ATMs also have great potential to reduce the cost structure of retail banking. This is especially true when they are used in conjunction with the new telephone banking services which only require ATM access and a few confirming letters to constitute totally 'branchless' banking. As we saw in the previous section, all-ATM branches are already being operated in a few locations, at least for the personal sector. As the machines become more sophisticated, they can be installed in more unmanned retail locations. In the longer term the cuts in the branch networks prompted by ATMs could well be drastic.

If this development is successful, the share of the market for personal customers could shift against the Big Four in favour of the smaller players who are skilled in technology and marketing. Retail banking is all about convenience. For many years the competitive edge enjoyed by the Big Four banks was due to the sheer density of their branch networks. Having the most branches in a district often translated directly into a disproportionate share of local deposits. Electronic delivery channels are not yet fully competitive with branch networks, but, as ATMs improve, the competitive power of a large branch system may diminish. On the other hand, new distribution channels require significant investment, and the Big Four may have the competitive advantage there, with their greater financial muscle.

As a result, we believe that management will have to decide which channels are to get the lion's share of new systems investment. Banks will have to manage choices carefully between systems investments to convert branches into effective retail outlets, as described in Chapter 7, and investments in electronic delivery systems that may make branches largely obsolete. In the past, a proliferation of delivery channels, traditional and electronic, could perhaps have been a strength to the banks – cash through the 'hole in the wall' ATM was an extra service to branch customers. In future, however, supporting these proliferating channels will become increasingly expensive.

Banks must locate the source of demand for branch services. Growth in the use of EFTPOS and ATM transactions will continue to reduce the use of paper cheques, and hence branch services, by individuals. However, personal sector customers are not the only source of branch costs and profits, as we have seen. It is the paying-in and paying-out activities of commercial customers that are important here. As we noted earlier, these are at present closely tied to the branch network. If, however, debit cards continue to produce a relatively rapid fall-off in the use of cheques and cash at the point of sale, commercial paying-in requirements will decline in proportion. They might be further reduced if businesses could pay in their receipts through an ATM without a human teller to count and confirm the deposit. There is accordingly an inherent and very important link between the discussion of payment systems and credit cards in Chapters 3, 4 and 5 and the discussion of delivery systems in this chapter. For the moment, there is no clear conclusion on the short-term implications of current trends for branches.

The banks should be able to better segment their branch delivery structure by customer and product, even though they are unable to force the pace in the development of payments systems and thus in creating all-electronic banking. There are already examples of automated branches in residential areas with virtually no demand for business services. If enquiry and customer service are taken over by telephone-based solutions on the First Direct pattern, and 'middle office' functions such as credit control are also centralised, bank offices might be tailored to support quite distinct mixes of customer and product. Technology and sophisticated marketing could produce a whole range of branch types, from little more than a few ATMs with a service phone or video link, to something resembling the full-service branch of today. Each type of location would produce quite distinct economies, the aim being to have the lowest-cost delivery system consistent with market effectiveness. Technology is not producing one answer, but rather a range of possible answers for the future of retail banking delivery channels.

Home banking in its various forms represents one subset of these answers, but the jury is still out. Initially it was much vaunted, but over 10 years after its inception sceptics remain. There is a common perception that home banking may be premature. There is no point in promoting a 'breakthrough in technology' as the solution, if the customers don't want to use it because there is no problem to solve.

However, First Direct represents a clean leap on to a new S-curve of branchless delivery which, despite its use of human operators (heavily supported by Stage B technologies for on-line processing and enquiry), has the essential characteristics of an electronic business system. In addition to operating independently of fixed opening hours and physical locations, it appears to represent a fundamentally lower and relatively fixed cost structure compared to conventional branches.

The fixed costs, over-capacity and pricing effects discussed in Part One could enter consumer banking, at least for the more standardised commodity products, if this mode of serving customers became prevalent in the personal sector or key segments of it. Competition can be expected to mushroom as the technology gets better and cheaper and customers become more comfortable with it. Midland gave First Direct a focused mission as attacker on this new S-curve, even if that put some of its own branch business in the line of fire.

Midland's strategy shows that banks can act as both attacker and defender, pursuing essentially independent roles. As well as attacking with First Direct, Midland is also defending its branch business – which is of course based on the previous S-curve – by spending over ten times more on increasing efficiency than its total investment in First Direct. It has pursued a major branch modernisation programme aimed at taking virtually all transaction processing out of the branches and upgrading their ability to sell other financial services. Since it is hard to conceive of the branch delivery system for the commercial and mass consumer segments being eliminated in the foreseeable future, this appears to be a well considered defender strategy. It is more likely that the nature of the business done through branches will simply change, as discussed in the next chapter.

How to decide what, if any, type of home banking system is right for the institution's customer base is a major challenge for senior management. How will it sit alongside existing and planned products? How can it be charged for? How does it affect existing data processing systems and schedules? What is the relationship with the ATM strategy? Adopting home banking in any form will clearly not guarantee success, but ignoring these vitally important advances in technology may result in banks missing out over the long term. It is not certain Midland's strategy as either defender or attacker will succeed and there is always the danger that such an approach is simply leading to high investment costs for evolving technologies while old forms of delivery have to be retained. But this dual strategic focus for managing the old and the new technologies in tandem does raise the possibility that the Big Four banks could avoid the risk that leaders in the old technology become losers in the new.

THE DIVERSIFICATION OF BRANCH SERVICES

Chapter 6 showed how services such as cash on demand through ATM machines and telephone banking have contributed to changing the role of the high-street bank branch. Allied to this, trends depressing current account margins, such as the payment of interest on current accounts already mentioned, have been pushing banks into a search for other, more profitable, banking products and services to sell to their account holders.

Selling insurance has been for many years one of the most profitable single activities of the UK high-street banks, and mortgage lending has been one of the largest sources of overall industry profits. Consequently, banks are making big investments in marketing systems built around customer information, and in automated sales support for branches, largely aimed at selling mortgages, insurance and allied investment products. The question is, will this automation combine with the increased competition for this business to erode margins in what seems at present to be an attractive diversification for the branch banks?

MORTGAGES: A BRIDGE TO PROFITABLE RELATIONSHIPS

The UK banking industry's rapid growth in assets and profits from the late 1970s up to 1986 was largely fuelled by the transition from cash to deposits, and by a consumer spending boom, driven by house purchases and the rapid expansion of mortgage borrowing against existing homes. The housing stock in the UK is almost static at 24.6 million units, of which 16.5 million homes (67%) are owner-occupied, an increase of more than 10% since 1981 (Figure 7.1). Rising incomes and family formation pushed up the price of houses by 40% in real terms between 1980 and 1989, when owner-occupied homes were valued at approximately £800 billion. In the years that followed values fell off, as did the number of homes in mortgage. It looks, however, as if this retreat is over, and it is believed that the combination of demographics, low rates of house building and shrinkage in the supply of rented accommodation will sustain a reasonably strong housing market and corresponding demand for mortgage finance.

Fig 7.1 Growth of mortgage lending in the UK
1981–96

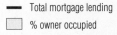

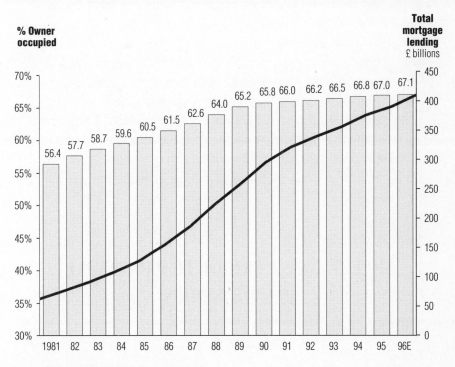

Source: Office for National Statistics, Dept. of Environment

At the height of the mortgage boom in 1991, loans outstanding against houses stood at £321 billion, representing a rise in real terms of 190% since 1981. During the 1980s the number of mortgages rose by 3.3 million. Not all this borrowing went to finance house purchase, since many house owners took out mortgages to tap the increase in value of their existing homes.

Mortgage borrowing was the leading factor in the rapid increase in personal sector debt (and corresponding fall in the personal saving rate) which characterised the 1980s and early 1990s (Figure 7.2).

Fig 7.2 Personal sector debt
1980–96

£ billions, percent

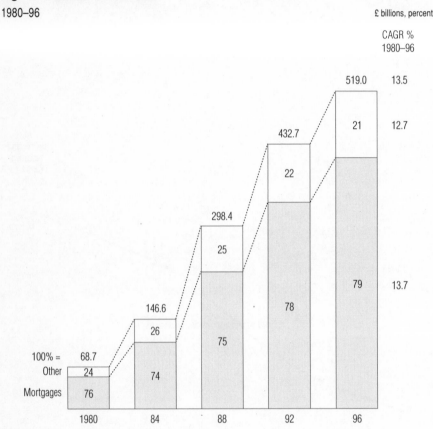

CAGR %
1980–96

Source: Office for National Statistics

The banks took advantage of the end of credit control in 1980 to compete directly with the building societies for house loans, and the building societies' share of outstanding mortgages declined (Figure 7.3).

Despite the entry of the banks into their formerly exclusive franchise, the building societies' assets and income grew significantly over this period. The societies, however, were at a disadvantage to the banks and emerging specialised mortgage firms, in that their shareholders and other depositors were their only source of funds. The banks had easy access to wholesale

Fig 7.3 Value of outstanding mortgages

1980–96

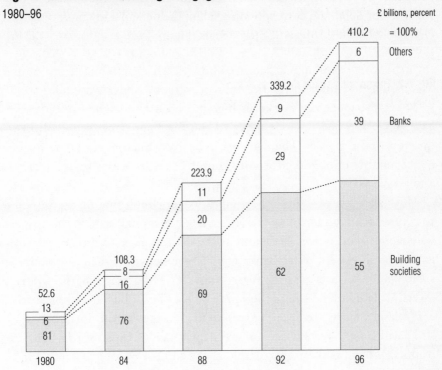

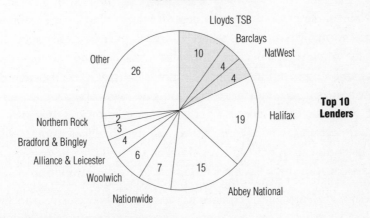

1996 mortgage lenders' shares
100% = £410.2 bn

Note: Until 1989, Abbey National is shown as a building society

Source: Office for National Statistics, Council of Mortgage Lenders, MMG analysis

funding and also took advantage of mortgage securitisation techniques first developed in the US. Building society deregulation was largely aimed at putting the building societies on a more equal footing with the banks in their ability to raise funds. The 1986 Act also prescribed a procedure through which building societies could convert themselves from mutual associations to banks, the course followed first by Abbey National.

Today, the mortgage market is highly concentrated. The top ten mortgage lenders, which include three of the Big Four banks, control three-quarters of the market. The market can be expected to consolidate further as the number of building societies continues to decrease through mergers and acquisitions.

Mortgages are of course the traditional stock-in-trade of the building societies (including for these purposes Abbey National), and in this respect they enjoy an edge over the banks as the natural place to turn for a mortgage. But all the Big Four banks have larger networks than any building society, and the success of the Big Four in selling mortgages in the 1980s is directly related to the size of their networks, as home buyers or home owners seeking a mortgage began to turn to the financial institution where they had savings or a current account. The presence of three of the Big Four banks (Midland is the laggard) among the top ten mortgage lenders indicates the distribution power of the branch bank.

Mortgages – especially during the 1980s – were not really actively sold. Before the banks undermined the building society mortgage cartel after 1980, the issue for consumers was finding a lender willing to extend a mortgage under any terms, and a deposit relationship with a building society was normally required to secure a place in the mortgage queue. Despite the entry of clearing banks and specialist firms, demand was far from saturated, and an institution willing to grant a mortgage could demand other business as well. The mortgage is not only an important product in its own right, but it serves to anchor a full customer relationship over its lifetime. Current accounts, savings, insurance and eventually pensions, wills and trust business can flow from a relationship centred on a mortgage.

These relationships have been reinforced by the promotion of endowment mortgages, which reached 60% of the market as a result of very aggressive marketing by lenders, who saw a chance to increase the safety of mortgage lending, cross-sell a life assurance product and promote a 'safe, affordable' mortgage to their customers. This was a major shift in the market, since as recently as 1985 42% of mortgages were still annuity (involving scheduled repayments of principal) in structure. Reaction to the selling practices of lenders has meant that endowment mortgages are not being pushed as much in recent years, but their importance has grown irreversibly.

An endowment mortgage is essentially an interest-only repayment mortgage linked to an endowment policy, which both ensures that the debt will be paid off in case of death or disability, and that the sum needed to pay off the mortgage (and in some cases a surplus, but possibly also a deficit) is accumulated through regular contributions to the policy. In other words, an endowment mortgage is really a combination of a conventional secured loan and an insurance and investment policy. It has strong effects on the profitability of mortgage lending since it is either brokered or underwritten by the institution making the loan, functions which can be as profitable as the mortgage loan itself or even more so. Unlike traditional life insurance, which has to be explained and 'sold' to the customer, endowment policies do not really have to be sold except as a way to obtain mortgage financing that might otherwise be less available or less affordable.

Other relatively straightforward insurance products can also be linked to the mortgage, most obviously the insurance of the house and its contents but possibly additional life insurance and savings plans as well. The mortgage thus promotes a host of potential, profitable relationships.

INSURANCE

Life insurance: how the banks compete

As we saw above, the mortgage product was in a sense the banks' bridge to distributing and underwriting simple lines of personal insurance, something that quickly became the most profitable single activity in retail banking.

Called *bancassurance* in French and *Allfinanz* in German, the combination of retail banking and insurance is a general European phenomenon. Europe's population is ageing, with the proportion of the adult population over 60 projected to reach 30% by 2030, up from just over 20% today. The ability of the state to provide adequate old age pensions is increasingly doubted, causing consumers to look to private insurance and higher returns on their savings. In most countries the tax system favours insurance and pension products; although the UK no longer provides tax relief on premiums (except for people over 60), there is no tax on pay-out, and pension schemes still qualify for tax relief. This demand favours insurance companies and puts pressure on bank deposits, where savings are taxed and yield is less. This pressure has been reflected, as we saw in Chapter 1, in relative holdings of assets. In 1980, the proportion of personal sector financial assets held in the form of bank and building society deposits was nearly the same as that held in the form of insurance and pension reserves, at 33–36% each. Today, more than 50% of household assets are held in the form of insurance and pension reserves and only 20% in financial accounts. There has been a clear trend towards professionally managed assets.

The UK represents about one-third of the entire EU life insurance market in terms of premiums, with per capita UK premiums at 135% of the EU average. About 30% of insurance held is basic life assurance that pays out only upon death, but the most widely held form of insurance is various types of endowment policies. Not surprisingly, the most popular endowment policies are those linked to a mortgage, either 'with profits' or 'unit-linked'.

Although the major life insurance companies, led by Prudential, still dominate the overall life insurance market, the major banks and building societies, and especially Lloyds TSB through its insurance subsidiaries, are among the top producers of annual premiums for linked life products, i.e., schemes where the premium is used partly to purchase life insurance and partly to purchase units in a unit trust or unitised fund. Banks and building societies in total accounted for 16–20% of all new individual life premiums in 1996 (Figure 7.4), with an even bigger share of 28% in the new single linked-life premiums segment.

There are at least four generic models or structures by which UK banks and building societies have entered the insurance market: exclusive marketing agreements, joint ventures, *de novo* companies, and mergers or acquisitions.

Whilst exclusive marketing agreements were very common, they have been increasingly replaced on the life side by other forms of participation. The main example remaining in life insurance is the link of Bank of Scotland and Standard Life. Some examples exist in general insurance, such as the link of Halifax with Royal & Sun Alliance, but these are also being replaced either by non-exclusive arrangements or by joint ventures.

Joint ventures have provided a learning step for many banks and build-

Fig 7.4 Distribution of new individual life insurance premiums

1996   Percent

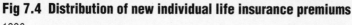

Yearly premiums   Single premiums

Source: ABI

ing societies, initially in life insurance and now in general insurance too, as
for example the case of the Abbey National joint venture with Commercial
Union. NatWest set up a joint venture with Clerical Medical and General
Life Assurance, and its sister company, National Westminster Unit Trust
Managers, to form National Westminster Life Assurance (NatWest Life),
which was launched in 1993. NatWest eventually bought out the other parties to have full ownership in 1996.

The outstanding *de novo* creation has been the TSB Trust Company,
which was the insurance, pensions and unit trust arm of the TSB Group
since its formation. Barclays Bank has also developed a strong *de novo*
insurance capability, while the entry of Virgin Direct in 1995 showed that
a *de novo* creation is still a viable option.

Lloyds' acquisition of majority control in Abbey Life, a first tier life company, is the prime example of the M&A approach. In 1996, Lloyds TSB
acquired Lloyds Abbey Life outright.

General insurance: the Direct Line model

As we mentioned above, mortgages have provided a springboard for selling other products, one of which is buildings and contents insurance, and
banks and building societies are major players in this market. But their
activities have been facing the challenge of direct writers (i.e., insurance
companies selling direct to policyholders, usually over the phone, thus
avoiding the costs of intermediaries) having better control of customer

information, and being generally able to price policies more accurately and on average lower. The direct writer phenomenon has extended to most lines of general insurance, but it started in motor insurance, with the entry of Direct Line, an event that was to lead to a major shake-up in the industry and which has been providing a model for several other operations, not only in insurance but also in banking, as we saw in the previous chapter.

Direct Line Insurance started in 1985 and is Britain's largest direct insurer. The business has grown dramatically. It now insures more than 2 million out of the 16 million motorists in the UK and has more than 800,000 home insurance policies in force. Its concept was to be the lowest-cost producer with the best service, targeting low-risk customers.

Its reputation for service is high. The customer telephones an operator – 90% of calls are answered within 10 seconds – who has an on-line computer to provide an insurance quote. Premiums can be paid by credit card. The service is available from 8 am to 8 pm Mondays to Fridays, and 9 am to 5 pm on Saturdays, and there is a 24-hour claims help-line and breakdown assistance. Direct Line was set up in Croydon but has since opened offices in Glasgow, Manchester and the Midlands. The multiple centres led to increased costs, but the number of premiums written in these areas rose too.

Direct Line achieved claims and expense ratios significantly better than for the rest of the industry in its first ten years; the expense ratio was around 10–15%, compared with the market average of 30%. It has managed to charge low prices because it controls operating costs and is very selective in its choice of policyholders: it does not insure young drivers, convicted drunk-drivers, owners of powerful cars, or residents of some inner-city areas. Direct Line has been retaining customers for an estimated eight years, compared with an industry average of about two years. This 'churn' may be because other insurers have intermediaries that are forced by competition to look around for the best price; or because such policyholders and intermediaries feel no loyalty to their insurer.

Recently, motor insurance has been undergoing a downturn in its cycle and Direct Line's profitability has been affected. Motor premiums have shown signs of saturation in the market and have fallen from their 1995 peak, as has the number of customers, while the number of claims has been growing. As a result, profit before tax in 1996 was just £26 million, compared with £112 in 1995. To some extent this downturn reflects the fact that Direct Line has become a victim of its own success. Based on its innovative service concept that technology made possible – both from a distribution and from an underwriting perspective, as we discuss in Chapter 9 – it transformed its industry and forced the other players to become more efficient. Direct Line may not be the star performer in an inefficient industry any more – the technology investment cycle may have caught up with it.

Nevertheless, the industry *is* cyclical and so Direct Line is likely to return to profitable growth; more so since it is unlikely that its competitive advantage has already been totally eroded. More important, for other players including banks, the message is now even clearer. Competing in general insurance has become much more challenging as a result of Direct Line's success.

TAILORING THE SALESFORCE TO THE SALES TASK

The TSB case study

The TSB arm of Lloyds TSB has longer experience of selling insurance, pension, and savings products than the other UK banks, and has developed a proven formula for success that other banks, and indeed Lloyds itself, have sought to emulate. TSB has specific sales strategies for each of its main product lines: life insurance and pensions, general casualty, unit trust, health insurance and commercial insurance. Except for its motor and commercial lines, where it acts as an independent broker, TSB designs, underwrites and sells its own products as a fully integrated business. All TSB insurance products are sold to the bank's seven million customers through one of three channels, all of which make extensive use of information technology to increase sales effectiveness while holding down costs.

The TSB Trust uses the TSB retail network as its tied agent under the terms of the Financial Services Act, but maintains two specialist salesforces of its own for more complex areas. The key to sales effectiveness is that products are sold through the cheapest channel consistent with their complexity and the degree of personal financial counselling entailed. All three channels use the same customer information systems, automation that has been layered into the branch system with minimal impact on core transaction and accounting systems.

The cheapest channel is *branch sales*, handled by customer service executives. They are usually counter staff who have been trained to sell standard products, using screens to lead customers through the features and benefits of various product options, pricing and other key selling points. Screen-based systems for applying for and approving standard mortgages have, among other things, eliminated the need for a bank manager to negotiate and approve individual requests. In addition, the screen-based sales are used for all mortgage-linked insurance products, such as the endowment policy, mortgage protection and house structure and contents cover, which are equally standardised. Other lines of general insurance, such as motor, travel and sundry protection policies, are also sold through the branch channel by retail bank staff. These policies are based on fixed premium rates and usually attached to an underlying credit facility or transaction, such as a car loan. They require little expertise to sell, and product information can be updated and new products added to the list via the branch sales support system. The same automation also tracks the productivity of the sales staff and is linked to sales incentive schemes.

For life insurance, pension products, and unit trusts, however, a well trained specialist salesforce is considered essential, since such products require competence in basic financial counselling and familiarity with complex Inland Revenue rules and rapidly evolving products. TSB tried at one point to use branch staff to sell such products, but concluded that branch sales are practical only for simple products, and set up its two specialist salesforces as a result.

The *Internal Salesforce* is based in the branches, and its staff spend much of their time talking to customers and establishing their credibility with branch staff. They depend entirely on branch staff for qualified leads, and do no prospecting on their own. The customer information database allows the bank manager to screen customers and pass the lead on to Internal Sales without revealing confidential information. Branch managers routinely write to their customers suggesting an insurance consultation; if a customer is interested, the salesperson simply confirms the appointment and makes the call. Most of the actual selling takes place in customers' homes in the evenings. Branches receive substantial commissions for successful introductions, which secures their active support for cross-selling. TSB Trust can afford to be generous in this respect because its sales commissions are very low (about a fifth) compared to traditional direct sales. However, with 34 contracts per salesperson per month, compared with an average of four or five per month for conventional insurance sales, the salesforce is well compensated and well motivated, especially as there are no upper limits on earnings.

The second specialist salesforce, *External Sales*, focuses on customers whom TSB serves primarily through electronic and home banking, and who thus have little direct contact with their branch. These customers' electronic transactions allow the bank to centrally generate a screened list of leads, which are provided to the External Sales force. They work throughout the country, independently of branches, and follow up the leads by telephone. At eighteen contracts per month, including non-life lines, again, the salesforce is extraordinarily successful compared to normal insurance industry experience.

TSB's success is all the more remarkable in that, with its quasi-public and 'people's bank' roots, it has an older, less affluent and probably more conservative customer base than any other bank. Using information technology to sift through the depositor base for worthwhile targets has been a critical factor in making TSB's insurance salesforce the most productive in the UK and possibly in Europe. Although very much a domestic retail bank in its focus, TSB teamed up with Cariplo, the leading Italian savings bank, and CNP of France in a joint venture to provide insurance products to Cariplo depositors. TSB could in principle develop many customer bases for its products as European integration proceeds. And the big opportunity, of course, is applying these skills to the Lloyds Bank customer base, an opportunity often stated as one of the rationales for the Lloyds TSB merger.

Should the Big Four emulate the TSB model?

TSB's success in selling insurance has been something of a model to the UK banking industry and has given credibility to the idea that the future of personal sector retail banking lies in cross-selling: selling more profitable financial products to current account holders.

TSB Insurance earned £191 million in the year ending October 1994, the last year it reported separately. In the same period the insurance activities of the Big Four banks earned approximately £700 million, even without the benefit of TSB's technology-assisted sales productivity. It would seem, therefore, that if they were able to develop good information systems about their customers, and design effective sales support systems, the Big Four could enjoy a remarkable increase in sales effectiveness and productivity. They could take share from the insurance and securities industries, and fend off retail competitors such as Abbey National and the building societies. With their massive branch networks and a pool of personal customers only slightly smaller than that of the building societies, and usually buying a more diverse range of financial services, the Big Four *should* be able to sell considerably more insurance, pensions, unit trusts and other relatively high margin products at little additional expense.

Already, the banks have an inherent advantage over other financial service providers of both insurance and mortgages in what they know about their customers; somewhere in their records they probably have the name, age, address, marital status, profession, car ownership, housing ownership, annual income, insurance coverage, financial obligations, net worth and spending patterns of most customers. An insurer or even a building society will have only a fraction of this data. Of course, banks do not have this information in a coherent and useful form, as most of their computing power goes to processing debits and credits to current accounts. It seems clear that banks ought to be organising their information systems around people rather than around accounts.

The large amount that the Big Four have been spending on technology to date has in part been inspired by a strategic vision of the customer file as the focus of a new core systems architecture, which would support the automation of accounts and credit authorisation, but much more besides. TSB, on the other hand, opted to focus on branch automation and local databases, to bring together information to support credit and product sales, without making changes to core processing and account systems. The TSB example suggests that the information needed to sell insurance products at least has little to do with the strength of banks' transaction processing capabilities. The most important aspects of TSB's systems investments were those that allowed a fundamental change in how branch staff and salespeople did their jobs. The technology itself was only a tool, albeit an important one, in a radical redesign of the business systems in the branches and insurance sales.

In the best of all possible worlds, banks would have instant access to all the information on a customer relationship which it had in all its product-specific and account systems, as well as the card files in branch offices and the mind of the bank manager. Taken together, this information would provide the basis of effective decisions on relationship management, credit and pricing, product sales and even new product development.

For dealing with large corporate and high-net-worth customers especially, banks would find such comprehensive information extremely valuable. However, for the great mass of personal and commercial customers in the branch system, it is questionable whether the value of fully automating and integrating current account and non-account information justifies the effort involved. The banks have to make critical choices about how to address the issue of accessing information on customers, recognising that they could spend all their revenues in pursuit of perfect information.

The banks must decide whether a central customer file or a decentralised information systems approach makes sense. Underlying this and all other such decisions are the key questions: Who would use the information, how and how often? And how much information is enough? A comprehensive, on-line, real-time customer file for quarterly current account reviews for the average branch customer makes no sense, even if it could be done at reasonable cost.

This in turn leads to the question of whether banks really have to rebuild their core systems, currently focused on the current account, to achieve a flexible IT structure based on the customer file. The value of the new structure may not exceed the cost of building it, given past experience of attempts to develop large and complex systems. It may well be preferable to maintain existing core processing systems, even quite old ones, far into the future, but simultaneously build links between old accounting software and new customer information systems. TSB has succeeded to a very large extent in doing just this, at modest cost.

It should be noted that TSB's starting point as a consumer-oriented bank recently created out of savings banks was probably a great advantage. Compared to a Big Four bank it had a very narrow product range, a relatively homogeneous customer base, and a far simpler and newer systems portfolio. The Big Four have far more complex products to sell and serve a much wider range of customers. In choosing how to move towards customer-focused systems, they may have to simplify the products they offer, perhaps narrow the customer segments they serve, and also redesign their business systems. For the time being, Lloyds TSB has decided to invest in a common new IT platform for the merged group, which however resembles more the Lloyds model than the TSB one. It remains to be seen how this choice will affect Lloyds TSB's efforts to apply the TSB model to the expanded customer base.

A QUESTION MARK ABOUT THE PAYOFF

Even if the Big Four were able to bring their inherent advantage in customer information to bear on this market, there are reasons to question
the scale of the strategic payoff. First, the TSB experience with specialist
salesforces illustrates that bank branches are not a very effective channel
for selling complex products. *Bancassurance* seems like perfect synergy for
large retail banks, but making it happen is very complicated, which indeed
is why the TSB example stands out.

Second, the market may be limited; hence possible oversupply could
frustrate banks' ambitions. Although per capita spending on life insurance
indicates that there are still nations with higher expenditure than the
British in this area, namely the Japanese and the Swiss, the British are now
spending 30% more than the Americans. The market for insurance and
mortgages is finite. These products are major 'sales' with long running
income streams, but once consumers have their endowment mortgage,
pension or unit trust in place, they may not need or want a similar product
for a long time, if ever. If many banks succeed in copying the TSB formula,
while the building societies are forming their own strategies and alliances
as well, the competition for market share is likely to grow increasingly
fierce. The UK public already spends a relatively high proportion of its dis-
posable income on housing and insurance. There is every possibility that
increasingly efficient product sales and marketing will lead to damaging
price competition in commodity products and recent poor results may well
be effects of such a development. The relatively high margins of products
such as life insurance traditionally reflected to some degree the difficulties
of explaining and selling to customers; if banks move towards electronic
systems for selling, these will require a degree of standardisation, and reinforce the commodity character of products. We simply do not know what
margins would look like in future conditions of abundant supply and efficient production and distribution.

Bank management should be wary, then, of two assumptions behind
cross-selling strategies based on customer information:

First, it is at least open to question that enough demand exists for banks
to solve the problems inherent in their cost structure by profitably selling
products such as insurance and mortgages to their traditional customers.
Second, strategic decisions, including how much to invest in the systems to
improve marketing and sales effectiveness, should not be based on the lev-

els of sales and margins available in these products today: banks must consider what their competitors are up to, and what the consequences will be. Substantially different competitive conditions will result if most large and capable players try to do the same things at the same time.

As noted at the beginning of this book, it is hard to find an example of technology simultaneously creating value for the customer while improving profits for the shareholder in retail banking. Profits overall have increased in recent years, as have customer value and technology investment, but a look at the pattern over a longer period and the sources of profitability makes the cause-effect relationship far from clear. TSB was a pioneer in bringing more systems power to bear on retail banking distribution, and was a leading technology 'attacker' in this arena of competition. If, however, all major competitors make similar use of the available technology, we are likely to see the more difficult competitive conditions and consequent unfavourable economic effects implied by our thesis. The transformation of the branch delivery system may forge an industry structure very different from that prevailing today.

PART

3

SUCCEEDING IN THE TECHNOLOGY REVOLUTION OF BANKING

From the perspective of banks, the previous chapters have painted a sometimes depressing picture of the likely consequences of technological change in banking. Management can, however, make a difference in how these developments affect their institutions. As in previous instances where technology has revolutionised industries, some firms will survive and prosper, new players will emerge and grow in strength, and other competitors will disappear. These outcomes are not predetermined. The ability to control the use of new technology, taking advantage of its positive potential and avoiding its pitfalls, will be decisive. This is a critical general management role. By general management, we mean the individuals directly responsible for all income and expense in a line of business, several lines of business or the institution as a whole.

Information technology is as central to the future of banks today as deposit money and cheque clearing were in Bagehot's day. It is worth remembering that when the new paper technology was putting an end to the era of old-established private banks, the proprietors of what became Barclays Bank embraced the new banking and formed one of the greatest joint-stock banks. Their fellow private banks are historical footnotes, having been acquired or failed. Management decisions, taken in time, do matter.

While general managers have a clear role in making these choices about future direction, technology managers are facing challenges of their own. For most technology managers the primary challenge is how to manage the transition from existing technology that supports the 'old' branch-based business model to new technology needed to support the 'new' business model: focusing on winning and holding customers through innovative services, devising new modes of decision-making, and disaggregating traditional banking activities. This challenge is further complicated by rapid changes in the capabilities and cost of new technologies. Banks today must choose from a bewildering array of new business opportunities and ways to fundamentally change the structure of existing IT costs and services, while also reconciling conflicting resource demands.

Each bank's ability to meet this challenge will be different. On the supply side, success will be shaped by the legacy of its existing systems and the efficiency with which new systems are added. On the demand side, the business managers will need to define their business needs clearly, and the technologists will need to interpret these requirements accurately and explain technology opportunities in an understandable way – a problem that has consumed much of the attention of information systems practitioners and writers. In general terms these practitioners have advised an approach of defining the business vision first before embarking on a methodically controlled system development cycle.

Big successes in these areas are thin on the ground, particularly when considering the major investment programmes the banks have undertaken. These shortcomings seem to have arisen across the board: projects don't deliver the benefits needed to cover the investments; or they fail for want of a clear business sponsor; or they fail because their scope grew beyond the capabilities of the technology or beyond the pockets of the investors.

The next three chapters address the three key challenges that bank managers have to face to succeed in the technology revolution of banking: optimising the current environment; developing a business and IT strategy for the longer term; and changing the culture of the organisation to foster an effective dialogue between bankers and technologists. In discussing these challenges, a set of frameworks is presented, developed to aid general management and technologists assess jointly the role IT can play in assuring business success today and in the future.

MANAGING
THE BANK
TODAY

Before deciding where to invest for the future, banks first must understand clearly the position they find themselves in now for each line of business: where they expend the bulk of their resources, and whether this expenditure is being applied to the most likely sources of improvement in the business. To help this understanding, a framework for categorising costs has been developed. This is called the technology management framework. This distinguishes between the 'generic' or 'commodity' technologies available to all banks and the 'value-added' technologies and activities specific to individual banks.

This understanding is essential if management is to be successful in a crucial task for today: reducing the cost and/or increasing the value of current activities, through business re-engineering. As an example, there is an analysis of how re-engineering was used to transform the economics of one bank's consumer business.

Technology, however, does not only transform industries by changing the operations and cost structures of the players. It can also become a powerful tool on the revenue side, enabling a fundamental shift in customer targeting through a technique described as customer lifecycle profitability marketing (CLPM). Using this approach, the analytical power of technology can generate dramatic improvements in the effectiveness of a bank's interface with the market.

The common theme behind these tools is that banks *can* become more effective in managing their business today, through the use of technology, but experience shows they rarely achieve their full potential. The secret may lie in taking an externally focused approach, where the market becomes the measure for any effort to improve the business.

UNDERSTANDING THE PRESENT POSITION: THE TECHNOLOGY MANAGEMENT FRAMEWORK

Generally, any business system for producing goods or services can be described in terms of three functions: core technology (F1); production (F2); and market-led product design (F3) (Figure 8.1). Together, the three functions contain all the tools, equipment, activities, and people that make the product; consequently, they represent 100% of the costs of producing it. The content of each function will vary by industry, by product, and by individual competitor, reflecting factors such as size and business mix.

In an ideal market-driven company, the customers' needs drive product design (F3), which drives the production function (F2), and ultimately dictates the shape of the technology (F1). The reality of the world is that market needs and product life cycles shift very quickly for many products (though scarcely at all for others); and the range of core technology options is almost overwhelming and increasing at a very rapid rate. This raises a major challenge for managers: how are they to respond to changes through an active product design (F3) function, given that previous decisions have constrained the shape of both production (F2) and core technology (F1)?

In banking, as in many manufacturing industries, the primary constraints arise from the production function, F2, because it is product-specific, containing both software and clerical skills inseparable from product knowledge. For this reason, F2 tends to be very complex, unique and consequently very time-consuming to change. An assembly process cannot be set up overnight, and neither can product-specific bank software systems. To make changes in this area takes large commitments of time and money, both usually in short supply. Where an F3 market opportunity may have a limited time window, and promise only modest returns, compromises must be made to ensure that the necessary changes can be made to the production function. In practice, no company, no industry can respond perfectly to market demands. In banking this ability to change core functions is frequently severely restricted.

F1 – The core technology function: competitively neutral

The core technology function is a collection of technologies and tools, not specific to the business or the industry, which are necessary to carry out the work of producing the final product. There is considerable labour and

Fig 8.1 The technology management framework

Theory

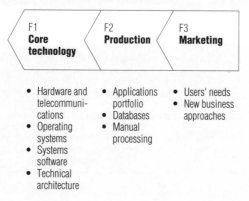

Reality

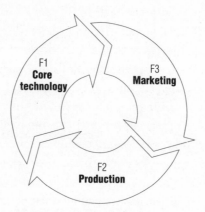

Adapted and reproduced from Thomas D Steiner and Diogo B Teixeira, *Technology in Banking* (Business One Irwin, 1990) with permission of The McGraw-Hill Companies.

Evaluating a new technology

Business needs drive production needs

Examples

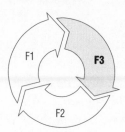

Business need
• New retail products offering more consumer choice, value and return
Impact on production
• Applications to support processing of individual deposit and loan products

Production needs dictate core technology capabilities

Examples

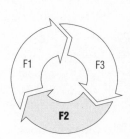

Production need
• Extra data for additional product parameters, e.g., variable rate consumer loans
Impact on core technology
• Additional capacity for processing transactions and on-line storage • On-line terminals for customer service

New core technologies create potential business threats/opportunities

Examples

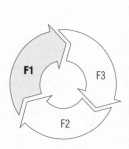

Core technology developments
• Internet • Neural network • Workflow
Potential opportunity/threat for business strategy
• New low-cost methods of payment transaction • Learning systems capable of defining own rules for, say, credit applications based on customer profiles • Flexible re-engineering environment

management content in F1, focused on the acquisition, installation, operation and maintenance of the tools. In manufacturing, these tools may be machine tools or rolling mills; in banking they largely consist of computers and the systems software needed to run them.

The core technologies and tools of F1 are by their nature entirely external to the banking industry. They are 'vendor-driven': created by corporations such as IBM, BT and Oracle, and by the academic and scientific community. Today these technologies can in most cases be bought off the shelf. While the operation and maintenance of F1 tools have traditionally been the responsibility of the businesses which have bought them, they are increasingly available from external vendors, including IT consultants, specialist contract staff, and 'outsourcers'.

Therefore, F1 technology is not a source of differentiation or competitive advantage; in fact, like all vendor-driven technology, it is competitively neutral. Nobody in financial services is totally, or for long, excluded from the whole range of F1. But, as in any other business, the biggest players with the deepest pockets can buy more and better tools than anyone else. They can also assemble high quality technical talent and specialised skills. In other words, they can commit themselves to being 'state of the art' in F1. While small banks and building societies simply do not have the resources to be tempted and will buy or share simple F1 tools, the largest banks, with strong and highly professional data processing staffs, are always pulled by the vendors and their own experts towards relentlessly upgrading their F1 technology. But even for these players there is always a wide gap between the existing F1 kit and the sort of kit they *could* have if they turned-in their old hardware, systems software and off-the-shelf packages for the latest releases. This gap grows almost daily.

While core technology is competitively neutral, the decisions involved in selecting and maintaining a highly capable and flexible F1 kit at a reasonable cost are critical to bank performance, both technically and economically. F1 decisions are highly technical and specialised, and the knowledge to make them is narrowly held. Consequently the decisions about when and where to upgrade technologies, and how to make trade-offs between low costs and desirable features, should be made by management with an understanding and an overview of the whole technology management framework, not by technicians who are expert only in narrow F1 issues. Investing too much or too little can seriously affect performance, because F1 can range from 5% to 10% or more of total bank expenses. Commit-

USING TECHNOLOGY TO REDUCE COSTS

Re-engineering current bank activities

As has been shown, most bank automation over the last thirty years has generally replicated paper processes which were themselves the product of custom and habit in F2b. There remains considerable scope for reducing the cost base through some form of business re-engineering. Re-engineering essentially means taking apart a transaction flow or a decision-making process, understanding why (and if) the work in each segment is necessary, and designing a simpler, better way of getting it done, linked to clear metrics. To see the potential for improvement, compare the differences in cost/income ratios of the Big Four with those of the building societies. Banks that pursue standard re-engineering and cost reduction initiatives can achieve savings of at least 15–30% of their baseline budget (equating to a 10–20 percentage point improvement in their cost/income ratios), even in profitable and efficient parts of the institution. The banks that re-engineer best and deliver real improvements in costs will move up the efficiency curve faster than their competitors, at least for a time. They can use that time to establish their options for the future, and to generate more money to fund further investments.

Re-engineering seeks to develop a very clear picture – literally a graphic representation or 'snapshot' – of the existing workflows, especially at the 'back end', where routine, high value transactions are processed. Then, the suggestions of the staff involved in each activity are combined with the top-down perspectives of managers who view the business process as a whole, in order to reduce the amount of work that goes into each transaction.

Work is reduced two ways. First, given the *ad hoc* way F2b processing practices developed, an examination of bank workflows almost always reveals many redundant procedures; e.g., the constant checking and rechecking for error, or the checks and balances to prevent loss or fraud that developed in paper-based banking. What serves no purpose is easily eliminated. Secondly, the remaining activities often involve doing things the hard way. They may be over-complicated; they may fail to take full advantage of existing automation. Often, they can be simplified quickly, without significant systems changes. Done well, re-engineering assesses how new systems features or the use of new and emerging technologies might fundamentally improve the F2a/F2b fit – that is, the marriage between application systems and transaction processing. This is an extremely complex task.

While most re-engineering initiatives have tackled transaction processes, the same concepts and methods can be applied to processes such as selling, lending and controlling/managing risk. These processes all involve a finite number of decisions, usually made according to accepted rules or norms. Re-engineering at this level of activity analyses how key decisions are currently taken, and at what cost, and looks for ways to improve not only overall productivity (i.e., how cheaply decisions can be made), but also overall effectiveness and quality (i.e., how well decisions can be made). Decision processes of this type can be reduced to rules which reflect best practice, and these rules can be embodied in relatively simple decision support software and expert systems.

Re-engineering in action: the TSB story

As discussed in Chapter 7, the case of TSB stands out in the way it reconstructed the way it did business. Before re-engineering, TSB branches were much like other high-street bank branches, with counter staff handling routine transactions and bank managers in charge of credit, marketing and administration. The bank wanted to reshape the branches into effective sales outlets for financial services, especially insurance. It had originally entered the insurance sales business by acquiring an established company; TSB bank managers were expected to provide qualified leads to insurance representatives, but had little reason to make much of an effort. Even where this was effective, it was costly, since the agents were paid conventional sales commissions. In addition to this retail thrust, the strategic vision of the bank was to expand into wholesale lending, something that its savings bank heritage left it ill-equipped to do, so it brought a large number of experienced commercial bankers into the bank manager function at competitive salaries. This was expensive; business lending of acceptable quality did not materialise and bad debts reached damaging levels, forcing a change of management and a thorough rethinking of strategy.

The new management team decided to fundamentally re-engineer branch banking, the traditional core business of the bank. TSB developed a screen-based insurance sales system, which supported the sales team structure described in Chapter 7 in some detail. This technology allowed relatively inexpensive staff to sell a high margin product effectively, a far more dramatic effect than just having a smaller number of lower paid staff engaged in transaction processing.

Even more radical was TSB's transformation of the bank manager role – traditionally, credit control, branch administration and the development of new business. These are mostly judgemental activities, conventionally viewed as requiring an experienced (and relatively well paid) person to perform them. Re-engineering challenged this proposition. Analysis of what really went on in these core business functions convinced TSB that the mass market personal sector could be served effectively without having a bank manager in most branches. Standard credit-scoring rules are more reliable than the average branch manager in controlling risk, and can be automated and placed in the hands of relatively junior staff through the same terminals that support product sales. Step-by-step screen displays showing features, benefits and pricing options can allow quite complicated products like mortgages to be sold by the same staff. The same systems can track the productivity of individual sales persons in the branch. As the branch becomes more automated, much of the reporting and administrative control role of the bank manager becomes redundant. Systems generate most of the data that higher levels of management require. This leaves the branch manager free to focus on new business development, building market information, and personnel and general oversight duties. But these functions, along with the servicing of relatively few complex commercial and upscale personal sector relationships, can be concentrated in the hands of a far smaller group of managers in regional offices that support multiple branches. As a result, TSB found that it could eliminate half of its middle management positions in retail banking even as it significantly improved its ability to cross-sell both banking and insurance products to its branch customers.

TSB's re-engineering effort fundamentally improved the economics of its consumer business. In 1990, TSB's retail banking pre-tax profits increased 40% to £258 million from £184 million in 1989. Insurance and investment services profits rose 37% from £83 million to £114 million, during which non-interest income increased by 26%, from £245 million to £308 million. Home mortgage outstandings, TSB's largest single asset category, were up 25%, in a very difficult housing market. This was accomplished with average staff numbers remaining flat at around 44,500. The full impact of re-engineering had clearly improved TSB's performance in the personal sector and had supported a change in overall strategy back to concentration on high-street banking.

The success of the TSB story lies in two key areas. First, the technical constraints faced by TSB were not as severe as those faced by its main high-street competitors. TSB's technologists had completed the development of their integrated banking system in the early 1980s and had done so around a core transaction-handling architecture. This architecture made it easier for the bank to change the structure of its business, to add new products and services and to extract customer data. Second, the management team was able to establish an effective dialogue relating business improvements to technical capabilities and constraints.

Successful re-engineering can generate substantial improvements in profitability. It requires, however, major organisational change and its focus is primarily on cost; it does not directly address the revenue side of the business. Yet, technology can be a powerful tool in improving the revenue stream of the business, by using an approach described here as customer lifecycle profitability marketing (CLPM).

USING TECHNOLOGY ON THE REVENUE SIDE: THE CLPM APPROACH

We have suggested that banks are in fact facing two major challenges: reducing their costs to compete with aggressive and more focused players, and sustaining their revenue streams, which are being threatened by the effects of technology-generated overcapacity. In their efforts to do the latter, the same technology can be a powerful tool, by enabling banks to become much more sophisticated in utilising the most important competitive resource they possess: their customer information base. Ignoring, for a moment, the potential constraints of existing F1-F2 systems, technology now makes it possible to determine each *individual* customer's profit contribution over the life of their relationship. With this customer lifecycle profitability information, F3 marketers can develop marketing initiatives to attract the best customers into the portfolio, increase the profitability of existing customers, and build loyalty among profitable customers. This focus is what is meant here by customer lifecycle profitability marketing.

Conventional thinking argues that customer-focused organisations should continually strive to deliver product and service offerings that better meet consumers' wants and needs – these needs are generally determined from market research, an inexact art form at the best of times. Using more scientific and exact predictive modelling techniques, however, CLPM can be used to create real and measurable lifetime value, by influencing customers to exercise more profitable behaviours, within the existing constraints of an organisation's ability to deliver. Effectively executed CLPM confers a first-mover's advantage, especially as it can pull customer treatment levers that will not be observed by competitors – which is why it can be described as 'stealth marketing'. Moving quickly is important, especially as customers can be changed much more quickly than organisations.

Becoming a CLPM marketer

Most marketers aspire to market to micro-segments of individual customers, generally based on some demographic or psychographic variables. While the prospect of micro-segment marketing is seductive, the organisational implications of getting there are daunting. Trying to pursue segments composed of individual customers is misguided. The aspiration of marketers should be to maximise the lifecycle value of their customers. And this objective has no built-in bias toward any particular size of segment, nor towards tailoring product offerings to customers versus influencing customers to change their behaviours.

The pivotal decision for the organisation is not whether and how to use information. It is finding the right balance between continuously changing the business and continuously changing the customer. On the one hand, a marketer could develop superior insights into customer needs by micro-segment, and then design customised product/service offerings to fulfil the needs of each segment. But delivering on the broad array of product and services promised would be challenging to say the least. On the other hand, a marketer could create incentives for customers to change their behaviour in a manner that aligns with the business's ability to fulfil its promises flawlessly. So, should a marketer try to transform the business or change the customer? The right answer involves a combination of both.

Successful businesses will do both, but their initial efforts will be directed at whichever option they can pursue more quickly and easily. Banks have some significant constraints on the speed with which they can change themselves. Consequently, it would make sense to focus the information and insight to change customer behaviours within the business's ability to fulfil its promises. Marketers will of course need to understand the capacity of their businesses to fulfil promises to multiple needs-based segments. Since more flexible businesses will get better leverage from CLPM, all businesses

221

should strive to reduce their constraining influences over time, in order to continue to build more profitable and more enduring relationships with customers.

Why aren't all organisations managing individual customers for increased profitability today? This is because marketers have been unable to measure individual customer lifecycle profitability, which can vary widely on the dimensions of volume of business, price, product mix, transactional pattern, service requirements, expected value of losses (e.g., insurance claims, loan defaults), and longevity (Figure 8.2).

Fig 8.2 Drivers of variability in customer profitability

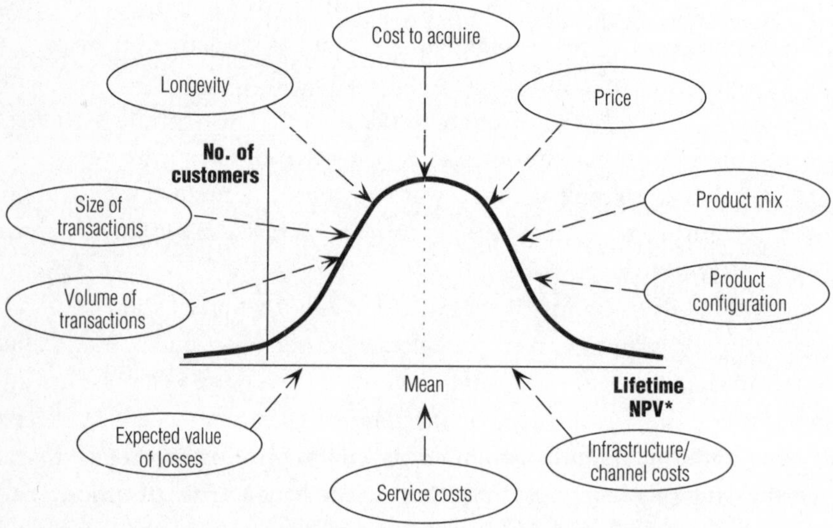

*Net present value

Typically, profitability is measured by product and then for a whole sector, e.g., personal. Also, most organisations are saddled with accounting systems that were designed to measure historical performance generally around the main organising unit of the bank, i.e., the branch. These systems are riddled with shared costs that are allocated on an arbitrary basis, fixed costs that are artificially treated as variable, and variable costs that are artificially treated as fixed. These accounting systems have been the barrier to marketers' building an economic model of their businesses, where revenues and costs are driven by customer behaviour. Furthermore, incentive schemes invariably are linked to short-term accounting measures rather than net present value, which takes into account future value income streams from the customer.

Measuring the true profitability of every customer along his/her whole lifecycle is a prerequisite to taking advantage of differences across customers and to tailoring products and services more precisely to customer needs. A fundamental change in organisational orientation and culture, however, is also essential, to enable the use of a different paradigm and the acceptance of decisions based on it.

The principles of CLPM

From an understanding of each individual customer's lifecycle profitability, an F3 marketer can develop optimal behaviour-influencing marketing initiatives to improve the customer base along the dimensions of mix, profile and longevity (Figure 8.3). Successful marketers will: identify and attract more profitable customers, and de-market inherently unprofitable customers; motivate existing customers to undertake more profitable behaviours; and retain profitable customers longer – recognising that customers with positive value over their lifecycle may well go through phases where traditional measures would make them appear undesirable.

After having successfully tackled the difficult first step to becoming a CLPM marketer – building the customer-centric economic model of the business – CLPM marketers will adhere to four principles:

1. Segment customers on profitability, as well as profit-related behavioural profiles (not just on descriptive or needs-based characteristics), and predict which customers will exhibit profit-maximising behaviours.

2. Influence specific profit-enhancing (not revenue-enhancing) behavioural changes among specific customers or segments with customised communication and incentives (within the business's capacity to fulfil the promises).

3. Use the stealthy profit levers, mix, profile and longevity, not just the signalling levers, price and share.

4. Manage marketing budgets just as any other investment (Return on Investment, Net Present Value), not as an expense, and create the reward systems that generate the right motivation for management.

Building from a solid foundation of the traditional marketing levers, the four principles of CLPM will enable marketers to optimise their total investment in marketing, analytically determining both how to invest and how much to invest, while simultaneously creating a sustainable competitive advantage.

CLPM in practice

Figure 8.3 illustrates an application of the CLPM approach in redesigning a marketing campaign for unit trusts. By focusing on the 'stealth' levels of

Fig 8.3 Impact of CLPM campaigns – Unit Trust case example

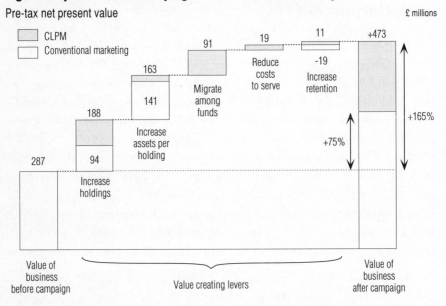

Pre-tax net present value

£ millions

Marketing objectives

Lever		Conventional objectives	CLPM objectives
Mix	Target attractive customers	• Target 10% across-the-board increase	• Target 0–50% increase based upon assets/profitability
Transactional profile	Get more assets from existing customers	• Target 100% increase in assets for 10% of all holdings	• Target 100% increase in assets for 0–25% of all holdings
	Migrate customers to more profitable funds	• None	• Target switch of 20% of Money Market assets to 'average' other fund for 50% of holdings
	Reduce costs to serve customers	• None	• Reduce variable costs by 25% for 40% of holdings
Longevity	Retain customers longer	• Target 10% reduction in churn for all holdings	• Target 0–50% reduction in churn based on assets/profitability

Source: MMG analysis

mix, profile and longevity, this institution was able to double the sales generated by the campaign, increase the size of every sale, increase the value of customers by migrating them between funds, reduce the cost to serve the customer base, and increase retention, leading to more than double the return that the conventional campaign would have achieved.

The application of CLPM can extend beyond the realm of marketing campaigns, by providing an individual customer behaviour perspective to critical business processes such as customer acquisition, credit line assignment and debt collections.

Using extensive databases for superior customer targeting, institutions such as MBNA Corp., the American credit card issuer, have been consistently able to identify and attract customer segments that in most years have a lower propensity to default than the average credit card customer. That ability both lowered loss provisions and cut operating expenses – for one thing, with lower losses MBNA needed many fewer collectors. Hence, it was possible to reduce prices in order to build volume while still maintaining and even adding to the bottom line.

Other card issuers have been able to achieve results comparable to those of MBNA via the same sort of database analysis. One institution used this approach to increase four-fold the creditworthy accounts approved by using a model to predict which prospective cardholders are most likely to generate target usage levels (Figure 8.4). Another model led to the reversal of a loss-making position by predicting the likelihood of write-offs and thus reducing the write-off rate from 12% to 7%. In another case, a predictive customer behaviour model enabled an institution to raise its yield on collections by up to 50%.

Another application of the CLPM approach has been at a large bank, which succeeded in singling out and attracting those mortgage applicants who were likely to create more value than the average mortgagor – because these customers were less prone to prepay their mortgage. This capacity enabled the bank to take pricing actions that increased volume and facilitated cross-sell while raising profitability or, more precisely, expected value per customer.

CLPM does not transform technology into a source of sustainable competitive advantage, but it uses it to exploit in a very powerful way the one source of competitive advantage banks have always relied on: information. Its focus on the customer is a major contribution to the management of banks today that has often suffered from a lack of market-driven objectives and measures.

Fig 8.4 Results of customer value techniques

Disguised credit card case examples

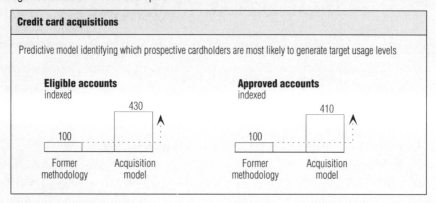

Credit card acquisitions

Predictive model identifying which prospective cardholders are most likely to generate target usage levels

Eligible accounts
indexed

Approved accounts
indexed

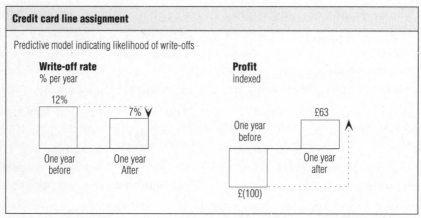

Credit card line assignment

Predictive model indicating likelihood of write-offs

Write-off rate
% per year

Profit
indexed

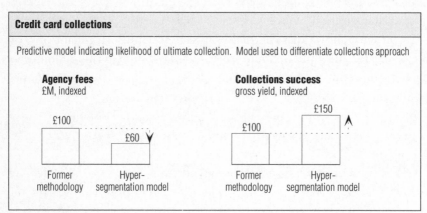

Credit card collections

Predictive model indicating likelihood of ultimate collection. Model used to differentiate collections approach

Agency fees
£M, indexed

Collections success
gross yield, indexed

Source: MMG analysis

PREPARING FOR THE FUTURE:
THE MARKET AS THE MEASURE

We can point to the successes of today's banks as they prepare for the future. TSB clearly stole a march on many of its competitors in the way it re-engineered its way of doing business, whether through the branch sales system or its change of branch and ATM servicing models. The Big Four have made major strides in centralising processing, out of branches, and in transforming branches from mini-banks into sales/service outlets. The question is, *could they have done more?* The reality is they remain high cost-to-serve businesses whose customer franchises will eventually come under sustained attack.

The re-engineering efforts undertaken by these large institutions have only scratched the surface of what is available. The programmes have tended to be excessively constrained by the legacy of past technology investments and have also been, most damagingly, too inwardly focused. It is no secret that most re-engineering projects do not deliver the promises – the TSB case may be the exceptional one-out-of-ten case. The reasons for under-achievement are quite simple: the targets tend to be too inwardly focused, a case of *microscopes vs. periscopes*; the projects seem to be no more than automation in disguise, frequently automating processes that make no sense anyway; and they often result in investments that deliver no better than me-too processes. In sum, these programmes tend to be no more than a case of shining up the *old* bank. The question is, what can be done, or is each institution limited to finding its own version of the TSB story?

Experience shows that the market is a powerful determinant of goals. Preparing for the future should start with an honest recalibration, overhauling and retuning against the metrics of the market. This can be thought of in three parts :

- Competitor-driven recalibration – i.e., for those competencies central to competitive advantage, what can be done to be best in class?
- Customer-driven recalibration – i.e., for those business parameters essential to sustaining customer relationships and positioning, what can be done to hold and retain the best customers? Clearly this is the domain and focus of CLPM, not only as regards marketing treatments but also as regards customer service delivery.
- Supplier-driven recalibration – i.e., for all other processes, are products

and services delivered or acquired to best-in-class market standards and prices? In a competitive supplier world, it makes no sense for an internal organisation to operate at worse than market prices or service levels.

Using this recalibration framework and pushing the boundaries of current resourcing models, the laggard banks and building societies have a vastly improved chance of starting their re-engineering programmes with sufficiently stretching targets. In particular, the winners will do more than match the leaders, and will avoid the main risk of me-too management, i.e. being no better than a mediocre competitor. While market-driven recalibration highlights more stretching 'periscope' targets, success still hinges on successful implementation – here the constraints of existing systems and capabilities remain the primary obstacle.

Pushed to the limits, supplier-driven recalibration may prove to be the 'golden egg' that delivers the true potential. Over the last fifteen years there has been a massive growth in the 'outsourcing' industry, an industry that is no more than the physical embodiment of 'supplier-driven recalibration'. Interestingly, and not surprisingly in a microscope-driven world, outsourcing is relatively under-utilised in banks. The dominant management philosophy over the last 30 years seems to have been that control of delivery resources is the path to control and cost-efficiency.

Even now, there is major resistance to outsourcing as a management device, driven mostly by management asking the wrong questions. Instead of asking, 'Why shouldn't we outsource an activity?' management tends to ask 'What should we outsource?'. This approach provides a conservative response. Taking the more aggressive line of questioning (Figure 8.5) reveals significant potential for outsourcing, with up to 60% of current bank activities outsourceable.

Successful outsourcing in the UK context will, however, require some effort to be put into developing suppliers, or into establishing joint ventures. For example, statement printing and mailing needs of the Big Four could not be met by any single supplier in the market currently. Alliance potential exists, e.g. between a utility like British Telecom and a Big Four bank.

Taken to its extreme, this approach could lead to the emergence of a radically disaggregated bank structure centred on a 'technical network' linking product factories and distribution channels (Figure 8.6). Perhaps this is what a new entrant electronic bank will look like.

Fig 8.5 Outsourcing decision screens

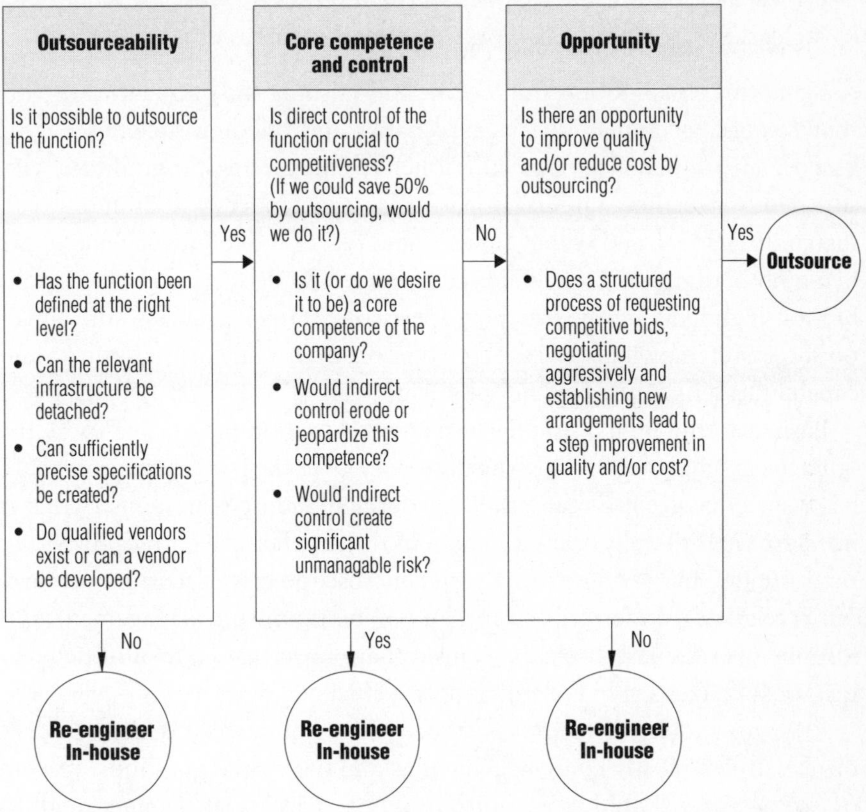

Outsourceability	Core competence and control	Opportunity	
Is it possible to outsource the function?	Is direct control of the function crucial to competitiveness? (If we could save 50% by outsourcing, would we do it?)	Is there an opportunity to improve quality and/or reduce cost by outsourcing?	

Outsourceability — Is it possible to outsource the function?

- Has the function been defined at the right level?
- Can the relevant infrastructure be detached?
- Can sufficiently precise specifications be created?
- Do qualified vendors exist or can a vendor be developed?

Yes →

Core competence and control — Is direct control of the function crucial to competitiveness? (If we could save 50% by outsourcing, would we do it?)

- Is it (or do we desire it to be) a core competence of the company?
- Would indirect control erode or jeopardize this competence?
- Would indirect control create significant unmanagable risk?

No →

Opportunity — Is there an opportunity to improve quality and/or reduce cost by outsourcing?

- Does a structured process of requesting competitive bids, negotiating aggressively and establishing new arrangements lead to a step improvement in quality and/or cost?

Yes → **Outsource**

No ↓ **Re-engineer In-house**

Yes ↓ **Re-engineer In-house**

No ↓ **Re-engineer In-house**

This model implies an ability to present and deliver a single, coherent view of the customer position with the bank across the product factories and to accept transaction input from multiple distribution channels.

In considering this model of a new retail bank – and the model will stretch a long way into the business sector – consideration should be given to whether emerging technology can be used to transform an old bank into the new model. As noted in the discussion of the product function, F2, most of the costs are locked up in product-specific 'stovepipes', reinforced by a high level of manual processes. The stovepipes tend to reach right through from the core branch accounting function to the customer service interface. For those customers holding more than the average 1.7 products, this new model is difficult to achieve without major systems investments or human intervention. However, for a single product customer a current

Fig 8.6 Retail bank business system

Case example

Traditional integrated business system

- All customers
- All products

**Disaggregated organisation serving
different distribution channels**

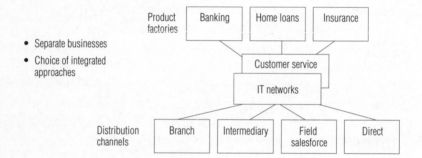

- Separate businesses
- Choice of integrated
  approaches

bank 'stovepipe' will deliver perfectly good value leaving the customer to integrate the bank or across banks unaided.

Technology and evolving thinking on IT architecture, especially around the client-server model, has produced some opportunities to work toward this new model. This needs to be considered at several levels.

- Front-end/surroundware tools allow for improved presentation and delivery of information to the point of customer contact, without changing the back-end processing. Further function can be added to the front end to aid things like cross-selling, scripting and on-line help, and even cross-system calculation to keep parallel databases synchronised.

- Network and telecommunication technologies allow for rapid deployment of data from centralised mainframe machines (the old world legacy systems) to the new front-end systems.

- Reverse engineering and code restructuring tools allow for some in-flight cleaning-up of core applications, for increased maintainability.

- Database technology, including predefined interfaces and data synchronisation and replication tools, enables organisations to set up new transaction and reporting databases alongside existing production data. These new databases can be used to support parallel (and new) information needs (e.g., risk management) and to supplement existing transaction data.

Used well, these technologies could provide a migration path from the old world to the new model in which legacy systems are first isolated and then progressively switched off.

While such a change may now be theoretically possible, no institution has yet been fully successful; the tendency has been to allow the core technologists – the F1 and F2 types – unbridled access to the corporate coffers in the pursuit of core systems replacement, rather than building migration routes. Elsewhere there is a progressive ossification of old legacy systems with new interfaces.

The next chapter is devoted to charting the future course. The key question posed is whether it is possible for the currently established market players to reinvent themselves and what the migration path looks like. Can it be one based on the legacy of the existing F1-F2 structures, leveraging these emerging technologies, or will it only be possible to start from a fresh start, clean sheet design abandoning the past legacy?

CHARTING THE FUTURE COURSE

In Chapter 8, it was argued that the challenge banks face in managing technology has more to do with managing the legacy of their existing production function (F2) than with managing the core technology (F1). The focus on technology for its own sake, rather than as a means of satisfying business needs, is the reason that many mid-80s projects to replace legacy systems failed to achieve their objectives. Meanwhile, earlier chapters demonstrated that banks are facing an increasingly hostile competitive environment, with the threat of long-term profitability decline as customers take more control of their own financial resources, and new competitors attack different lines of business.

The chances of success in the search for new profit improvement opportunities will be determined by how effectively each bank integrates technology thinking into its general management framework, how successfully each bank is able to harness technical and process innovation in the pursuit of the new dominant designs and how successfully the technologists are able to relax the constraints imposed by the interwoven nature of the core technology and production functions (F1 and F2).

These challenges give rise to the following key questions.

1. At the level of overall business direction, how should the bank think about technical innovation – i.e., how should it think about true product innovation?

   - In that context, how should the banks think about the challenges to their traditional product lines from outside competitors. Further-more, how seriously should they take the actions of non-traditional players, like technology and communications companies?

   - More specifically, are the developments in electronic commerce so pervasive, so fundamental and so imminent that they, in fact, will force a transformation for the banks?

2. Within the context of existing technology structures and specifically, the core F1 and F2 functions, how should the technology and business managers approach the issues of more integrated and less spaghetti-like legacy systems?

- To what extent should these managers need to take cognisance of cross-institutional and cross-industry process changes?
- What criteria govern these decisions, some of which could entail mammoth investments?

3. In making investments in innovative improvements, how can banks determine whether to go it alone and push proprietary enhancements and products?

- In which cases does it make sense to work with peer institutions, either to form consortia to provide services, or to purchase such services from third-party providers?
- At certain points in time, does it make sense to pursue simultaneously both proprietary development and shared ventures?
- If so, what criteria determine when to shift emphasis from a proprietary structure to a shared structure?

4. With regard to the respective roles of the technology and business managers, how should the general management function interact with the technology management function?

- To what extent can clear lines be drawn around areas requiring tight control?
- To what extent should policy be more flexible in certain areas, allowing for looser adaptation?
- How should a bank think about establishing such policies at particular points in its evolution?

These questions need answers. The techniques described below are aimed at building the dialogue between general managers and technologists in devising future strategies. Any such discussion, however, needs to be accompanied by a warning: the far future will not resemble the present, and banks need to invent their future today if they are not to be overwhelmed by the pace of change.

INVENTING THE FUTURE BANK:
HARNESSING INNOVATION

Effectively managing the bank's existing businesses only helps fight half the technology-driven battle for survival. Few will escape the logic of the thesis of this book. Increasing systems intensity inherently involves more fixed costs, over-capacity and exposure to predatory pricing and shrinking margins. In the short term some businesses may be sheltered temporarily by a productivity or service quality advantage, proprietary software, or a strong position in a hard-to-penetrate market niche. While as much profit as possible should be extracted from these advantages, at the end of the day all existing banking business will become more efficient. It will thus become much harder to extract acceptable profits from any one business, as systems intensity increases and unit costs fall. Many will become obsolete and disappear altogether.

This requires that general management establish two very distinct but equally important and accountable senior roles. One role has as its single and relentless focus the reduction of bank costs, using any and all tools made available by technology. The other role, which ought to be detached from the existing way of doing the day-to-day business of the bank, is to invent the future bank. Its goal must be to create, *de novo*, and without the constraints inherited from paper-based deposit banking, the most efficient and effective financial services business which current and emerging technologies will support (Figure 9.1).

Taking direct banking as an example, the decision to shutter significant parts of the branch network in favour of a non-traditional, branchless bank is very difficult for a 'traditional' Chief Executive of a UK domestic bank to make. Yet this is the course that Midland Bank embarked on in setting up First Direct, but then Eugene Lockhart was not a 'traditional' executive, having come to banking from management consulting.

The great advantage of this type of long-range vision will become apparent when the focus shifts to paring down or getting out of existing businesses and products, generally a very messy process. These businesses and products always have their defenders, and exiting always has its costs. Shared cost structures and shared customer bases further muddy the decisions. It is clearer and cleaner to look at current demographic, social and economic trends and the evolving technologies and decide which businesses are emerging (or can be created), which are objectively attractive

Fig 9.1 Charting the future

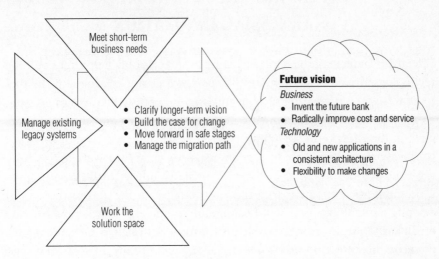

now, and which are likely to be in the future, than raking through the legacy of past decisions. This analysis, together with a clear-eyed assessment of the strengths and weaknesses of the organisation and its competitors, forms the basis for designing the business portfolio of the future.

It might well be asked what the 'inventor of a future bank' would do and when he or she would know that the work was complete. Clearly one approach could be to spend time with technology companies to understand new technologies and to guess how they might be applied to transform banking. From here the intrepid inventor could move to pilot the new technologies; the NatWest pilots on Interactive TV and Mondex probably fall into this category.

The key question to be explored is whether the lessons of 'dominant design' and the concept of technology diffusion accelerators and decelerators can be used to lay out a path. The challenge is whether an existing bank can behave like an attacker and improve the success rate of its innovation effort.

The innovation challenge

Utterback and Foster have shown that defenders are vulnerable to attackers who can exploit radical innovations and demonstrate real value to new customers. It is also known that the IT investment cycle does not always make every attacker a warrior and every defender a weakling. Utterback also shows that quite often short-term results disguise long-term effects. For example, as unprofitable early adopters shift their custom to a new attacker, the profits of the defender may increase, if only temporarily. In the long term, today's unprofitable customer may end up creating a positive net present value for his or her provider, which may not be the defending institution.

Empirical evidence collected by Utterback and confirmed by innovations in the US financial services markets suggests that established leaders often fail to recognise the potential threats from innovation early enough. They also frequently fail to act rapidly and decisively when they do recognise the threat. There are a number of reasons for this, some of which may be unique to the financial services world:

- Anticipating the emergence of the dominant design is difficult. In the early stages of innovation a large number of participants are experimenting with new designs. Even if one could look at all the designs, one could not know about the parallel discussions going on across the market participants that could trigger design combinations. For example, it was difficult for Lloyds Bank (and IBM) to anticipate some thirty years ago that their nervousness about locating IBM-branded ATMs outside branches was not shared by Barclays. There is also a high risk for an established player that the intelligence is filtered out by the lack of fit with the established order.

- The weight of the installed base holds the idea back, particularly where the innovation potentially cannibalises the existing infrastructure. Interestingly enough, in banking there are examples on both sides. For example, the implementation of the smart card is being held back by the installed base of EFTPOS and ATM card readers. On the other hand, banks have invested quite readily in new channels (e.g., telephone banking) without actively managing-down the cost of the installed base. The more relevant impact of installed-base blindness is where an innovation is rejected because it does not fit the delivery mechanism optimised to deliver the old design.

- Rigid organisation structures frequently suppress all experimentation or starve experimentation units of needed resources. Frequently this rigidity is reinforced by excessively risk-averse decision making, which rejects new ideas in the belief that old profit streams renew perennially.

- Back-logged application development resources will also hold the innovation back, either by failing to provide resources to develop the ideas or simply by discouraging innovation completely. Of course, this is a major problem for the larger institutions with long-established infrastructures and the consequent long list of indirect projects, e.g., adjusting to EMU or the year 2000, absorbing new regulations and adjusting to frequent reorganisations.

- Sometimes the capital budgeting processes impede decisive responses to attacks. In the cases reviewed by Utterback, net-present-value techniques systematically favoured narrowly defined, incremental initiatives over the less certain returns from radical new technologies. This mixing of uncertainty and risk results in cases being presented with cash flow bearing little resemblance to what may actually happen. Where decisions are framed in option values, the choice between expanding resources in new ideas versus improving on old infrastructures becomes clearer. Ideally one would seek a judicious balance between novel ideas and those that represent merely improvement of the existing technology, especially where the improvement ideas reinforce any of the IT investment decelerators.

Before considering how to apply these lessons to invent the future bank there is value in testing whether a radical technical innovation could transform banking. Utterback's thesis for the class of industries he studied is that it is not a question of 'will it?' but of 'when?'. The concept of decelerators and the dominant role of banks in payments in the UK suggest a less certain outcome.

Electronic commerce and banking

These questions can be illuminated and the way in which innovation may affect banking can be illustrated by considering how Utterback's framework relates to the emerging phenomenon of electronic commerce described in Chapter 4. Electronic commerce was described there as the exchange of goods and services for payment, using an emerging electronic infrastructure for functions related to trade, such as exchange of information, transmission of payment and distribution. By emerging electronic infrastructure is meant the networking of computers across consumers and small, medium and large businesses through the Internet and Intranets.

This emerging infrastructure may redefine the dominant design of how commerce is conducted, thereby creating a platform for non-traditional players to attack the banking industry. Clearly, the electronic commerce industry is very much in the early, fluid stage of innovation. This stage is characterised by a large number of infrastructure, access and content providers experimenting intensely with new technologies, formats and value propositions. Internet access as a component of the new dominant design provides an example. A large and increasing number of on-line service and Internet access providers are engaged in a fierce battle for market share. Similarly the fight for the dominant access device has barely begun and features the PC, the network computer, TV set top boxes, screenphones and other devices as contenders. Other characteristics of the fluid stage are the lack of a well-defined regulatory framework (e.g. consumer protection, privacy laws) and a proliferation of underlying communication technologies, as the telecom and cable companies experiment with different protocols and 'cables' to get the content delivered cheaply and reliably.

What may be the impact of the new platform once a dominant design emerges? While nobody can answer this question with any certainty, several scenarios are plausible. A benign scenario is that retail banking will not be affected significantly at all. Although an increasing number of customers may want to conduct their banking electronically, they may do so by using traditional banks. For the banking industry, this scenario would result in a temporarily higher cost base, as banks develop their on-line offering, while maintaining their traditional channel infrastructure. As retail banking becomes progressively independent of geography, banks may begin to face customer loyalty erosion as customers experience more offers while 'web surfing'. However, these developments would represent changes in degree rather than the kind of radical innovation described by Utterback, because the foundations of banking that are payments and risk assessment remain unchallenged.

A more radical scenario would have attackers exploiting the new platform to create radically new value propositions with which banks cannot easily compete. Tripod Inc., a US-based affinity association catering to 18- to 34-year-old people in transition from college to work life ('the transition generation') provides information and guidance on topics such as career, managing personal finances, community, travel, etc. through a World Wide Web site and a magazine with a circulation of 1,000,000. In May 1996 Tripod entered an alliance with Security First Network Bank, the first Internet-based bank, to establish an interactive, full service personal finance centre tailored to the needs of Tripod's target group and hyperlinked to the

Tripod web site. In November 1996, Tripod reported that its membership exceeded 116,000 and was growing at 10,000 a month. According to PC-Meter, Tripod was the 31st highest ranked website in the world in the fourth quarter of 1996.

This example illustrates how a new value proposition built around an electronic interface platform might erode the traditional banks' franchise. It also demonstrates the difficulty that a defending player faces in recognising the potential threat arising from such a new offering.

A defending bank reviewing this example would be foolish to be complacent about the threat imposed by the newly acquired franchise, especially if the bank was optimised to serve 50-year-olds. The question is whether a defender would necessarily be excluded from responding. The worrying part of this example is that the electronic infrastructure allows a new entrant, who already has a customer franchise, to attack the cross-sell product potential so easily accessible by traditional banks using their existing channels. The real concern arises when the valuable products and customers move away from the banks, leaving only the high-cost low-margin transaction products (i.e. the payments infrastructure).

Consider further the implication of e-cash, the digital equivalent of cash. E-cash provides a secure method for an Internet user to complete transactions by paying in e-cash, previously downloaded to the hard disk. The challenge for banks is that any company can become an e-cash issuer, although, to date, the current issuers are banks, namely Mark Twain Bank in the US, Deutsche Bank in Europe, and Advance Bank in Australia. An electronic-commerce supplier could elect to issue e-cash and control both transactions and payments. How much of a challenge this is to banks will depend on a number of key factors:

- Will customers overcome their fear and hold e-cash accounts outside of banks?
- Will enough companies accept e-cash to provide scope for an e-cash acceptor to use e-cash for its payments?
- Will banks stay out of e-cash issuance?
- What will be the attitude of bank and government regulators, considering the importance of money creation to controlling monetary policy and the control of money laundering?
- Are there other changes that in combination could reinforce this trend, e.g., supermarket banking?

- Will new product entrants assume the control banks currently exercise over credit?

UK experience offers some key differences that may improve the chances for defenders. For example, regulation is in some respects looser and in other respects tighter. A bank can offer a full range of products and is not faced with Glass-Steagall type restrictions. The Bank of England will seek to regulate the behaviour of new entrants, as happened to the Antigua-based European Union Bank when it started offering high-rate deposits across the Internet. We do see the Federal Reserve acting in the same way, for example, in restricting foreign banks from issuing dollar cheque accounts cleared through US banks.

UK banks dominate and share the payment system through industry owned and operated infrastructure. It is this control of cheque clearing, electronic funds transfer (BACS and CHAPS), debit and credit card switching, and Giro payments that may allow the banks breathing space to defend in the electronic commerce battle. An ancillary factor is that the banks continue to play an important role in credit provision, driven by the flexibility of the current account overdraft and their significant share of credit-card-based trading.

With this tradition, and with the significant market power of the banks, it would be surprising to see the major banks choose not to be involved in electronic commerce, and it is difficult to believe they would not have a chance against most attackers. However, complacency would be folly, particularly if the infrastructural cost disadvantages outlined in Chapters 1 and 2 allowed more nimble attackers to steal a march.

Against this background, how can established players respond to the threats from technology-driven innovation, let alone capitalise on opportunities? Action clearly is needed to overcome or at least mitigate the inherent disadvantage defenders have against attacking firms.

There are probably no easy answers. However, it is possible to find effective ways to manage innovation. Success will require a concerted investment in keeping up with emerging designs and in reacting to new technologies and applications.

Monitoring and experimenting

Close observation of technological and market developments is critical to the early recognition of successful innovations. While predicting dominant design may be impossible, observing it, and reacting rapidly and decisively, can make the difference between the survival or the demise of the defender. Just tracking the evolution of existing technologies, competitors or customers is insufficient. For example, radical innovation often emerges from unexpected players or networks of players, as the US examples in the credit card and mutual fund (unit trust) businesses show. Also, asking existing customers of established leaders will tend to generate answers confirming the current dominant design, rather than pointing in the direction of a new one.

Hence, continuous monitoring of the environment and staying alert to emerging offerings is crucial. To be effective, it should be complemented with controlled experimentation.

Given the uncertainty of the timing and shape of an emerging dominant design, it is unwise for established players to invest heavily into any one end-game scenario. Rather, established players should invest moderately in structured experiments with new value propositions and technologies. These experiments, if well designed, serve a number of key purposes. First, they allow an incumbent to hedge bets for the future. Second, they enforce the need to monitor market developments and test hypotheses about emerging innovations, and in general help keep one's ear to the ground. Third, experiments represent a good vehicle for developing future core capabilities (for example, measuring lifecycle profitability) and participating in shaping the future rather than waiting for it to happen.

Such continuous experimentation is important to managing innovation and to preparing to defend against radical innovation. However, successful defence will depend more often than not on committed investments into one or the other stream of experimentation. Too often have we seen bank strategies fail for want of consistent investment. Choosing correctly depends on how well the idea fits the customer's needs, how deeply the bank adds to its competence and how well the ideas are carried through to execution.

Developing an ideal business design

As already noted, existing business infrastructure and architecture can be a drawback in the innovation process. However, it can also be the source of strength and cashflow. Recognising that the *status quo* is transitory is a key first step in maximising the value that an established player can derive from the installed base. Adapting it continuously is the second step. Given the unpredictability of radical innovation, this process has to be evolutionary and grounded in today's reality. 'Clean sheet' redesign techniques, pioneered by the business process re-engineering practitioners, are helpful in this regard, as they demand an unbiased view of new potential approaches and processes as a starting point. However, they become grounded in the reality of the present, once the analysis turns to planning the migration.

Starting with a 'clean sheet', an established bank would devise an 'ideal business system design' based on an in-depth knowledge of the external environment. This design ought to depict in detail key architectures of the business system: the overall business architecture (corporate strategy, product markets, value propositions etc.), the process architecture (end-to-end value chain), the social and organisational architecture (organisation design and culture) and the systems and physical architecture (IT systems, channel and other physical infrastructure). The design should be devised in such a way as to be operational within the currently prevailing (rather than some envisioned future) business environment and constraints. For example, it should be achievable with currently available technology and reflect current customer behaviour. As the environment evolves, the design should be updated dynamically.

Based on the ideal design, banks can begin to critically assess their resource focus. How much resource is really committed to achieving the ideal design? For example, the balance of technology investment in maintaining and updating legacy systems vs. spending on new technologies should be examined. Banks should also contrast the ideal design with the existing business architecture, identify gaps and develop programmes to acquire or develop missing capabilities, restructure business processes and migrate towards the evolving ideal design. As new ideas emerge from the continuous monitoring discussed earlier, these can be tested against the ideal design.

The ideal business system design provides a structured approach to evolving an established leader's installed base, keeping it agile without negating the value that is derived from it.

Setting up independent structures

Some established players have started independent organisations to experiment with new formats and value propositions, thereby effectively becoming attackers themselves. These new structures often compete directly with the defender's main business.

The most notable and successful example of this approach in the UK banking industry is Midland's start-up of First Direct, which was set up alongside Midland Bank, the old bank, with new processes, new people, a very different culture and a new customer proposition. The parts shared with the old bank were largely infrastructural, did not 'touch' the customer and were already honed to the level of efficiency demanded by the customers. It is not surprising that First Direct has been very effective at attracting new customers (more than 75% are not Midland Bank customers) and that word-of-mouth referrals have been high; this is the new design for high service banking. What is of even greater interest is to recall the reaction of the competing banks, who went to some lengths to deny the success of the new format, even while First Direct cherry-picked the attractive high-net-worth customers. Fortunately for those banks, First Direct did not tackle the market as aggressively as it could have and was not followed by any more aggressive attackers.

The case of Banco Commercial Portugues is equally interesting as it shows that a new bank could be built without reliance on the existing bank's infrastructure. BCP was started as a new bank using standard technology and targeting high value customer segments with highly tailored product offerings. It was this combination of customer focus and offering flexibility that proved unassailable to the competing banks. The story does not end here, as BCP developed new formats to tackle new segments, each time using the 'new bank' concepts. For example, Banco Nova Rede aims at younger customers and looks and feels quite different to BCP, with its younger image carefully reflected in branch decor and advertising.

Utterback points out that setting up independent structures is one example of how market leaders have been able to defend themselves. However, such an approach will not enable the defending part of the business to escape its challenge. Numerous examples, including Xerox's Palo Alto Research Park and GM's Saturn division, prove that reintegration of such an independent structure into the parent organisation is all but impossible. The deep cultural gaps between the organisations tend to frustrate any attempts to merge the start-up with the main business. In fact, when Gene Lockhart launched First Direct he went on record with a statement that in time the old bank could be 'switched off'.

Implications for banks

These approaches to managing innovation are not meant to be exhaustive. However, if implemented, they should go some way to addressing the cen-

245

tral issue posed at the beginning of this book: how can banks bridge the gap between general managers and technologists? It should be clear from the discussion in this chapter and throughout this book that innovation occurs at the intersection of the marketplace and technology. A radical new technology that fails to create a measurable, immediate benefit for a significant customer base has no chance of developing into a successful business. Stated the other way round, a technology that delivers this benefit to customers has a shot at evolving into a new dominant design and, if radical enough, transforming the industry. The challenge for management, then, is to develop a deep understanding of the link between customer benefit and technology. The key to this understanding is the notion of innovation. In the end, application of technology *per se* is unlikely to create lasting competitive advantage. Applying technology to drive innovation in the marketplace, on the other hand, has the demonstrated potential to create massive customer value and competitive advantage. Remaining competitive in the short to medium term depends on managing technology effectively, reducing costs aggressively and exploiting revenue opportunities, as we saw in Chapter 8. In the long term, however, the players who manage innovation, rather than technology, are likely to win.

What does this mean for UK banks? Analysis would seem to indicate that the Big Four are vulnerable to attack especially while they operate at a cost disadvantage; this is already happening on the margins as more flexible players cherry-pick more valuable customers. They are also vulnerable where more rigid organisation structures restrict their ability to respond to new attacks; this is happening even in cases where 'new bank' concepts have been implemented.

However, analysis also seems to suggest that the pace of change may not be as rapid as in US banking and that the existing banks can defend their franchise. To do this, they will need to harness the powers of innovation to reinforce the decelerators referred to in Chapter 2. In particular, we expect to see defenders leveraging customer data and brand power to further reinforce customer loyalty and to use proliferating product features to reinforce customer inertia (if such a concept makes sense). By the same token we also expect to see further alliances between banks and other franchise holders, for example, between Royal Bank of Scotland and Tesco, Abbey National and Safeway, or NatWest and British Airways. What these do is give shared access to the customer franchise and share some of the margin without giving up the banking franchise.

BUSINESS IT VISION:
HARNESSING THE TECHNICAL INFRASTRUCTURE

Much has been written and spoken exhorting managers to base IT strategy on business strategy. This is not always as simple as it sounds, especially when the rate of technical innovation is high: sometimes the rate of change in the industry demands frequent changes in strategic direction and positioning – often before the previous generation systems have been implemented. Sometimes business strategy and IT strategy are developed in tandem – for every constraint removed, what business opportunities open up? Too often, the general practice is that today's business strategy just perpetuates what went on yesterday, over-investing in new F1 technologies that do not facilitate any new competitive strategies.

Basing the vision on a renewed dialogue

Furthermore, the gap between the high-level F3 strategy and the necessarily detailed F1-F2 IT development strategy is too wide for the latter to reliably achieve the aims of the former. The way to deal with this is to build a dialogue between the business managers (the F3 types) and the technicians (the F1-F2 types), based on a shared vision as shown in Figure 9.1. This involves:

- Articulating and sharing a *business/IT vision* that captures the essence of the business objectives (e.g., simultaneously reducing costs and increasing product penetration) and the technical environment this implies (e.g., old and new applications working together in a consistent way) . While this may appear to be a simplistic concept, it is essential to shaping the subsequent detailed analyses supporting properly articulated investment decisions.

- Getting to grips with the *technical 'solution space'* – that is, with the realities of the current F1-F2 structures – to understand the constraints likely to be imposed on achieving the business vision. These constraints do not have to be taken as given – removing them has simply to be justified.

- Making a clear *business case for change* for each investment decision, combining quantified statements of expected benefits, expected costs, likely timescales and potential risk. In the same way as any other investment (e.g. lending to a third world country) has to be justified on economic grounds, IT investments should be no different.

- Managing the *migration from the current to the future*, focusing particularly on managing the level of risk implicit in any project (in particular, so as not to combine high levels of technical and operational business risk).

- Managing the *core F1-F2 functions* with aggressive cost and customer service targets, thereby ensuring that business results are achieved with economic use of technical resource.

Working towards a vision: the BITE framework

This process of linking business and technology change can be summarised in the business improvement/technology evaluation (BITE) framework shown in Figure 9.2.

Fig 9.2 Linking business and technology change

The BITE framework

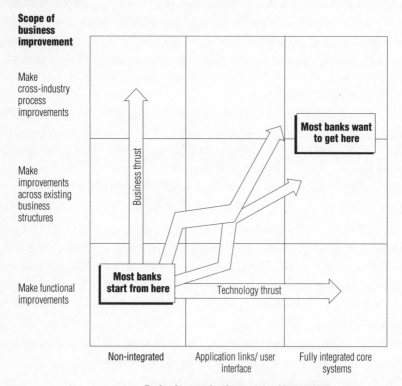

Technology evaluation: scope of integration

The business improvement axis shows the primary types of improvement available to any business without changing its core products and markets. These are the types of business improvement most frequently encountered and most frequently constrained by the existing technology base. For example, geographic expansion can, in most cases, either be achieved with existing technology or be built up on an independent (and often new) technology base.

The simplest and most frequent business improvements are *functional improvements*, i.e., changes within the existing F2 operational structures of the business, such as improved processing automation in branch back offices. Such improvements are the most frequently identified, tend to be easier to implement and are in many instances fairly well exhausted by routine line management attention. Consequently they are usually small, and typically will yield no more than two to three percentage points improvement in the overall cost/income ratio of the bank.

The next level of improvements apply *across existing business structures* but within the confines of the existing business boundaries – that is, changing the existing applications/transactions (F2) structures. The main aim of any cross-business improvement programme is to eliminate the inefficiencies that invariably arise through the year-by-year extensions and modifications to the basic business functions. The primary mechanism for getting at these inefficiencies is to study the way the business delivers its product or service from beginning to end of the process. Because of their wider scope, these improvements are harder to identify (although they are frequently easily identified by outsiders, particularly customers) and harder to capture (as they require concerted action across the lines of traditional organisation structures and procedures).

The final category of business improvement included in this framework is *cross-industry process improvements*, where the limits of the existing business boundaries are relaxed, e.g., to create a new F3-F2 structure. Numerous examples of such improvements exist in the manufacturing sector. For example, many businesses have progressively redefined industry boundaries to redesign supply chain processes, by building suppliers' end-to-end processes directly into the core manufacturer's end-to-end processes. In UK banking the earliest example of such thinking was the creation of joint clearing, which is now the heart of the industry's payments system.

The technology axis of the BITE framework represents the likely stages of the evolution of software applications. Most businesses, and banks are no exception, started their IT journeys by installing *applications specific to the current business*. For mainline manufacturing companies, these are likely to have taken the form of functional applications such as invoicing, sales, inventory, finance, production. For banks, these are likely to have been some mixture of functional applications (payments, accounting) and product applications (deposit processing). In most cases the applications portfolio has grown through the addition of new applications to meet new automation or product demands. Most of these additions will have been made without tying into the existing set, other than to ensure the base technology platform remained largely consistent.

It is this continual addition of applications that created the need for many, if not all, of the businesses to go through the second phase of *cross-linking the applications*. This cross-linking has taken many forms and served many purposes, for example:

- A savings account linked to a current account by using the payments system to handle the transfers.

- Branch terminal programs written to 'front end' multiple product processing systems in order to provide uniform access for clerks or tellers, frequently requiring extensive use of (hard to remember) key codes.

- A product usage database created to identify which products a customer uses.

- Programs written to download management information on to spreadsheets, e.g., for further analysis by finance or risk management.

These cross-links have resulted in a plethora of system interfaces, many of which were designed for single purposes. For each change to the underlying applications, the technology manager needs to be sure that the affected interfaces will continue to operate satisfactorily. For each new application built or, even more critically, replaced, new interfaces may have to be built and the potential impact on connected applications fully understood. Notwithstanding these limitations, cross-linking applications continues to offer a fast and relatively inexpensive way to add new functionality.

Whereas the tangle of interfaces resulting from cross-linking applications has been the bane of the technology manager's existence, the *fully integrated system* has been the real enigma. The concept of integrating a set of systems so that everything can be accessed is appealing. With a fully integrated system, users could, for example:

- Access all processing functions from a single access structure such as a menu, with data shared across functions.
- Link back all data about a customer to a single customer profile.
- Tie back cost and revenue information, at appropriate levels of abstraction, to customers, products, or organisational units.
- Analyse appropriate risk and other control information centrally by exposure type, e.g., by market, country, sector, instrument, currency, counter-party.
- Log and track all customer contacts centrally or remotely.

There is undoubted intellectual appeal in connecting the key aspects of a system, thereby limiting the need for future change, and it is easy to establish a substantial list of business benefits to justify the large investments, not the least on the cost side. Indeed, in one case it could be shown that a fragmented infrastructure cost one-and-a-half to two times as much as a theoretical best-case integrated architecture. In reality, however:

- Technologists have been dazzled by the intellectual appeal and have not always correctly assessed the technical risks associated with such large projects and with the technologies needed to run these new systems.
- Business benefits used to justify the investments often have not been specifically linked to the IT investments, or they have been double-counted with other non-IT projects and have subsequently not been realised.
- The business requirements definition has exploded in scope because specifiers, lured by the potential, have built in a very wide range of options, leading to a requirement for super-flexibility. In our experience, this has translated into projects that are super-expensive.
- Building the interfaces needed to allow phased migration to the new system has proved more expensive than building the original system. Projects have overrun, particularly because of the time needed to test the impact of the new system on existing applications and interfaces.

The result has been the creation of some very large projects, the complexity of which has continued to grow with each day of detailed definition work. Many have failed or been cut back so that what was finally delivered was significantly less than the original promise, and any benefits expected remained theoretical. Actually, an integrated environment in a bank with a large number of different lines of business, like any of the Big Four, can lead to increased complexity and costs or loss of business opportunities, as the dialogue between business managers – who think in business line terms – and technicians – who think in application terms – becomes much more difficult.

Notwithstanding these experiences, there are examples of banks who do work with well-integrated systems. For example, some of the building societies and Other Retail banks (e.g., Nationwide, Abbey National) started their automation programmes later than the banks and have a more limited set of products and processes to integrate (e.g., no small business customers, no non-secured lending products). Clearly, any new bank or building society has an opportunity to strike directly for an integrated systems solution from the outset, e.g., by using a software package, as done by Banco Commercial Portugues in Portugal. The closest example of this in the UK is the case of Direct Line, which, although an insurance company rather than a bank (but part of Royal Bank of Scotland and now offering banking products itself), provides a good example of the technology-driven design of a new operation. With systems that enable it to provide superior customer service and to manage its business more effectively than the traditional players (e.g., by adjusting its underwriting intra-day as its portfolio of risks develops), it succeeded in becoming the biggest motor insurance writer in just a few years and, as we saw in Chapter 7, achieved profitability superior to that of its competitors who had been in the market for the best part of this century.

The BITE framework is a useful device to describe where a particular business is today and to map where the current initiatives will take it. There are two independent thrusts in operation in each business. One is driven by the business managers, looking to drive business improvements through some form of end-to-end process re-engineering initiative; the other is driven by the technologists, looking to implement some form of integration solution, very often on a new technical platform. It is this insight that starts the more valuable dialogue between the two groups as to where the business-improvement value lies (and how valuable it is) and what the technical opportunities and constraints are. The purpose of the dialogue is to agree on a target point on the matrix that delivers an appropriate business case – a quantification of the benefits, costs, delivery timescales, and risks, and appropriate statements about non-quantifiable attributes like flexibility, learning and extensibility. Once this target point is agreed, the debate can shift to the issues that affect the realities of delivery.

Achieving this type and level of dialogue has been a challenge for most businesses, including the UK banks. Business managers should be the owners of the business case and should be continually testing the business ideas against the 'solution space' – that is, the feasible range of change, whether of systems, processes or organisation. For their part the technologists should be evaluating the realities of the technical 'solution space', to identify options for extending it to create new business opportunities and to clarify specifically the risks involved in the projects required.

In the first part of this book it was argued that in the electronic era banks must compete in a more selective manner, in arenas in which they can hope to enjoy some competitive advantage. The dialogue prompted by the BITE framework will help business managers and technologists develop a joint strategy for the future that both fixes the bank today and sets a new direction for the future bank, but also focuses on the migration challenge.

DECIDING WHERE AND HOW TO COMPETE: THE TECHNOLOGY STRATEGY GAMEBOARD

In this section, a framework is presented for assessing whether a bank ought to go it alone or to share the building work with other market participants. Quite clearly the degree of innovation required will predetermine some of the opportunities.

In order to get a sense of what alternatives exist, a framework called the technology strategy gameboard presents competitive position along two dimensions (Figure 9.3). The vertical axis of the gameboard asks the bank to choose which customer groups it will target – *where* it will compete. The horizontal axis asks it to decide *how* it will compete – which products it will offer, and how these should be delivered.

Banks traditionally provided many services to many customer groups through a paper-based, labour-intensive branch system. The emergence of lower-cost technology is forcing almost all banks to look at the services they provide, and to choose one of four possible ways of competing in each.

Type 1 competitors invest heavily in developing their own electronic delivery systems and new products. To keep their costs low, and to realise

Fig 9.3 Competitive position following full impact of technology

The technology strategy gameboard

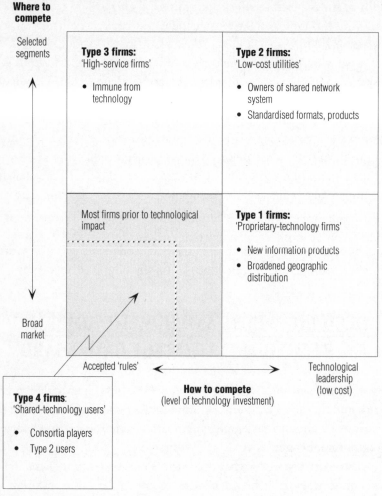

Adapted and reproduced from Thomas D Steiner and Diogo B Teixeira, *Technology in Banking* (Business One Irwin, 1990) with permission of The McGraw-Hill Companies.

the economies of scale inherent in the technology, they try to push as much volume as possible through the electronic delivery system. The favoured tactics for gaining this volume are to attract a wider range of customers, and to reduce their prices. To be successful as a 'high-volume low-cost' Type 1 company, it is probably necessary to move first, and quickly. To a large extent the Big Four have followed Type 1 strategies, although none has really achieved leadership. For example, Lloyds Bank was the first bank to install ATMs on a large-scale proprietary network, but failed to sustain their market share gain. Type 1 firms should constantly review their cost competitiveness and value proposition, both against other Type 1 companies, and against any Type 2 utilities, and be ready to act when they fail to meet these external benchmarks.

Type 2 competitors develop the new technology and either sell it to others or share it with them. The leaders in this 'develop and share' strategy become information utilities, providing standardised formats and least-cost public networks to firms that have not built proprietary systems. In funds transfer, for example, SWIFT (the Society for World-wide Financial Telecommunications) is a classic Type 2 example, as are Visa and Master-Card in credit cards. Type 2 shared networks can extend beyond the boundaries of banking, as technology enables the co-operation with other kinds of institutions, such as retailers and employers in the payments area, to create value for customers. The direct debit scheme in the UK could be considered an example of such an arrangement.

Type 3 firms take a very different approach. They insulate themselves from the new technology, and its uncertainty and expense, by concentrating on services that are not available electronically. For example, Coutts Bank provides wide-ranging personal banking services targeted at rich individual customers. Such firms hope to maintain relationships with customers who want such services, and are willing to pay more for them even when they have less expensive alternatives to hand from Type 1 and Type 2 firms. These 'premium service' businesses are very attractive economically because they are simply staying close to their customers and saving the high cost of technology investments. However, over the long term, Type 3 businesses may become increasingly vulnerable to technology, especially where customers come to expect services or convenience that the Type 3 banks cannot provide.

Type 4 firms often cannot afford the investment required to build the systems that a Type 1 competitor has; nor is their competitive position with their customers strong enough to allow them to take a Type 3 approach. Most of the building societies and the Other Retail banks fall into this category. Their best chance of staying in the game may be as 'piggyback players', using the information utilities of the Type 2 firms, or sharing their networks. For example, several of the building societies issue Visa or MasterCard credit cards, and use the credit and processing services of the Bank of Scotland and the clearing bank services of one of the clearers, particularly the Co-operative Bank.

For most institutions, especially the larger banks, no single answer is appropriate for all lines of business. Whether to be a supplier, participant or user in each will depend, for example, on the strengths of the other Type 1 competitors, how powerful the Type 2 utility has become, the viability and importance of the customer service offered in a Type 3 approach, and whether a Type 4 supplier taking a 'piggy-back' approach can retain control over its customers.

Further, the right answer for any one line of business will vary at different stages of its development. So it may be a good thing to be a Type 1 developer of proprietary systems before shifting focus to become an initiator (even as part of a consortium) of Type 2 shared services offered to other participants. The Technology Strategy Gameboard plots a dynamic, not a static, world.

This chapter has addressed three of the four questions posed in charting the future course for UK banks. Because the answers to the fourth question, 'how should the general management function interact with the technology management function?' apply whether one is charting the future course or managing the bank today, they are dealt with separately in the next chapter.

PEOPLE: CHANGING THE CULTURE

The aim of this book has been to show how technology is restructuring banking and threatening to destroy the profitability of current activities. Survival will depend on managing the different parts of the bank's activities so that they work better together, or on building a new operational model with new cultures living alongside the old. And we believe that the key to this survival is to promote dialogue between bankers and technologists, a dialogue that few banks have successfully pursued. In this chapter, we consider two human-resource issues raised by this potentially profound transformation in banking.

First, what steps can bank management take to manage across the various cultures now necessary to operate a successful bank? We suggest a short-term solution, and a long-term programme to create a cadre of technologically aware, skilled bankers for the future.

Second, what decision-making framework will resolve the dilemma apparently inseparable from IT management: how to balance the need for centralised control of data-processing resources with the management desire for a degree of IT autonomy?

MANAGING ACROSS THE CULTURES

The UK clearing banks traditionally had a unified culture. They hired and trained school leavers and other young people as clerks. In each bank, on-the-job training was specific to the transaction processing practices (F2b) developed over the years, with the Institute of Bankers' courses and exams setting a general professional standard. All senior bankers were 'tried in the detail of the business', having been rotated through various departments throughout their careers. The long, hard process of promotion through the ranks produced many capable bank managers who ran the thousands of individual branches. Almost all senior general managers came from branch management. At its best, this culture produced exceptional *administrators*, senior clearing bankers very strong in the F2b skills of running large organisations efficiently and with strict attention to detail. However, these skills were only of limited help when information technology began to permeate bank business systems.

Information technology introduces a second culture to banks, one which is not, of course, unique to banks. It has its own knowledge and skills. The skills of the applied *technologist* who works on the F1 core technology relate to that technology, not to banking or any other business. Unlike the administrator, who focuses on getting the work of the bank done, the technologist focuses on tools, i.e., on the technology itself. Administrators might know in general what they wanted the technology to do, but rarely had any useful understanding of it. When called upon to define their requirements for technology, their first response was to direct that the paper-based business system be replicated in a computer application.

To further complicate the culture of a bank, the applications systems themselves all had to be custom-built until very recently, and in many cases still are. This required the services of yet a third cultural type, the *crafter*. At the high end of the computer programming field, the designers of software systems are creative, more like artists than technologists. They rarely make good administrators, and the brightest and most creative of them don't want to manage. They want to make the best software their skills and the available tools will allow them to make. The 'craft guild' culture of F2a could not be further removed in temper and outlook from the clerk culture of F2b, but those were precisely the people who had to work together to introduce automation to the banks. Although systems development methodologies were developed fairly early in the automation process, translation problems between users and developers persist.

With increasing competition and more extensive product lines, the administrators in general management turned to yet another culture, that of the product *marketer*. Sometimes this meant hiring marketing professionals from outside banking, sometimes it was a matter of telling trained bankers – that is, administrators – that they were now responsible for marketing. Marketing, the F3 skill, came late to the UK banks, and fitting it into the core administrative culture was uncomfortable at first, no matter how it was introduced. Good general marketers were by definition lacking in knowledge of specific products and services (though as banking products have proliferated, this has become a serious problem for the traditional bank manager as well). On the other hand, conventionally trained bankers rarely took to marketing with great success. Worse, product management and marketing tended to grow up as support functions, outside the central structure of the bank, which remained the branches and their direct infrastructure. To sell to the market, marketers had first to sell to the experienced and sceptical bank managers. The bank managers knew from years of dealing with customers that their product – a foreign term in itself – was 'a good banking service', full stop. The marketing experts were convinced that the bank had scores if not hundreds of products, and had produced promotional material accordingly.

Barriers between cultures

Stepping back, it is clear that all of these cultures and their associated skills are necessary to a competitive business. It is equally clear that they are specialities, having little in common. Worse, they come to have less in common as time goes on, and they tend to fragment further. For example, the F1 world of generic technologies has become too complex for even the most capable technologist to track all the relevant advances, especially as the PC and LAN developments and mainframe technology move ahead on separate tracks. However, the skills of those in this area probably remain more broadly-based and thus more transferable than in the other parts of the business system. By contrast, the base of shared knowledge and skills of those writing specialised applications in F2a is already narrow, and shrinking further. The types of systems required by banks vary enormously today, both because banks have many more products and because more technology can be put into them; each crafter therefore can know very few systems. The work of the bank clerk in F2b has also changed beyond recognition, partly through the advent of IT, and partly because banks now offer more products. Even the work of the marketers in F3 is becoming specialised: managing consumer marketing is very different from managing wholesale products. In each market segment, complex products and intense competition force further specialisation, as in cash management services.

Gaps in perception and communication between the cultures will continue to widen. Their internal cohesion and shared comprehension breaks down in all large banks as tools proliferate, languages diverge, products become more differentiated, and market segments served become more tightly defined.

This dispersive trend has to be confronted and, if not reversed, at least contained. Banks compete product by product, across whole business systems. The proportion of the costs and customer value arising in each function might vary by product, but every product draws on them all. It is widely recognised that technology decisions must be effectively integrated with both operational realities and business opportunities and threats. The challenge for general management is to get the cultures to work together effectively to keep the bank competitive. In addition to this, general management needs to foster innovation, in pursuit of dominant design and to make choices about which innovation threads to follow. Often management attempts to address this need through formal strategic planning processes, or committees to review technology plans and expenditures. However, such formal organisational approaches rarely manage to solve the dispersion problem.

There is no simple answer. In the best of all possible worlds, the general manager of the bank (or of a large business within the bank) would at least be conversant with the culture and knowledge specific to each function in the business system. He or she could play the co-ordination role at the top, and this could be replicated where appropriate at lower management levels. The problem is that very few of the current generation of senior managers are sufficiently conversant with all cultures, their unique vocabularies and skills, to play such a role. The rotational training system within the bank does not build such learning, as the rotations tend to be too narrowly focused on particular skills and cultures.

A management and accountability problem therefore arises. Technology issues are very threatening to many senior general managers. With very little experience to draw on, they may have to make critical decisions involving vast investments and material business risks. Feeling uncomfortable with technology issues, general managers tend simply to distance themselves from the problem.

Such distancing can take the form of placing almost all such decisions with a single managing director who has a strong background in data processing and operations, normally the Finance Director. Alternatively, since it is seldom practical for all technology issues to be addressed in a central function, they may be dispersed into the major lines of business. Or – radically – a manager with a technology background might even be put in charge of a traditional line of business which absorbs the lion's share of technology spending. But the bank's cultures remain distinct, no matter

261

what the formal organisation chart looks like. Co-ordination and communication problems will still persist.

There are only two reliable ways to bridge the cultures effectively, one short term and one longer term.

Short term: a general manager collective

The short-term solution is to recognise that no single person at the general manager level can actually manage the business system across all functions and their cultures. Instead of asking individuals to cope with the impossible, banks should focus on building a collective 'general manager function' for each major line of business, or for the bank as a whole. This can be either a highly formal or an *ad hoc* arrangement, although we have found a formal Information Management Council operating at board level to be enormously valuable. What matters is that each function in the business system is effectively represented in, and controlled by, the general manager collective. In practice, the managers involved must be senior enough to discuss the key business issues arising in and cutting across the F1, F2a, F2b and F3 functions in a mutually comprehensible fashion, even if their subordinates cannot. They must also have enough detailed knowledge of their own function to ensure that it acts according to the common direction laid down by the general manager collective.

This does not necessarily mean that four people are involved in the collective role. One manager may handle the more technical F1 and F2a portfolios and another wear the F2b and F3 hat. What is important is the communication between them. The people who understand and manage the key resources in the business system must talk to each other regularly to agree where the business is going, how it is going to get there and what role technology is to play. Some managers will inevitably have great demands made upon them, especially the rare senior technologist who understands business issues or the equally scarce senior banker who understands technology. That can't be helped. We know of a chief information officer in a large US corporation – very business-oriented and technically capable – who wears the F1 and F2a hat in three general manager functions, ranging from consumer banking to global treasury. It is not easy, but it works. There are not yet enough such managers in the industry.

The general manager collective (or Information Management Council) will operate more effectively if it is not required to deal with the detailed IT questions facing the business lines – that is, if it is able to focus on the more strategic business issues. Some banks have had good results from appointing Business Information Managers in each business line. These managers, who need to be technology-literate in some measure, are responsible for developing and monitoring the business cases for IT investments in the business line, and for managing communications with the experts who provide the IT solutions. Where the right skills have not been available, many banks supplement the role with a counterpart in the IT organisation (sometimes called a Technical Information Manager), who focuses on defining solutions and generating opportunities for using technology.

Long term: managers with wider experience

The longer-term solution is to see that in future there are more of such technically competent and business-oriented managers. Here, the UK clearing bank tradition of a common point of staff entry and broad exposure to all key banking tasks is a good foundation. But this foundation has been eroded as the banks' increased needs for specialists has led them to recruit more graduates and others with technical qualifications. Setting such people to work sorting cheques is obviously not practical in this day and age. Nor is it practical to make highly specialised managers assume positions of responsibility in a culture alien to them. Cross-fertilisation is important, but we have seen senior credit officers in large banks put in charge of operations and technology, yet unable to understand or control what their nominal subordinates really did. The way to avoid this banking version of 'Yes, Minister' is to develop younger managers through meaningful assignments in all the banking cultures before they move to more senior levels of responsibility. Frequently the most rewarding way to do this is to assign bankers to technology projects, as either project managers or 'business analysts'. As application development technologies become more 'presentation' oriented, these 'business analyst' positions will increasingly come to be filled by people who can play both the IT role (the crafter) and the banker role (the administrator and marketer).

This new breed of managers, familiar with all the cultures, need not be culturally omnipotent. They do not have to write code in the 'craft guild', but can have a substantive role in managing a development project. In the armed services there is sophisticated electronic technology everywhere, and many officers who understand it because of the education and practical assignments which made up their career path. Banks too should recognise that the 'detail of the business' is now largely technological and will become more so. Their managers do not need to be computer scientists; most of the information technology banks use is not so arcane. As Bagehot pointed out, the people trained in the paper-technology of a century ago learned it as one would a language, by working with it. Only by working in all the relevant disciplines and cultures of the contemporary bank's more elaborate business system can the general managers of tomorrow be properly trained to co-ordinate the demands of the business with the capabilities of the technology available to them.

Managing across the cultures as described above should ease communication problems in the longer term; but it will not entirely resolve another cultural issue that banks face – who is to control IT resources, and how far can IT decision-making be delegated?

CONTROLLING TECHNOLOGY RESOURCES

Few general managers are comfortable with the current state of technology in their banks at any given time. Typical concerns include the level and trend of total systems expenditures, the inability to demonstrate that the cost improvements or incremental revenues which justified expenditures are being achieved, complaints of unresponsive central data processing functions by the users, who often also complain of excessive development costs, and unacceptably high (and often inexplicable) data processing charges. On the other hand, the technologists (and 'crafters') often are concerned and frustrated by the lack of commitment and comprehension among general managers and users of what they are trying to do for the bank.

Traditionally these issues have been viewed as organisational problems, basically a question of delegation. When information technology was new, crude, and by nature hard to use, general management designated a technology 'supremo', to whom they delegated the job of building and maintaining the bank's data processing infrastructure. This supremo decided what made sense from a processing and security viewpoint and the users had to live with it. As technology became more compact, flexible and easy to use, such delegation to a central function came to make less and less sense to businesses whose cost structures and products had a high technology content.

There were at least two reasons to seek substantial autonomy. One was the ability to control product-specific development, especially where competition demanded quick response and constant improvement in features and benefits. More rarely this might extend to the ability to control processing quality and availability. The second reason to seek autonomy was to escape the large, ever-growing costs of the central data processing function. This was not helpful to the overall numbers of the bank. If one business can escape from an allocation by running its own shop for less, it may improve its numbers. Allowing individual businesses to control their data processing function can get very expensive unless the central functions shrink in proportion. The central data processing costs allocated out to users are real, and so is any additional spending by businesses trying to avoid them.

With the advent of PCs and LANs, technology permeates banking with everything from word processing systems to spreadsheets available to all managers and their support staff. Often these people, as departments or even as individuals, buy directly from vendors. Also they want to access and manipulate bank data, both internal MIS and specific customer information. As more innovative tasks can be performed, many generalists get excited about technology for the first time. The problem is that little or none of this expanded use of standard technology is documented or consistent, and issues of data integrity and security become serious.

This is a natural progression: the technology gets both more advanced and easier to use, the systems intensity of businesses increases, technology spreads into all aspects of bank work, and banks evolve from the tyranny of the data processing supremo to a more broadly delegated responsibility for developing and using IT.

Of course things are not that simple. Banks use a complex of differing technologies simultaneously. They are currently using systems that were developed in automation Stages A, B and C (see Chapter 2), many of which will have to remain centralised even if they are redone in Stage D. The core accounting system of the bank is the most obvious case. Other technology, such as dealing-room automation, is often more driven by market and external connectivity requirements and has to be highly devolved to the users. A typical bank has at any moment a complex portfolio of technologies with different characteristics and uses, of different ages and quality and with different degrees of importance to the safe and orderly running of the bank. These technologies have different stakeholders: some have little impact beyond the business or department using them, some are critical to the performance of many businesses. Some require scale, some require flexibility. The complexity and diversity of this portfolio will only increase over time.

The need for control is clear to general management. How to go about it is less clear. The classic levers of control are organisational and are usually discussed in terms of centralised versus decentralised data processing and development. There are also the planning and architecture approaches to controlling technology direction and spending. When the data processing function had to be centralised, the organisation issue was simply who it should report to, and there can be many equally valid answers to this as long as the data processing department takes direction from general management. Later, the organisational issue became how much and under what restraints and standards development or business-specific processing can be devolved to the businesses. Again, there are many valid solutions, depending on the specific circumstances. However, as the performance of business systems in a bank continues to grow more technology-sensitive, the number of concerned parties and vocal stakeholders in technology decisions grows. Organisational levers become increasingly inadequate.

To an extent they can be reinforced by a planning process that links technology planning to business strategies across the bank, but this seldom yields clear decisions. Banks can also set up committees to bring together users and data processing and development people, but these can easily get bogged down in their own process without producing either consensus or improved communication. Finally, there is 'architecture', an overarching design and set of standards intended to define how data processing and development can be integrated into an efficient and yet flexible whole. But 'architecture' begs the question of who gets to design it and who gets to vote on it. Moreover, it is more likely to remain a direction and intention than to become a reality. Things are moving too quickly in core technology, 'production' and the market for a detailed architecture to shape and control them.

General management requires a second lever to effectively exercise control: policy quite easily defined as guidelines for thinking and action. A policy defines general management's expectations of how people or organisations will do things independently in the absence of specific orders from above. It helps ensure that the actions of employees support the corporate objectives in consistent and predictable ways. Clearing banks have always had numerous policies on a range of issues but rarely have clearly defined policies on the use of technology.

The tight–loose matrix

It is possible to develop a policy-driven approach to controlling the data processing resource. This approach, which is described as 'tight–loose', is represented by a two-dimensional, four-box matrix (Figure 10.1). Each box is a generalised abstraction of the approach a bank might adopt on a specific technology control issue. Each quadrant defines a type of policy approach – from very restrictive to very broad – which is most appropriate to overall management ends in the particular circumstances. The answer to the control issue is not either to centralise it or to decentralise it, but rather do some of each, depending on circumstances. Because of the nature of different business needs, technologies and integration requirements, a bank will to some extent be in all four quadrants at once.

Fig 10.1 The tight–loose matrix

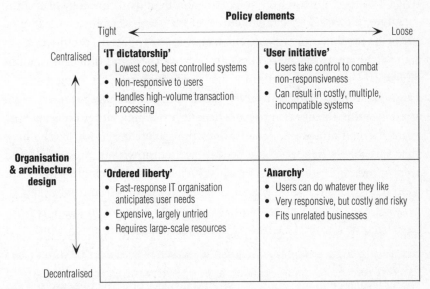

Adapted and reproduced from Thomas D Steiner and Diogo B Teixeira, *Technology in Banking* (Business One Irwin, 1990) with permission of The McGraw-Hill Companies.

The term 'tight–loose' means that corporate systems policy cannot (and should not) specify how actions are carried out in all cases. Rather a policy should set some standards and procedures but also allow users the latitude to make their own choices when applications do not need to adhere to bank-wide standards. For example, a bank's policy for its traders might be that they can develop their own applications as long as bank-wide information exists to manage risk and fund positions. Standards to implement this policy could include: one network for all trading desks, common database management software, standard formats for position data, and limits on which application packages can be employed.

Each box in the tight–loose policy matrix needs to be considered separately.

- *IT dictatorship*. This has been the traditional approach for banks, and it continues to be broadly applicable, particularly for high-volume transaction processing. Even for more distributed applications, some projects need to be placed here. Networks and network interface are a good example. A bank-wide network needs to be rigorously consistent, and its operation must be centralised. It must be under tight policy control. There is no room for looseness in defining interfaces.

- *User initiative*. How users accomplish that interface is a different issue. They can get impatient if the purchase of PCs or workstations, for example, is too tightly controlled. 'User initiative' is a better way to give users the flexibility to choose which equipment to install, provided it can handle the interface. A strong central data processing function remains in place, but users can, within policy guidelines, take the initiative on a range of things that matter to them. They will pay for their own initiatives and of course enjoy any benefits or suffer any problems arising from them. Initiatives outside policy guidelines can result in a lot of incompatible hardware and software in a bank, so policies have to be strictly upheld.

- *Anarchy*. When banks embark on decentralisation without policy, the business units soon end up making all the key data processing decisions. This can create costly, incompatible and hard to maintain data processing environments very quickly. Anarchy is destructive when users can buy and build things which cannot be networked with the parts of the bank which need to interface with them. However, in other cases anarchy can be constructive – as when traders and corporate finance personnel model spreadsheets.

- *Ordered liberty*. One way to avoid destructive anarchy is to combine tight policy with decentralised organisation. This gives users autonomy of action within a framework of bank-wide definitions and standards. You can do department computing if you meet tight definitions of compatibility and timeliness of information required elsewhere in the bank and use standard formats. There is on balance at least as much order as there is liberty, perhaps more. But users feel more in charge, and in ways important to them.

A model for ordered liberty can be found in the constitutions of some federal states, such as the USA; the role of the centre is clearly defined as the minimum to ensure protection from external dangers (so, for example, risk management should be done centrally), and to enable communications/commerce between units (e.g., exchange of customer information to assess creditworthiness). Policies and standards are clearly set, but, within those, units operate independently. As described in Chapter 9, this solution will theoretically lead to higher costs than a centralised one, but this cost disadvantage is likely to be made up by the reduction in complexity, the increase in flexibility, and the closer alignment of the interests of technologists and business unit managers.

None of the four boxes on the matrix is the best solution for everything. Ordered liberty is not always good, nor is a measured tyranny or a little anarchy always a bad idea. Using a policy matrix like this significantly increases general management options for controlling technology. A complex development project may have some elements that fall in all four quadrants. Different technology management functions may also require different approaches. F1, with its standardised nature and high economies of scale, is likely to be better if centralised, and indeed probably outsourced altogether. F2, however, may be better decentralised, provided the 'federal state' roles can be carried out. If such a mixed structure is adopted, the key risk to watch is the creation of several unnecessary levels of interface between the centralised and the decentralised elements.

EPILOGUE
LOOKING INTO THE FUTURE

In this book it has been shown that:

- The cost of large-scale information processing has been declining by orders of magnitude (as in Bagehot's time).

- Banks are creating processing over-capacity and reducing the barriers to entry as technology becomes more widely accessible, e.g., through utility operations, and reduces the scale required for low-cost operation.

- Consequently, and as in the US, technology investments by banks in the UK are actually creating value for bank customers and eroding bank profit potential.

- Technology impact varies by line of business and by institution. It is greatest in traditional banking products and allows those who are not burdened with paper-based cost structures to thrive.

- The potential exists that radical innovation could undermine traditional banking and that defenders are unprepared and vulnerable.

No institution dare try to stop technology investments, as it would then undoubtedly be left behind. However, in this new environment, banks' profits will surely drift away, as their cost structures are not changing fast enough to allow them to generate the required returns. Under pressure from virtually all sides, the banks will be forced to find some way out of this trap and 'either adapt or die' – just as in Bagehot's time.

The way forward for banks may lie in accelerating rather than resisting the tendency of technology to disaggregate the highly integrated business systems which emerged in Bagehot's day. Ironically, one immediate possibility for banks is a 'back to the future' reversion to real bills banking. The conventional model of commercial bank credit extension looks almost exclusively at a snapshot of the financial position of the borrower – no matter how sophisticated the models used by the risk management experts.

The quality of a borrower's cash flows and commercial counter-parties are not taken into consideration – *at least not in real time* – but in principle there is no reason why banks could not, over time, revert to financing discrete transactions. This would require the marriage of electronic data interchange with financing as well as payment to create electronic bills of exchange, a perfectly feasible development given available technologies and infrastructure (as, indeed, is an efficient market for such bills). This would enable banks to reduce borrowing costs for small businesses (eliminating high-cost overdraft facilities in favour of bill discounting) while improving their own profitability. Unfortunately, it is hard to conceive how this opportunity can be effectively confined to banks.

Another 'back to the future' possibility is to jettison the existing cost structure of the paper-based era and start afresh. Essentially, if it is inevitable that new competitors with very large cost advantages are going to cherry-pick the best customers, as did Direct Line in insurance (as shown in Chapters 7 and 9), banks may as well face up to this reality and start new operations aimed at cannibalising their own (and their competitor's) customer base. General Motors adopted much the same strategy in its launch of Saturn (whose performance results and customer satisfaction have validated that decision) as have many insurers who have launched direct subsidiaries. The most mature example of this in UK banking is First Direct, which, since September 1989, has created a business with over half a million affluent customers and a reputation for excellent service. While a number of banks have started down this road, the real challenge will be to reduce the cost of the existing branch network as customers adopt the alternative delivery channel. In the worst case they could end up by simply duplicating their existing cost structures.

A third option is for banks to focus on exploiting their most valuable assets – their brand, their customer base, their detailed customer information, and their increasing financial muscle in the marketplace. In this model, banks would have to do little more than manage a brand franchise and their own risk profile, essentially acting as assemblers of products and services for their clients and packagers of risks that were not transparent in the marketplace. This is clearly the path Barclaycard and other card issuers are following. This may be what NatWest intended in its recent decision to drop 'bank' from its name. By making use of the potential promised by database marketing and micro-segmentation against their customer data (especially transaction history), banks would understand their customers better than any other company that shared them and so would be in the strongest position to market to them. Banks would then use the financial power that their sheer capitalisation arms them with to dominate the marketing arena. We see this as a core factor coming out of the US industry consolidation – the Chase name is becoming an irresistible powerhouse. The challenge is to acquire skills in an area where banks have generally been deficient, i.e., retailing. Banks may find that their brands do not easily attract customers to non-traditional bank products – it is easier to see Marks & Spencer or Tesco offering a current account than Barclays offering high-street fashions or groceries. On the other hand, Barclaycard is now the second largest Ford seller in the UK through tying its loyalty scheme to discounts on Ford vehicles.

An apocalyptic view of the future might go further and conclude that there is no practical limit to the extent to which banks as institutions will be dismantled and replaced by markets. This will include the creation of money itself through the development of international networks and private payment systems beyond the reach of regulation as the availability of information reduces the risk currently associated with unregulated payment vehicles.

Of course, many existing banking institutions will survive in some shape or form by adopting courses of action which may or may not be related to those above. But if these have a common thread it lies, perhaps, in their close links with the payment system itself – the last redoubt of the traditional banking franchise. The best chance of any effective response to the technological transformation of the banking environment may lie in the exploitation of the customers' traditional reliance on the banks for the accurate, secure, rapid and guaranteed transfers of value.

This book has outlined a number of methods and techniques that may be used by an organisation to establish a dialogue as to the correct, maybe dynamic, strategy that is right for the moment. As any masterful and battle-scarred general knows, no battle-plan survives the first contact with the enemy!

LIST OF ABBREVIATIONS

ABI	Association of British Insurers	FDR	First Data Resources
ACH	Automated Clearing House	GEIS	GE Information Services
ADP	Automatic Data Processing	HOBS	Home and Office Banking Service
ANSI	American National Standards Institute	HSBC	Hongkong & Shanghai Banking Corporation
APACS	Association for Payment Clearing Services	ISIS	Interbank Switch Issuer Service
		ISSC	Integrated Systems Solutions Corporation
APR	annual percentage rate	JCCC	Joint Credit Card Company
ATM	automated teller machine	LAN	local area network
BACS	Bankers' Automated Clearing Services	LDC	less-developed country
		LID	line-item detail
BBA	British Bankers' Association	M&A	mergers & acquisitions
BCP	Banco Commercial Portugues	MBNA	Maryland Bank of North America
BITE	business improvement/technology evaluation	MICR	magnetic ink character recognition
		MINT	Midland NatWest TSB
BOLP	branch on-line processing	MIS	management information systems
BSA	Building Societies' Association	MMG	Mitchell Madison Group
BT	British Telecom	MORI	Market and Opinion Research International
CAGR	compound annual growth rate		
CASE	computer-aided software engineering	NOP	National Opinion Polls
		NPV	net present value
CD	certificate of deposit	NYCE	New York Cash Exchange
CHAPS	Clearing House Automated Payment System	OCR	optical character recognition
		PDQ	Process Data Quickly
CHIPS	Clearing House International Payments System	PIN	personal identification number
		PISCES	Petroleum Industry Services for the Clearance Electronically of Sales
CLPM	customer lifecycle profitability marketing		
CNP	Caisse Nationale de Prévoyance	PTT	post-telephone-telegraph
EDC	Electronic Debit Card	RTGS	real-time gross settlement
EDI	electronic data interchange	SAP	Systems Applications and Products in Data Processing
EDIFACT	EDI for Administration Commerce and Trade		
EDS	Electronic Data Systems	SCUG	Switch Card Users' Group
EFTPOS	electronic funds transfer at point of sale	SWIFT	Society for World-wide Financial Telecommunications
EPSS	European Payment System Service	T&E	travel and entertainment
FDIC	Federal Deposit Insurance Corporation	VAN	value-added network
		VAT	value-added tax

INDEX